First World War
and Army of Occupation
War Diary
France, Belgium and Germany

51 DIVISION
154 Infantry Brigade
Gordon Highlanders
4th Battalion
1 March 1916 - 31 March 1919

WO95/2886/2

The Naval & Military Press Ltd
www.nmarchive.com
Published in association with The National Archives

Published by

The Naval & Military Press Ltd

Unit 10 Ridgewood Industrial Park,

Uckfield, East Sussex,

TN22 5QE England

Tel: +44 (0) 1825 749494

www.naval-military-press.com

www.nmarchive.com

This diary has been reprinted in facsimile from the original. Any imperfections are inevitably reproduced and the quality may fall short of modern type and cartographic standards.

© Crown Copyright
Images reproduced by permission of The National Archives, London, England, 2015.

Contents

Document type	Place/Title	Date From	Date To
Heading	WO95/2886/2 4 Battalion Gordon Highlanders		
Heading	51st Division 154th Infy Bde 1-4th Bn Gordon Hdrs Mar 1916-Mar 1919		
War Diary	Mervieux	01/03/1916	06/03/1916
War Diary	Doullens	07/03/1916	08/03/1916
War Diary	Ivergny	09/03/1916	09/03/1916
War Diary	Duisans	10/03/1916	10/03/1916
War Diary	Ecurie	11/03/1916	16/03/1916
War Diary	La Sabliere	17/03/1916	22/03/1916
War Diary	Etrun	23/03/1916	28/03/1916
War Diary	Sabliere	29/03/1916	31/03/1916
War Diary	La Sabliere	01/04/1916	03/04/1916
War Diary	Ecurie	04/04/1916	09/04/1916
War Diary	La Sabliere	10/04/1916	15/04/1916
War Diary	Etrun	16/04/1916	21/04/1916
War Diary	La Sabliere	22/04/1916	27/04/1916
War Diary	Ecurie	28/04/1916	03/05/1916
War Diary	La Sabliere	04/05/1916	09/05/1916
War Diary	Etrun	10/05/1916	15/05/1916
War Diary	La Sabliere	16/05/1916	21/05/1916
War Diary	Etrun	22/05/1916	22/05/1916
War Diary	Ecurie	23/05/1916	27/05/1916
War Diary	Sabliere	28/05/1916	31/05/1916
War Diary	La Sabliere	01/06/1916	03/06/1916
War Diary	Etrun	04/06/1916	08/06/1916
War Diary	La Sabliere	09/06/1916	15/06/1916
War Diary	Ecurie	16/06/1916	21/06/1916
War Diary	La Sabliere	22/06/1916	28/06/1916
War Diary	Etrun	29/06/1916	30/06/1916
Heading	154th Brigade 51st Division 1/4th Battalion The Gordon Highlanders July 1916		
Heading	1/4th Battalion The Gordon Highrs War Diary Volume No.17 From 1-7-16 To 31-7-16		
War Diary	Etrun	01/07/1916	04/07/1916
War Diary	La Sabliere	05/07/1916	10/07/1916
War Diary	Maroeuil	11/07/1916	13/07/1916
War Diary	Villers Brulin	14/07/1916	15/07/1916
War Diary	Ivergny	16/07/1916	16/07/1916
War Diary	Bernaville	17/07/1916	20/07/1916
War Diary	Nr Becourt	21/07/1916	21/07/1916
War Diary	Highwood	22/07/1916	23/07/1916
War Diary	Support Trenches Bazentin Le Grand	24/07/1916	26/07/1916
War Diary	Support Trench	26/07/1916	26/07/1916
War Diary	Becordell	27/07/1916	31/07/1916
Heading	154th Brigade 51st Division 1/4th Battalion Gordon Highlanders August 1916		
War Diary	Becourt	01/08/1916	01/08/1916
War Diary	Becordel	01/08/1916	06/08/1916
War Diary	D 18.b	07/08/1916	09/08/1916
War Diary	Bailleul	10/08/1916	11/08/1916

War Diary	Wallon Cappel	12/08/1916	14/08/1916
War Diary	Armentieres	15/08/1916	15/08/1916
War Diary	Subsidiary Line	16/08/1916	21/08/1916
War Diary	No 1/3 Trench	22/08/1916	26/08/1916
War Diary	Nr Bailleul	27/08/1916	31/08/1916
Heading	1/4th Battalion Gordon Highlanders War Diary Volume 19 September 1-30 1916 To Headquarters 154th Inf Brigade 1/10/16		
War Diary	Nr Bailleul	01/09/1916	02/09/1916
War Diary	Soyer Farm	03/09/1916	08/09/1916
War Diary	Armentieres	09/09/1916	09/09/1916
War Diary	Trenches 84/89	10/09/1916	15/09/1916
War Diary	Armentieres	16/09/1916	22/09/1916
War Diary	Fort Rompu	23/09/1916	25/09/1916
War Diary	Estaires	26/09/1916	30/09/1916
Heading	1/4th Battalion The Gordon Highlanders War Diary Volume 21 October 1916 To Headquarters 154th Inf Brigade 1/11/16		
War Diary	Autheux	01/10/1916	03/10/1916
War Diary	Sarton	04/10/1916	04/10/1916
War Diary	Bus Les Artois	05/10/1916	06/10/1916
War Diary	Courcelles	07/10/1916	08/10/1916
War Diary	In The Trenches	09/10/1916	12/10/1916
War Diary	Colincamps	13/10/1916	16/10/1916
War Diary	Louvencourt	17/10/1916	17/10/1916
War Diary	Forceville	18/10/1916	18/10/1916
War Diary	Lealvillers	19/10/1916	22/10/1916
War Diary	Forceville	23/10/1916	30/10/1916
War Diary	Raincheval	31/10/1916	31/10/1916
Operation(al) Order(s)	Operation Order No. 1 by Lt Col S.R. McClintock Commanding 1/4th Gordon Highrs	16/10/1916	16/10/1916
Miscellaneous	Report On Raid By 4th Bn Gordon Hrs On Enemy Trenches At K.23.d.75.50	16/10/1916	16/10/1916
Map	Map		
Heading	Boyaux Arriere 7/10,000		
Miscellaneous	Defence Scheme For No.1 Subsector		
Heading	War Diary 1/4th Battalion Gordon Highlanders Volume No.22 November 1916 To Headquarters 154 Infantry Brigade 1/10/16		
War Diary	Raincheval	01/11/1916	03/11/1916
War Diary	Trenches	04/11/1916	07/11/1916
War Diary	Mailly Wood	08/11/1916	13/11/1916
War Diary	In The Trenches	13/11/1916	13/11/1916
War Diary	Trenches	14/11/1916	19/11/1916
War Diary	Mailly Wood West	20/11/1916	23/11/1916
War Diary	Hedauville	24/11/1916	24/11/1916
War Diary	Puchvillers	25/11/1916	26/11/1916
War Diary	Ovillers Post	27/11/1916	29/11/1916
War Diary	Ovillers Huts	30/11/1916	30/11/1916
Heading	1/4th Bn The Gordon Highrs From 1st To 31st Dec 1916 War Diary Vol 22		
War Diary	Ovillers Huts	01/12/1916	03/12/1916
War Diary	Trenches	04/12/1916	06/12/1916
War Diary	Dugouts	07/12/1916	09/12/1916
War Diary	Bruce Huts	10/12/1916	10/12/1916
War Diary	Senlis	11/12/1916	16/12/1916

War Diary	Bruce Huts	17/12/1916	27/12/1916
War Diary	Bouzincourt	28/12/1916	31/12/1916
Miscellaneous	4th Gordon		
Miscellaneous	1/4th Gordon Hrs Provisional Defence Scheme		
Heading	1/4th Bn Gordon Highrs War Diary For Month Of January 1917 Volume No.24		
War Diary	Bouzincourt	01/01/1917	01/01/1917
War Diary	Bruce Huts	02/01/1917	07/01/1917
War Diary	Wolfe Huts	08/01/1917	09/01/1917
War Diary	Trenches	10/01/1917	12/01/1917
War Diary	Rubempre	13/01/1917	13/01/1917
War Diary	Candas	14/01/1917	14/01/1917
War Diary	Maison Rolland	15/01/1917	15/01/1917
War Diary	Sailly Bray	16/01/1917	17/01/1917
War Diary	Bonnelle Huts	18/01/1917	29/01/1917
War Diary	Nouvion	30/01/1917	31/01/1917
Heading	War Diary Volume No.25 1/4th Bn The Gordon Hrs February 1917		
War Diary	Nouvion	01/02/1917	05/02/1917
War Diary	Canchy	06/02/1917	06/02/1917
War Diary	Gueschart	07/02/1917	07/02/1917
War Diary	Bachimont	08/02/1917	08/02/1917
War Diary	Hericourt	09/02/1917	09/02/1917
War Diary	Chelers	10/02/1917	11/02/1917
War Diary	Bethonsart	12/02/1917	21/02/1917
War Diary	Frevillers	22/02/1917	27/02/1917
War Diary	Bois De Maroeuil	28/02/1917	05/03/1917
War Diary	Trenches	06/03/1917	11/03/1917
War Diary	Maroeuil	12/03/1917	14/03/1917
War Diary	Hermin	15/03/1917	31/03/1917
Heading	1/4th Battalion Gordon Highs War Diary Volume No.24 April 1917		
War Diary	Hermin	01/04/1917	05/04/1917
War Diary	Bray	06/04/1917	12/04/1917
War Diary	Laresset	12/04/1917	15/04/1917
War Diary	Blangy	16/04/1917	21/04/1917
War Diary	Trenches	22/04/1917	24/04/1917
War Diary	Arras	25/04/1917	25/04/1917
War Diary	Gouy En Ternois	26/04/1917	27/04/1917
War Diary	Tinques	25/04/1917	30/04/1917
Operation(al) Order(s)	Operation Order No. 1 by Lt Col S.R. McClintock Commanding 1/4th Gordon Highrs	22/04/1917	22/04/1917
Heading	War Diary For May 1917 Of 1/4th Gordon Hrs Vol 27		
War Diary	Tinques	01/05/1917	11/05/1917
War Diary	Y Huts Etrun	12/05/1917	13/05/1917
War Diary	Arras	14/05/1917	15/05/1917
War Diary	Railway Cutting H23.c.9.9	16/05/1917	19/05/1917
War Diary	Trenches H14 C 2.1 & H 20 C 7.8	20/05/1917	20/05/1917
War Diary	Trenches	21/05/1917	24/05/1917
War Diary	Railway Embankment H13d9.9 (Map Ref. Sh 51b N.W)	25/05/1917	30/05/1917
War Diary	Arras	31/05/1917	31/05/1917
Heading	War Diary Of 1/4th Battn. The Gordon Highlanders June 1917		
War Diary	Tournehem	20/06/1917	21/06/1917
War Diary	Lederzeele	22/06/1917	30/06/1917

War Diary	Arras	01/06/1917	01/06/1917
War Diary	Magnicourt	02/06/1917	03/06/1917
War Diary	Marest	04/06/1917	05/06/1917
War Diary	Matringhem	06/06/1917	07/06/1917
War Diary	Tournehem	08/06/1917	19/06/1917
Heading	War Diary For July 1917 Of 1/4th Gordon Hrs		
War Diary	Lederzeele	01/07/1917	08/07/1917
War Diary	'A' 30 Central Camp	09/07/1917	11/07/1917
War Diary	Trenches	12/07/1917	15/07/1917
War Diary	A 30 Central	16/07/1917	30/07/1917
War Diary	A 30 Central Camp Ref. Sh. 28 N.W.	31/07/1917	31/07/1917
Heading	War Diary Of 4th Gordon Hdrs For Aug 1917 Vol 31		
Miscellaneous	Headquarters 154th Infantry Brigade	01/09/1917	01/09/1917
Miscellaneous	A.30. Central	01/08/1917	01/08/1917
War Diary	Support Line	02/08/1917	03/08/1917
War Diary	Front Line	04/08/1917	07/08/1917
War Diary	St. Janster Biezen	08/08/1917	09/08/1917
War Diary	Nortleulinghem	10/08/1917	23/08/1917
War Diary	St. Janster Biezen	24/08/1917	29/08/1917
War Diary	Morat Camp	30/08/1917	31/08/1917
Heading	War Diary Of 4th Battn Gordon Hrs For September 1917 Vol 31		
War Diary	Morat Camp	01/09/1917	04/09/1917
War Diary	Dirty Bucket Camp	05/09/1917	06/09/1917
War Diary	Canal Bank West	07/09/1917	09/09/1917
War Diary	Line	10/09/1917	12/09/1917
War Diary	Siege Camp	13/09/1917	19/09/1917
War Diary	Line	20/09/1917	21/09/1917
War Diary	Siege Camp	22/09/1917	23/09/1917
War Diary	Poperinghe	24/09/1917	28/09/1917
War Diary	Courcelles	29/09/1917	30/09/1917
Miscellaneous	Report on Action From 20/9/17 To 29/9/17 Astride Keerselare-Poelcappelle Rd	22/09/1917	22/09/1917
Operation(al) Order(s)	Operation Order No. 7 by Lieut Colonel J. Rowbotham M.C. Commanding 1/4th Battalion The Gordon Highlanders	17/09/1917	17/09/1917
Miscellaneous	Addenda No.1 To Operation Order No. 7		
Heading	1/4th Battalion The Gordon Highs War Diary-Volume 33 October 1917		
War Diary	Courcelles	01/10/1917	04/10/1917
War Diary	Neuville Vitasse	05/10/1917	12/10/1917
War Diary	Line	13/10/1917	20/10/1917
War Diary	York Lines	21/10/1917	28/10/1917
War Diary	Lattre-St-Quentin	28/10/1917	31/10/1917
Heading	1/4th Bn The Gordon Highs War Diary-Volume No.34 November 1917		
War Diary	Lattre-St-Quentin	01/11/1917	17/11/1917
War Diary	Ytres	18/11/1917	19/11/1917
War Diary	Metz	20/11/1917	20/11/1917
War Diary	Cantaing	21/11/1917	24/11/1917
War Diary	Metz	25/11/1917	25/11/1917
Miscellaneous	Report On Action 30th To 34th November 1917 and Capture Of Cantaing By 1/4th Battalion The Gordon Highlanders		
Miscellaneous	Report On Medical Arrangements In The Recent Action	27/11/1917	27/11/1917
Miscellaneous	Sheet 4	26/11/1917	26/11/1917

Type	Description	Date From	Date To
Operation(al) Order(s)	Operation Order No. 18 by Lieut Colonel J. Rowbotham M.C. Commanding 1/4th Battalion The Gordon Highlanders	19/11/1917	19/11/1917
War Diary	Rocquigny	01/12/1917	01/12/1917
War Diary	Old British Line	02/12/1917	02/12/1917
War Diary	Trenches	03/12/1917	05/12/1917
War Diary	Fremicourt	06/12/1917	16/12/1917
War Diary	I 17 B	17/12/1917	22/12/1917
War Diary	Fremicourt	23/12/1917	31/12/1917
Operation(al) Order(s)	Operation Order No. 28 by Lieut Colonel J. Rowbotham M.C. Commanding 1/4th Battalion The Gordon Highlanders	04/12/1917	04/12/1917
Heading	1/4th Bn The Gordon Highs War Diary Volume No.36 January 1918		
War Diary	Trenches	01/01/1918	07/01/1918
War Diary	Fremicourt	08/01/1918	15/01/1918
War Diary	Trenches	16/01/1918	18/01/1918
War Diary	Fremicourt	19/01/1918	19/01/1918
War Diary	Courcelles	20/01/1918	20/01/1918
War Diary	Bailleulval	21/01/1918	31/01/1918
Heading	1/4th Battalion The Gordon Highs War Diary Volume No.35 December 1917		
Heading	War Diary 1/4 Battalion The Gordon Highlanders Volume No.37 February 1918		
War Diary	Bailleulval	01/02/1918	02/02/1918
War Diary	Logeast Wood	03/02/1918	13/02/1918
War Diary	Lindop Camp Fremicourt	14/02/1918	20/02/1918
War Diary	Trenches	21/02/1918	28/02/1918
Heading	51st Division 154th Infantry Brigade War Diary 1/4th Battalion Gordon Highlanders March 1918		
War Diary	Trenches Support Line	01/03/1918	04/03/1918
War Diary	Front Line	05/03/1918	09/03/1918
War Diary	Lebucquiere	10/03/1918	15/03/1918
War Diary	Trenches Front Line	16/03/1918	25/03/1918
War Diary	Colincamps	26/03/1918	26/03/1918
War Diary	Pas	27/03/1918	27/03/1918
War Diary	Barly	28/03/1918	29/03/1918
War Diary	L'Ecleme	30/03/1918	31/03/1918
Miscellaneous	4th Battalion Gordon Hdrs Operation Order No	08/03/1918	08/03/1918
Miscellaneous	1/4 Battn Gordon Highlanders Report On Operations	01/04/1918	01/04/1918
Operation(al) Order(s)	Operation Order No. 13 by Lieut Colonel J. Rowbotham M.C. Commanding 1/4th Battalion The Gordon Highlanders	14/03/1918	14/03/1918
Miscellaneous	Defence Scheme Battalion In Rest	10/03/1918	10/03/1918
Miscellaneous	1/4th Battalion The Gordon Highlanders Defence Scheme		
Miscellaneous	1/4th Battalion The Gordon Highlanders Provisional Defence Scheme		
Miscellaneous	Addendum To Provisional Defence Scheme	01/03/1918	01/03/1918
Map	Map		
Miscellaneous	1/4th Battalion The Gordon Highlanders Defence Scheme		
Miscellaneous	Instructions On Preceding To Trenches	14/03/1918	14/03/1918
Miscellaneous	Scheme For Occupation Of Defended Locality Of Sailly-Labourse By 154th Infantry Brigade	02/04/1918	02/04/1918
Miscellaneous	Operation Order	04/04/1918	04/04/1918

Heading	51st Division 15th Infantry Brigade War Diary 1/4th Battalion The Gordon Highlanders April 1918		
Heading	1/4th Battalion The Gordon Highlanders War Diary Volume No.39 April 1918		
War Diary	L'Ecleme	01/04/1918	04/04/1918
War Diary	Auchel	05/04/1918	14/04/1918
War Diary	Robecq	15/04/1918	21/04/1918
War Diary	La Miquellerie	22/04/1918	22/04/1918
War Diary	St Hilaire	23/04/1918	30/04/1918
Miscellaneous	History Of Operations	17/04/1918	17/04/1918
Heading	War Diary 4th Battalion The Gordon Highlanders May 1918		
War Diary	St Hilaire	01/05/1918	04/05/1918
War Diary	To Ecoivres	05/05/1918	06/05/1918
War Diary	Roclincourt	07/05/1918	07/05/1918
War Diary	Reserve Trenches	07/05/1918	07/05/1918
War Diary	Roclincourt	08/05/1918	10/05/1918
War Diary	Res Trenches	11/05/1918	16/05/1918
War Diary	Front Line	17/05/1918	31/05/1918
Heading	War Diary For June 1918 Of 4th Gordon Hrs		
Miscellaneous	Headquarters 154th Infantry Brigade	30/06/1918	30/06/1918
War Diary	Trenches	01/06/1918	06/06/1918
War Diary	Front Line	07/06/1918	15/06/1918
War Diary	Ecurie Wood Camp	15/06/1918	22/06/1918
War Diary	Front Line	23/06/1918	28/06/1918
War Diary	Ecurie Wood Camp	29/06/1918	30/06/1918
Heading	154th Brigade 51st (Highland) Division 1/4th Battn The Gordon Highlanders July 1918		
Heading	War Diary Volume No. 41 July 1918 1/4th Battalion The Gordon Highrs		
War Diary	Ecurie Wood Camp	01/07/1918	05/07/1918
War Diary	Front Line	05/07/1918	11/07/1918
War Diary	Anzin	12/07/1918	12/07/1918
War Diary	Ostreville	13/07/1918	14/07/1918
War Diary	Bryas Train	15/07/1918	15/07/1918
War Diary	Nogent	16/07/1918	16/07/1918
War Diary	Chouilly	17/07/1918	18/07/1918
War Diary	Bellevue	19/07/1918	31/07/1918
Miscellaneous	Report On Operations	08/08/1918	08/08/1918
Heading	War Diary Volume 43 August 1918 1/4th Battalion The Gordon Hrs		
War Diary	Nanteuil	01/08/1918	01/08/1918
War Diary	Bellevue	02/08/1918	04/08/1918
War Diary	Berles	05/08/1918	15/08/1918
War Diary	Trenches	16/08/1918	18/08/1918
War Diary	Roclincourt	19/08/1918	25/08/1918
War Diary	Trenches (North bank of Scarpe)	25/08/1918	25/08/1918
War Diary	Trenches (Div. Res)	26/08/1918	28/08/1918
War Diary	Front Line Trenches	29/08/1918	31/08/1918
Heading	1/4th Battalion The Gordon Highlanders War Diary Volume 44 September 1918		
War Diary	Front Line Trenches	01/09/1918	01/09/1918
War Diary	Greenland Hill	01/09/1918	03/09/1918
War Diary	Roclincourt	04/09/1918	11/09/1918
War Diary	Mont St Eloy	11/09/1918	24/09/1918
War Diary	Trenches Greenland Hill	25/09/1918	30/09/1918

Heading	1/4th Bn The Gordon High War Diary October 1918 Volume No.45		
War Diary	Greenland Hill Support Tr	01/10/1918	01/10/1918
War Diary	Camp Mont St Eloi	02/10/1918	07/10/1918
War Diary	Inchy	08/10/1918	10/10/1918
War Diary	Iwuy	11/10/1918	11/10/1918
War Diary	Support Trenches Iwuy	12/10/1918	12/10/1918
War Diary	Front Line (St. Amand)	13/10/1918	14/10/1918
War Diary	Thun St Martin	15/10/1918	16/10/1918
War Diary	Trenches Avesnes Le-Sec	17/10/1918	17/10/1918
War Diary	Front Line Avesnes Le-Sec	18/10/1918	19/10/1918
War Diary	Front Line Fleury	20/10/1918	20/10/1918
War Diary	Support Fleury	21/10/1918	21/10/1918
War Diary	Support Round Fleury	22/10/1918	22/10/1918
War Diary	Douchy	23/10/1918	24/10/1918
War Diary	Support In Front of Fleury	25/10/1918	25/10/1918
War Diary	Front Line Maing	26/10/1918	26/10/1918
War Diary	Front Line Famars	27/10/1918	27/10/1918
War Diary	Reserve Maing	28/10/1918	28/10/1918
War Diary	Maing Douchy	29/10/1918	29/10/1918
War Diary	Douchy	30/10/1918	31/10/1918
Miscellaneous	1/4th Battalion The Gordon Highlanders	24/10/1918	24/10/1918
Miscellaneous	1/4th Battalion The Gordon Highlanders	30/10/1918	30/10/1918
Miscellaneous	Schedule "A"		
Miscellaneous	1/4th Battalion The Gordon Highlander Report On Operations	17/10/1918	17/10/1918
Miscellaneous	1/4th Bn. The Gordon Highlanders History Of Operations		
Miscellaneous	1/4th Battalion The Gordon Highlanders Map Reference	30/10/1918	30/10/1918
Miscellaneous	Schedule "A"		
Map	Disposition Map		
Heading	War Diary Of 1/4th Batt. The Gordon Highlanders From 1st November To 30th November 1918 Volume No.46		
War Diary	Cambrai	01/11/1918	30/11/1918
Heading	1/4th Battalion The Gordon Highlanders War Diary For December 1918 Volume No.50		
War Diary	Cambrai	01/12/1918	31/12/1918
Heading	1/4th Battalion The Gordon Highlanders War Diary 1-31 January 1919 Vol 47		
War Diary	Cambrai	01/01/1919	10/01/1919
War Diary	Houdeng	11/01/1919	31/01/1919
Operation(al) Order(s)	1/4th Battalion The Gordon Highlanders Operation Order No. 93		
Miscellaneous	1/4th Battalion The Gordon Highlanders Amendment To Operation Order No. 93		
Miscellaneous	1/4th Battalion The Gordon Highlanders Operation Order No. 93 Administrative Orders	10/01/1919	10/01/1919
Miscellaneous	Table Z		
Heading	War Diary Of 1/4th Gordon Highlanders Vol From 1st Feb 1919 To 28 Feb 1919 Vol 48		
War Diary	Houdeng	01/02/1919	22/02/1919
War Diary	Manage	23/02/1919	23/02/1919
War Diary	Vlatten	24/02/1919	28/02/1919
Heading	War Diary Of 1/4 Bn Gordon Highlanders From 1st March 1919 To 31st March 1919 Volume		

War Diary	Vlatten	01/03/1919	04/03/1919
War Diary	Vlatten-Buir	05/03/1919	05/03/1919
War Diary	Buir	06/03/1919	31/03/1919

WO195/8886/2

4 Battalion Gordon Highlanders

51ST DIVISION
154TH INFY BDE

1-4TH BN GORDON HDRS
MAR 1916 - ~~JAN~~ MAR 1919

FROM 3 DIV
8 BDE

154/51

WAR DIARY or **INTELLIGENCE SUMMARY**

Army Form C. 2118

1/4 Gordon Highlanders

Jewel Bn 25.2.16

Instructions regarding War Diaries and Intelligence Summaries are contained in F.S. Regs., Part II. and the Staff Manual respectively. Title Pages will be prepared in manuscript.

(Erase heading not required.)

Place	Date	Hour	Summary of Events and Information	Remarks and references to Appendices
MERVIEUX	1.3.16		Battn. — in billets. Coys went for short route march in afternoon.	
"	2.3.16		Ordinary training.	
"	3.3.16		" "	
"	4.3.16		Very bad weather. Snowed most of day.	
"	5.3.16		Church Parade. Fine. Got orders to move following day.	
"	6.3.16		C.O. & Adj. left at 2 am. 5 motor lorries went & sent transport at 9 am & arrived DOULLENS at 1.30 pm. Coys 1, 2 & 3 on French. B.M. paraded at 9 am & marched to see trenches, on route march. Battn. in buses etc the same by. Major Mackinnon & left Bandsmen went 5 miles from to see trenches.	
DOULLENS	7.3.16		Battn. marched to IVERGNY at 9 pm arrived at 4 pm snow by 3. Fine. 17.30 pm	
"	8.3.16		Left at 8.30 pm marched to DUISANS arrived at 3.30 pm. 16 miles cold wind snow. B.O. had lorries on road. Coys arrived of 6 trucks at 8 pm.	
IVERGNY	9.3.16			
DUISANS	10.3.16		Divisional Inspection. Left at 8 am and marched to ECURIE with 2 Companies Chocolats and relieved French Regt no 138. 2 Corps to ARRAS CENTRALES relieved 2 Corps of French Territorial Regt.	

1/4 London Div.

Army Form C. 2118

WAR DIARY
or
INTELLIGENCE SUMMARY
(Erase heading not required.)

Instructions regarding War Diaries and Intelligence Summaries are contained in F. S. Regs., Part II. and the Staff Manual respectively. Title Pages will be prepared in manuscript.

Place	Date	Hour	Summary of Events and Information	Remarks and references to Appendices
FEU RIE	11/8/15		Very quiet. Fine weather. Resuming position, a lot of work required to put right. Working hard improving position - very quiet.	
	12/8/15		Fine day, very quiet. Working hard improving CTs	
	13/8/15		Some shelling in morning mostly on CTs of PEURIE - there at work on CTs Very quiet.	
	14/8/15		Very quiet. Some shelling report 11am near Bn HQrs one shell landed just behind HQrs no matter of any DB. August - no damage	
	15/8/15		Fine weather - very quiet. Relieved 4th Seaforth in front line & Seaforth Trenches tonight.	
La Fallin	16/8/15		Still night. A little shelling during forenoon. New Zealand were arrived today.	
	18/8/15		Very fine weather. Fine quiet as usual. Offr. & men arrived tonight. One of them Capt. R.J. FORMAN to try to ruptured by Pullet (machine gun rifle) in left county of inquiry held good opinion that would are wilful.	

1875 Wt. W593/826. 1,000,000 4/15 J.B.C. & A. A.D.S.S./Forms/C. 2118.

Army Form C. 2118

WAR DIARY
or
INTELLIGENCE SUMMARY
(Erase heading not required.)

Instructions regarding War Diaries and Intelligence Summaries are contained in F. S. Regs., Part II. and the Staff Manual respectively. Title Pages will be prepared in manuscript.

Place	Date	Hour	Summary of Events and Information	Remarks and references to Appendices
La Sablière	18/9/16		One cyclist officer killed and one cyclist officer wounded tonight whilst in charge of working party in trenches	
	19/9/16		Very quiet after 4th tunnel near Wyn about 9am.	
		10.55	Lce/Cpl Jones wounded in L check by bullet this morning	
		13.55	Sgt Spencer found dead in dugout. Asphyxiation.	
		18.10	8th M.T.M.Bty committed on Chook by ??. Shell a misfire	
	20/9/16		and 2nd morning. Very quiet. 9pm. Tptl a mitrailleuse wounded to toilet in front tonight	
	21/9/16		Very quiet. Enemy used trench mortars 1595 and 9.2 Garden wounded in leg by Grenade	
	22/9/16		2nd. Very quiet. Our spying by 4 Seaforth tonight. 5pm. moved just unfortunately & killed in ETRUN. All Convoys up and inspection of equipment	
ETRUN 23/9/16	24/9/16		Sunny, humid. 2 men sent to R.B. at ANZIN and & officers sent to work on BOYAV ANZIN	

WAR DIARY
or
INTELLIGENCE SUMMARY

Army Form C. 2118

(Erase heading not required.)

Instructions regarding War Diaries and Intelligence Summaries are contained in F.S. Regs., Part II. and the Staff Manual respectively. Title Pages will be prepared in manuscript.

Place	Date	Hour	Summary of Events and Information	Remarks and references to Appendices
ETRUN	27/2/16		Snow disappearing today. Usual fatigues and training.	
	28/2/16		Church services notified owing to inclement weather.	
	29/2/16		Cold weather. Usual fatigues and parades.	
	2/3/16		Cold today. Training for trenches. C.O.'s inspection of whole Battn. Between 3 & 5pm. Relief completed by 11pm.	
SAILLY	29/3/16		Fine clear weather. A little shelling over the Mtyrs during morning otherwise very quiet.	
	30/3/16		Fairly clear. Light shelling during day. One of our aeroplanes brought down by enemy shell fire at 10.25 am about 2000 S.E. of our right front.	
	31/3/16		Enemy exploded a mine on our left front at 2.35 am. Short hostile airlight 4 gun sniper clear during day. Very quiet. Hardly any shelling.	

John N Morgan
a/adj t. 76 9 hwls ton-dn 76/3/16

WAR DIARY / INTELLIGENCE SUMMARY

Army Form C. 2118

Place	Date	Hour	Summary of Events and Information	Remarks and references to Appendices
La Sablière	1/6/16		Dull cold. Very quiet. 2/Lt Smith D Coy wounded on return by sniper mortar.	
	2/6/16		Cold, clear. Man putting by enemy on our right at 2 pm in retaliation to our own trench mortars fire. Quiet.	
	3/6/16		Cold, dull. Relieved by 4 Seaforths in Habris [?] Centrale and MAPS Coy. C.O. to ECURIE [?]	
ECURIE	4/6/16		Dull. A, C and part of Sheervich [?] sent in to ETRUN then morning. B Coy working for Sappers. C.O. ½ Coy working under R.E. at ECURIE.	
	5/6/16		Cold, very quiet. Working as above. Col. Allan sent to 2 Ayrshire during night of suffering from neuritis. Major ... working as above.	
	6/6/16		" "	
	7/6/16		" "	
	8/6/16		Bright, clear. Working as above.	
	9/6/16		" " Relieved the 4 Seaforth at La Saulière this evening. Very quiet during relief.	
La Sablière	10/6/16		Bright, clear. Enemy's artillery very active today. Three 7.7 shells were landed in Chemin. ... Dugout about 5pm badly wounding 2/Lt [?] Sergeant and slightly wounding Lance Cpl [?] William.	

WAR DIARY
or
INTELLIGENCE SUMMARY
(Erase heading not required.)

Army Form C. 2118

Place	Date	Hour	Summary of Events and Information	Remarks and references to Appendices
La Sablière	11/4/16		Dull raining all day. 2/Lt S.C. Kerchin slight shrapnel wound just over the jaw. Apparently bullet wounds through thigh.	
	12/4/16		Enemy here and there active again evening & about noon, troubled in left front line. Inclining too RE's and also enemy evidently the [?] and Duncan in C Coy. the Serjt. RAG killed at night by bullet when just on front trench.	
	13/4/16		Bright very quiet.	
	14/4/16		Dull rainy. Enemy sent over a good deal of heavy shell onto RICINCOURT about 11 am.	
	15/4/16		Dull highly quiet. Relieved by 2 Lingerie this evening and battalion marched back to billets in ETRUN.	
ETRUN	16/4/16		Bright. Cleaning up. Major McClintock took over command this morning.	
	17/4/16		Dull quiet. 145 men employed on various fatigues.	
	18/4/16		Raining. " " " "	
	19/4/16		Dull " " " "	
	20/4/16		Bright clear. 204 men employed on various fatigues and military practice.	

WAR DIARY
or
INTELLIGENCE SUMMARY

(Erase heading not required.)

Army Form C. 2118

Place	Date	Hour	Summary of Events and Information	Remarks and references to Appendices
ETRUN	31/3/18		Very foggy W. wind, German aeroplanes crashed this morning. Relieved 4" Suffolks at La Sablière this evening. Trench very deep.	
La Sablière	1/4/18		Raining all day, very quiet. Trenches in a very bad condition.	
	2/4/18		Bright and dry - very quiet	
	3/4/18		Very bright. Very many enemy 'planes over. Very heavy enemy bombardment shortly with S.O.S. at 8" Stubb between Somewhat "generally heavily with	
	4/4/18		Very bright. Many shells. Much machining. Very bright at 6.45 & 7.30pm on Tyn Ford. to enemy.	
	5/4/18		Very bright moon. Relieved by 4 Suffolks tonight. "C" Coy went forward to ETRUN DG of ABRIS CENTRUE.	
	6/4/18		Relieved 4th High Sts General repeatedly and B. Coy. & Adam.	
ECURIE	7/4/18		...pts at 7 am in area. Training exercises on front of 150m Rifle. Heavy firing for over an hour each night. Very bright quite away daylight	

Army Form C. 2118

WAR DIARY
or
INTELLIGENCE SUMMARY

(Erase heading not required.)

Instructions regarding War Diaries and Intelligence Summaries are contained in F. S. Regs., Part II. and the Staff Manual respectively. Title Pages will be prepared in manuscript.

Place	Date	Hour	Summary of Events and Information	Remarks and references to Appendices
FEURIE	28/4/16		Very bright. Saw a German aeroplane brought down near a ruin. A good deal of heavy fire on either side of our own front.	
	29/4/16		Very bright & warm. Considerable number of small shells & shrapnel landed near Ypres today.	

John Chilcomer Jr.
of Adjutant
& Arthur Drew Hughes

WAR DIARY or INTELLIGENCE SUMMARY

Army Form C. 2118

1/4 Gordon Hrs Vol 15

Place	Date	Hour	Summary of Events and Information	Remarks and references to Appendices
ECURIE	2/5/16		Very bright. At 8.30am shell dropped near Churches ECURIE wounded. At 9.30am shell exploded near Mens R.E.S. Guardroom & number of shell wounded near HQn the forenoon. Lt Guy of A Coy being killed by piece of shrapnel. Was alarm in K2 Sects received at 6.35pm & not nothing developed.	
	2/5/16		Bright nothing to report. Some 5.9 or 8" shell sent across & reconnaissance about 4.30pm, otherwise comparative quiet during the day.	
	3/5/16		Still very quiet. Relieved 4" Seaforth at LA SABLIERE this afternoon. Enemy sent off shelling and mortaring about 6.30pm.	
LA SABLIERE	4/5/16		Bright morning, fairly quiet. Lt A.D. Kyd killed by trench mortar at night.	
	5/5/16		Very warm. Considerable amount of shelling and mortaring overnight, also from 1pm to 5pm. Cpl Balmanno killed by T mortar in afternoon. Ten Heavy shelling and mortaring from 6 to 7pm. Lt Boyne of A Coy killed by T mortar and 2 wounded.	
	6/5/16		Warm. Considerable mortaring from 4am to 9am. 2 men of B Coy wounded. Mortaring more or less whole day.	

WAR DIARY or INTELLIGENCE SUMMARY

Army Form C. 2118

(Erase heading not required.)

Place	Date	Hour	Summary of Events and Information	Remarks and references to Appendices
La Sabrière	7/5/16		Fairly quiet overnight. Good days work mostly raining and shelling during afternoon. Two Church C.S. wounded by shrapnel.	
	8/5/16		Colder this morning and raining heavily for short time.	
	9/5/16		Cold wet. very quiet. Relieved by 2 Seaforths this evening. marched back to Etrouns to billets in ETRUN.	
ETRUN	10/5/16		Warm. Preparing kits, men on various fatigues. Remainder cleaning up.	
	11/5/16		Warm same fatigues. remainder on various	
	12/5/16		" " "	
	13/5/16		Wet	
	14/5/16		Drill - Church Parade	
	15/5/16.		Drill and getting ready for trenches. Relieved 4th Seaforths at La Sabrière this afternoon.	
La Sabrière	16/5/16		Quiet overnight during day. One man slightly wounded by trench mortar last night and one suffering from shell shock	

WAR DIARY or INTELLIGENCE SUMMARY

Army Form C. 2118

(Erase heading not required.)

Instructions regarding War Diaries and Intelligence Summaries are contained in F.S. Regs., Part II. and the Staff Manual respectively. Title Pages will be prepared in manuscript.

Place	Date	Hour	Summary of Events and Information	Remarks and references to Appendices
La Sablière	17/5/16		Bright, warm morning. Hostile artillery fairly active during morning.	
	18/5/16		Warm. Hostile artillery active today. Several small red balloons sent up from Thelus slightly over Frelinveut. No amount of shelling by enemy.	
	19/5/16		Bright, fine. Two men wounded by shell early in morning.	
	20/5/16		Bright, warm. Very quiet.	
	21/5/16		Very quiet. Two Bombers wounded by A. Grenade. Relieved by 4 Suffolks in afternoon. A B C & D Coys returned to ETRUN. D Coy & after operation went out to K ECURIE in afternoon.	
ETRUN	22/5/16		A Coy Coy. went out to K ECURIE. D Coy sent back from ETRUN	
			B Coy left in ETRUN.	
ECURIE	23/5/16		About 3/10/16 A Coy sent to SNKFKRVAD. D Coy from ETRUN to 4 BRI at ABRI MOUTON. B Coy from ETRUN to 4 BRI CENTRALE. C Coy & Schenelisk left in ECURIE.	
	24/5/16		Very quiet. Raining most of day.	

1875 Wt. W593/826 1,000,000 4/15 J.B.C. & A. A.D.S.S./Forms/C. 2118.

Army Form C. 2118

WAR DIARY
or
INTELLIGENCE SUMMARY
(Erase heading not required.)

Place	Date	Hour	Summary of Events and Information	Remarks and references to Appendices
ECURIE	25/5/16		Very quiet. Wiring done round B and XIII M.G. emplacements. Accident at Grenade School (Brigade) one officer killed and four men wounded.	
	26.5.16		Some shelling at Ecoivres camp at 6 am with 4.2". Pte Burr killed and Pte Birch wounded, both of the transport, by accident. The mule pulling the trolley on the XVII Corps line at ST ELOY kicked a dud trench mortar which exploded and caused three casualties. The mule is no more. Quiet day. Some 4.2" Zerwitzer shells landed near H.Q. Visit of	
	27.5.16		Sir Charles Bergne, who had just taken over command of Corps, along with Brig. Gen. Gerrard and G.S.O. 1 51st Divn. Relieved 4th Seaforth Highlanders with our front line allotted with just over the LILLE road. Wiring relief the Hun shelled with H.E. the BARRICADE causing much annoyance but no casualties.	
SABZIERE	28.5.16		Very quiet all day. Our night front line was shelled by eight 4.5" Zerwitzers in the afternoon. At 8.30 p.m. our artillery 6 "Zerwitzers, 4.5" Zerwitzers and 18 pr. carried out a scheme of bombardment of the	
	29.5.16		Hun front and Support lines. The scheme was carried out in three phases of a few minutes each. The fourth phase, which was not on the Artillery schedule was the retaliation on our trenches — the Hun that strafed us most in the scheme. The his "Zerwitzers dropped several shells about 100 feet in and behind our trenches twice.	

WAR DIARY
or
INTELLIGENCE SUMMARY
(Erase heading not required.)

Army Form C. 2118

Instructions regarding War Diaries and Intelligence Summaries are contained in F.S. Regs., Part II. and the Staff Manual respectively. Title Pages will be prepared in manuscript.

Place	Date	Hour	Summary of Events and Information	Remarks and references to Appendices
SABLIERE	30.5.16		Rain at night. About noon several whizz-bangs were sent over H.Q. and during the afternoon a 3" howitzer shell dropped in front of left COLLECTEUR. From 5p.m. to 7p.m. the left front company (B) was heavily bombarded by aerial torpedos fired at a range of 900 yds from the N. side of the LILLE Road. Coy. S.M. Italie was killed by one of these trench mortars. Our snipers located the position of the mortar and our 4.5" howitzer fired 54 rounds at it. This stopped its firing for some time.	
	31.5.16		Aerial torpedos started again at 6 a.m. and during the morning our 4.5" howitzers and 18" Somnien threw on them the latter scoring three direct hits which stopped the nuisance.	

Capt.
Revr. Hughes
101st Bn. Can. Grenr. Highrs.
2/0cy.

WAR DIARY or INTELLIGENCE SUMMARY

Army Form C. 2118

1/4 Gordon HH Vol 16

Place	Date	Hour	Summary of Events and Information	Remarks and references to Appendices
LA SABLIERE	1/6/16		Our 8" Hows fired 20 rounds at 7.M. emplacement causing 2 mortar to cease fire. Considerable hostile T.M. activity during afternoon. L/Cpl Sharp M. Innes Osborn killed by T.M. bomb.	
	2/6/16		Enemy trench mortars	
	3/6/16		Hostile large T. mortar fired a few rounds but ceased on retaliation by our 18 Pdrs. Reference to 4 trench mortar batteries in ECRPN.	
ET RUN	4/6/16		Night cleaning up	
	5/6/16			
	6/6/16		Nowt [?] trouble and fatigues	
	7/6/16			
	8/6/16			
La Sabliere	9/6/16		Relieved 4" Seaforths in trenches this afternoon. Several trench mortar bombs fell in L22 about 5 pm killing Sgt Donnell (sniper), Sgt McNeill 'C' Co, Pte Brown (M. Gun) and wounding Sgt Pearson + men of E Coy and 1 man of M. Guns. Pte A. Morrison ale Seaforth wounded and 3 men of 'C' Coy suffering from shell shock	

Army Form C. 2118.

WAR DIARY
or
INTELLIGENCE SUMMARY.
(Erase heading not required.)

Instructions regarding War Diaries and Intelligence Summaries are contained in F. S. Regs., Part II. and the Staff Manual respectively. Title pages will be prepared in manuscript.

Place	Date	Hour	Summary of Events and Information	Remarks and references to Appendices
La Sabliere	10/9/16		Fairly quiet. Head form to C.C.T. this morning, food sent this afternoon and mustards in evening.	
	11/9/16		Sent early tent fatigue out, good deal of shelling & machining from 2 to 3 p.m.	
	12/9/16		Quiet. Raining most of day	
	13/9/16		Wet period. Quiet. Lot of machining at night.	
	14/9/16		Dull and Quiet. Had tent forward and hour at 11 a.m.	
	15/9/16		Still quiet. Relieved by 4 Tenforth afternoon. A Coy to Dunk Road. B Coy to Abri Central. D Coy to Abri reproduction and C & S Coy. to ECURIE.	
ECURIE	16/9/16 17/9/16 18/9/16 19/9/16 20/9/16 21/9/16		Coys. Working under RE and supplying various fatigues	
	22/9/16		Took over trenches L¹ from 4 Tenforth this afternoon. Quiet at night	

Army Form C. 2118.

WAR DIARY
or
INTELLIGENCE SUMMARY.
(Erase heading not required.)

Place	Date	Hour	Summary of Events and Information	Remarks and references to Appendices
Fallière	22/9/16		Fallincourt bombardment opened about 3 am and turned fiercer about 5/6 hour. There appeared places with explosions every 3/5 minute experienced that 2 men had been hit amongst carrying station (one man belonging to 2 Suffolk and an R.E.)	
	23/9/16		Left Support line. Shells went 5.9 from 6.20 to 8.30 pm. Our duty with them blown in but and went out all night. Oldhampton officers. And also thrown right the two officers got out at night. Enemy recommenced shelling with s.g at 11.45 am. Some of the shells landing very near our dug Sgt Hilliard Stapleford exploded almost at the feet of the mortar sentry especially wounding him and damaging mess of the waiter branch	
	24/9/16		Only morning. Heavy bombardment heard in the South	
	25/9/16		A Contested scheme with our artillery and T.M.ors commenced today at noon and is to be carried on for 4 days	
	26/9/16		Our bombardment still continuing at regular hours throughout day & night off ? Men are beginning to show	

Army Form C. 2118.

WAR DIARY
or
INTELLIGENCE SUMMARY.
(Erase heading not required.)

Instructions regarding War Diaries and Intelligence Summaries are contained in F.S. Regs., Part II. and the Staff Manual respectively. Title pages will be prepared in manuscript.

Place	Date	Hour	Summary of Events and Information	Remarks and references to Appendices
Lafeyfun Ridge	27/6/16		Regt. of enemy of new army seen with strong rifle shots. Are likely the only troops on the line in front line.	
	28/6/16		Scheme had continuing, but not for Phase afternoon was cancelled at last minute then afternoon. On the whole the raiders by enemy own very slight. We had only 1 killed & 1 wounded. Br. should have been returned & they, but ashy was too quick till today as I am satisfied that enemy might know of any arrangements for any Bn. from a clear field by a man (or Bn. on our left) who were captured the day before. Relieved by 4 Sanforth this evening and Bn. marched back to Billets in ETRUN	
Etrun	29/6/16		Cleaning up & ca.	
	30/6/16		Warm parade fatigue.	JC Wyman Lt Col Ath R.M. Ford'm Highles

154th Brigade.
51st Division.

1/4th BATTALION

THE GORDON HIGHLANDERS

JJLY 1 9 1 6

Vol

1/4th Battalion The Gordon Highrs.

Volume No 17

WAR DIARY

From 1-7-16
To 31-7-16

4 Batt/ London Regt

WAR DIARY
INTELLIGENCE SUMMARY.

Army Form C. 2118.

Place	Date	Hour	Summary of Events and Information	Remarks and references to Appendices
Etrunyes	1/9/16		Usual Parades and fatigues.	
"	2/9/16			
"	3/9/16		Paraded afternoon and returned to Enforth in trucks in course of evening. Found 2 Coys of 2/21st London Regt. in for instruction. Very quiet.	
"	4/9/16			
La Sablière	5/9/16		Very quiet still	
"	6/9/16		Raining heavily. Front trenches very wet do. with several having standing about 2 feet of water in front trenches and deep mud not improving.	
"	7/9/16		Shortening in front trench to 9" round. 2/13" London Regt relieved the Coys in front to 2nd Coys to trenches here, one Coy to A.B.C.D. E got today and 2nd Coy to MORTON. Centrale and , Coy to MORTON.	
"	8/9/16		Bright warm today. Trenches improving.	
"	9/9/16		Hostile artillery more in evidence today. B. S. Bomb burst tremendously at West[?] gun tonight injuring the Cullin alr Sgt Young (1/13 London) slightly and severely wounding 1 Sgt Horner.	
"	10/9/16		Quiet today. Relieved by 4th Linforth in afternoon + marched by platoons to new billets in MARUEUIL.	

WAR DIARY
or
INTELLIGENCE SUMMARY

(Erase heading not required.)

Army Form C. 2118.

4 Batt Northn Hghrs

Place	Date	Hour	Summary of Events and Information	Remarks and references to Appendices
MARDEUIL	12/9/14		Cleaning up and doing various fatigues for Brigade & getting ready for a move.	
	13/9/14		Left MARDEUIL by Platoons at 9 am and formed up as a Battalion on Ep Pk – Road near HAUTE AVESNES. Left this point at 11.15 am and marched to VILLERS BRULIN arriving there about 1.30 pm Rested during afternoon (A & B Coys got rum & jam of agjoining village. (GUEST REVILLE) Received orders at 6 pm that Brigade would move at 8 am tomorrow in motor lorries and that officers kits had to be reduced to 35 lbs weight that kit so had to be disposed of at our OMC till supplies kit & co. Packed up and got ready to move.	
VILLERS BRULIN	14/9/14		Cleaning up	
	15/9/14		At 2 am received orders to be at a point overmain road near TINCQUES at 3.30 am Sounded reveille at one and got breakfast marched off at 3.30 am Reached assembling point at 5 am – in friends of time Entrained men in motor lorries (25 ea end) – about for an hour and then left about 6 am and reached IVERGNY about 8.30 am. Resting during afternoon.	

4 Batt Gordon Highrs

Army Form C. 2118

WAR DIARY
or
~~INTELLIGENCE SUMMARY~~

(Erase heading not required.)

Place	Date	Hour	Summary of Events and Information	Remarks and references to Appendices
IVERGNY	16/9/16	7.30 am	Got orders at 4 am to trek to BOCQUEMAISON at 7.30 am. Had breakfast and marched off at 6.15 am from Bocquemaison marched to BERNAVILLE reaching there about 1.30 am. Men very tired and many cases of bad feet. Resting during afternoon.	
BERNAVILLE	17/9/16		Route march of about ½ mile during forenoon. Good number of men fell out with bad feet.	
do	18/9/16		Company route marches during forenoon and drill in afternoon. Men's feet improving.	
do	19/9/16		Route march during forenoon and drill so during afternoon. Men's feet almost all right again. Transport to move received at 6 p.m. Transport left at 8 pm. Later ready to move received at ... orders received to move off at 1.30 am. Reveille about 12pm midnight.	
			CANDAS	
do	20/9/16		Left BERNAVILLE at 1.30 am and marched to ~~Berry~~ when informed about 5 am. Reached MERICOURT at 8 am. Detrained there water on roadside for an hour and then marched to BECOURT, reaching there about 1 pm. Men had had breakfast and in bivouacs. Transport arrived about 5 pm.	

WAR DIARY or INTELLIGENCE SUMMARY

Army Form C. 2118

(Erase heading not required.)

Place	Date	Hour	Summary of Events and Information	Remarks and references to Appendices
BECOURT	2/9/16		Men resting and cleaning. At 8 p.m. received orders that Battn had to proceed to Trenches taking only 20 Officers. Marched off at that hour by Coys through BECOURT and past MAMETZ WOOD and to HIGH WOOD, where we took over trenches from W. KENTS. Guides were waiting at edge of MAMETZ WOOD. From there to Trenches Battn had to walk through a communal and heavy barrage of artillery fire. The last Coy (A) had to walk thro' a barrage of tear shells and have put on 9/11/3 Coy can to trenches, be casualties on way up to Trenches. There were on S.E. edge of HIGH WOOD. D Coy in touch on S.W. of wood, and C. Coy in trench running through cover end of wood. B Coy in edge of E. A. C. chains to dig trench 150 yds to rear	
HIGH WOOD	3/9/16		3.30 a.m. when our artillery commenced orders till about 7 a.m. Enemy at once replied on our trenches to shell wood heavily. Capt Reid with Byrne slightly wynd and with H.3 shells. C.O. were sent for by the Brigadier and were informed that the Battn had to try and take enemy trench in front of HIGH WOOD at night. A Good deal of telling throughout the day. Our artillery commenced shelling of the enemy at 4 p.m. and at 10.30 p.m. B.C. made a small attack on enemy trench on right of	

WAR DIARY

Army Form C. 2118

INTELLIGENCE SUMMARY

Place	Date	Hour	Summary of Events and Information	Remarks and references to Appendices
HIGH WOOD	2/9/16		HIGH WOOD attack failed.	
	3/9/16		At 12.30 am an attack was made by Division on our left at 1.30 am our artillery suffered and our attack advanced in lines of Coy. C. Coy. leading. An attack was made in front of German trench and the attack failed. It was found fire trench and the supports strong front was empty shell holes that in a few minutes (C) Co suffered up with shell holes more or less but no Coy all sense of direction was lost and trench or S.W. was reformed and the trench in map of Bath Jeanville + S.E. sides occupied by what was left 250 YR was heard to be firing and about 12 officers and about 250 YR ran to previous afternoon our Coy. to Support Key then sent up to support us and at midnight another Coy came up.	
			From 6 am to 7.30 am our own artillery turned a considerable number of shells in and around trench on SE edge of High Wood causing about 30 casualties to 4th Gordons and to our T.G. team there. In evening we received orders that we were to changeover to support trenches nr BAZENTIN G GRAND and at 11 pm we were relieved by 4th Seaforths and marched back by Coy to	

WAR DIARY or INTELLIGENCE SUMMARY

(Erase heading not required.)

Army Form C. 2118

1st Batt Gordon Highlanders

Place	Date	Hour	Summary of Events and Information	Remarks and references to Appendices
Support trenches	13/7/16		Support trenches. The augment of my Shylew their got returns from front about midnight	
Support trenches BAZENTIN LE GRAND	14/7/16		Quiet during day. Enemy during evening began burning trenches. Sentry at our back of their trenches found front to them about 2 pm. C.O. to Brig. afternoon. (phoned) Brought from Bell and 4 sections of enemy was leaving trenches and moving on Euforche. That enemy was leaving trenches and moving on within side of HIGH WOOD. At 8.35 pm our artillery and M. Guns opened on HIGH WOOD. At this time our artillery and M. Guns stopped & heavy Turk of German line and Church afterwards enemy barrage opened between High Wood & Support line. This continued till 9 pm. Every one standing to.	
	15/7/16		At 1 am B Coy was sent up to support or reinforce at Euforche. At 2.30 am sent 5.10 & 3.0 in support of reinforce. At 2.30 am sent Bell order D Co was sent out to dig new trench across about 100 yds S. of & after of HIGH WOOD. D Coy returned about 10 am having completed work at 1 am. C.O. was sent out to reconnoitre south of High Wood. Henry Shilling by recall artillery during afternoon recon had to shift often along to right of trench.	
	16/7/16		Sent off A Coy at 1 am to support & Euforche - only D Co	

WAR DIARY or INTELLIGENCE SUMMARY

Army Form C. 2118

(Erase heading not required.)

Place	Date	Hour	Summary of Events and Information	Remarks and references to Appendices
Support Trench	10/7/16		Only D Coy left in support trench. D & B Coys returned about 5 pm to S system and marched back to Bivouac at BECORDEL arriving about 8 pm, got things together without any casualties. Found draft of 80 NCO's had arrived. A.C. Coys were relieved at HIGH WOOD about 9 pm and marched to bivouac after midnight. All very tired. That favourites apart and sniping officers. 13th OR Batt at	
BECORDEL	11/7/16		Cleaning up and making deficiencies	
			MEAULTE	
	12/7/16		Cleaning up and recurring deficiencies	
	13/7/16		Very warm. Short parade for physical drill and bayonet fighting. Draft of 20 men arrived 11 pm.	
	30/7/16		Very warm. Church service 10.20 am.	
	31/7/16		Very warm. Short parade in forenoon.	
			Still very warm.	
			Men at bath again.	
Casualties	21/7/16 July			
Officers	Missing 2			
Killed 2	Wounded 9	O.R.		
Wounded 9		Killed 37 Wounded 214		
Missing 1		Died of Wounds 1 Missing 59		
		Wounded to Bn 1 Missing 2	314	

J.G. Thomson Lt Col
t BnM Order Wylie

154th Brigade.
51st Division

1/4th BATTALION

GORDON HIGHLANDERS

AUGUST 1 9 1 6

WAR DIARY or INTELLIGENCE SUMMARY

Army Form C. 2118

No 21 (A) DIVISION

674

Place	Date	Hour	Summary of Events and Information	Remarks and references to Appendices
BECOURT BECORDEL	1/8/16		Still in bivouac. Only 1 tent left for O/R men. All officers men in bivouac - very warm. Supplying 430 men daily on fatigues at Dug outs and DIV. REAR H.Q.R.	
	2/8/16 3/8/16 4/8/16		Very warm. 430 O/R on fatigue daily	
	5/8/16		Very warm. Usual fatigues. Whilst D Coy's fatigue party was covering railway near TRICOURT on way to fatigue a shell landed between No. 15 & 16 Platoon injuring L/Sgt J. M. KYNOCH killing 5 O/R wounding 28 O/R of which one died of wounds in ambulance, and slightly wounding 9 O/R, a total of 46 casualties with the one shell in D Coy.	
	6/8/16		Batt. left Bivouac at 12 noon and marched via DERNANCOURT to field at D.18.2. Arrived there at 2 pm and pitched Bivouacs. 15 tents handed over to Batt by the Brigade. Very warm.	

WAR DIARY or INTELLIGENCE SUMMARY

1st Batt Gordon Highrs

Army Form C. 2118

672

Place	Date	Hour	Summary of Events and Information	Remarks and references to Appendices
D18Z	7/8/16		Very warm. Parades in forenoon and men marched to near DERNANCOURT in afternoon to wash.	
	8/8/16		Very warm. Transport left this afternoon at 2 pm, everything sent with transport except Pack Gear, Hand cart, leaving only what could be carried in pack.	
	9/8/16		Reveille 4 am. Batt funded at 6 am and marched to MERICOURT Station where entrained. Very warm. Arrived LONGPRE 12.20 pm detrained there and marched off to BAILLEUL (13 kilos) at 12.30 pm. Exceedingly warm and some men began to fall out. Reached BAILLEUL at 4.30pm. 55 men fell out. Found only an open field for men but in an hour had had arranged Barns for nearly the whole Battalion. All men who had fallen out reported in course of the evening. Transport arrived at 10pm.	
BAILLEUL	10/8/16		Cooler and raining slightly. Men resting and bathing feet. Capt Otto, 2 officers & 100 men from A Co. and billeting	

Army Form C. 2118

2 Batt Gordon Highrs

WAR DIARY
or
INTELLIGENCE SUMMARY

(Erase heading not required.)

Instructions regarding War Diaries and Intelligence Summaries are contained in F.S. Regs., Part II. and the Staff Manual respectively. Title Pages will be prepared in manuscript.

673

Place	Date	Hour	Summary of Events and Information	Remarks and references to Appendices
BAILLEUL	10/8/15		Party left at 11 p.m. for PONT REMY Station to entrain there for STEENBECQUE	
BAILLEUL	11/8/15		Transport left at 6.15 am and Batt. at 8 am for PONT REMY Station when when entraining left there 11 am and reached STEENBECQUE station at 8.30 pm detrained there and marched to WALLON CAPPEL reaching there at 10.15 pm took over billets there, most of the Batt. being under cover.	
WALLON CAPPEL	12/8/15		Warm. Men cleaning up.	
	13/8/15		Joint Church service with 7th & 9th H.L.I. in forenoon. CO and small reconnoitring party went up to the trenches near ARMENTIERES.	
	14/8/15		Transport left at 5 am to travel by road to ARMENTIERES. Batt. paraded at 10 am marched to EBBLINGHEM Station entrained there at 12.20 pm and arrived STEENWERCK Station at 1.45 pm. From there marched to ARMENTIERES arriving there about 4.30 pm. Transport arrived	

WAR DIARY or INTELLIGENCE SUMMARY

Army Form C. 2118

1 Batt Gordon High[landers]

674x

Place	Date	Hour	Summary of Events and Information	Remarks and references to Appendices
Sass	4/8/16		Church afternoon. Took over billets in one large building. Billets taken over from 3rd Battn of 3rd Bde of N.Z. Div.	
ARMENTIERES	15/8/16		Cooks this morning. C.O. officers and NCO from each Coy proceeded to tender this morning as a preventitive party. Town shelled about 6 km. about 30/35 casualties civilians. Snipers went up to the advanced other Battns. In afternoon the Signallers and running grooms trenches. C Coy went up at 6 km. Rest of 13 attatchm from each Coy. At 10:30 pm marched off to platoons stood over paraded at 10:30 pm in supporting line from Coy. B at 11pm 1st N.Z. Bde at 11:30 pm. Very quiet. 4 Infantry holding the front line which is about 1500 yds from our trenches our platoon holds a strong point from Rydal Redoubt one of our platoons holds a strong point from Rydal Redoubt one Coy in reserve other, my right, mentioned Batth and another under left Batth. both for work and in case of attack.	
Saturday	16/8/16		Not a single shell. Trenches in good order.	
Lina	17/8/16		Quiet a few light shell landed behind the line near house in chapelle somewhere, one man of C Coy killed and another wounded by mortar bomb. Interior wiring in between the lines. Brothers Farm strong point taken over.	

1 Batt Gordon Highrs

Army Form C. 2118

WAR DIARY
or
INTELLIGENCE SUMMARY

(Erase heading not required.)

Place	Date	Hour	Summary of Events and Information	Remarks and references to Appendices
Intgydiem Line	18/8/16		Patrols last night reported all quiet. Heavy rain at night	
	19/8/16		Quiet. Good weather. Slight shelling of village	
	20/8/16		As movement of civilian noticed in PERENCHIES. Searchlight turned on our towards from direction of WEZ MACQUART.	
8th	21/8/16		Relieved by 1 Seaforth in front line. Heavy shelling at nyt. One man wounded slightly.	
No 13 Tunnellers	22/8/16		Weather good. Situation quiet. Formidable went for gas, and Welsh buried in alert position.	
Res.	23/8/16		Neither very quiet. Aeroplanes shelled. Aeroplanes off at 5 am a shell from sh.nr battery (A112 mm ?) cater. Road immediately over our MG and expended our territory Sgt.	
Res	24/5/16		Mushroom. Artillery active on both sides about 8 am one of our aeroplanes was brought down just behind support line of Battn on right.	
Res	25/8/16		Artillery active on both sides. Good deal of trench mortaring both sides also.	
Res	26/8/16		Both Alys. of Shells ammunition shelled about 10 am and again in afternoon — my minenwerfer. Relieved in afternoon by 6 Seaforths. Batt. left trenches by march - thence to NIEPPE where we		65/4

WAR DIARY
or
INTELLIGENCE SUMMARY
(Erase heading not required.)

Army Form C. 2118

676+

Place	Date	Hour	Summary of Events and Information	Remarks and references to Appendices
	26/8/16		Companies reformed and thereafter marched to Training Camp 1 mile S.E. of BAILLEUL. Bath parties then to 11 p.m. Good Camp and french tents	
BAILLEUL	27/8/16 Sun		Church Service in forenoon. Men employed in cleaning kit, equipment, inspections.	
	28/8/16		Company parades &c. Rehearsal of Brigade parade for H.R.H. the Prince of Wales attd. for inspection of incoming of Divisions. Sent details for 5'6, 7' form allotted to divisional Band. Rain nearly all day.	
	29/8/16		Physical drill in morning. Parade of Brigade at 11 a.m. for inspection by General PLUMER. 11 a.m. Marched past Minister is coming. 3 mile march to Bath parades in afternoon. Rainy rain heavy after 2 p.m. Parades in evening.	
	30/8/16		Physical drill in morning. A.B.C. Coys marched to STEENWERCK the Baths. D.G. Coys went for route march. Very heavy rain from mid on onwards.	

Army Form C. 2118

1st Batt Gordon Highrs

WAR DIARY
or
INTELLIGENCE SUMMARY

(Erase heading not required.)

Instructions regarding War Diaries and Intelligence Summaries are contained in F. S. Regs., Part II. and the Staff Manual respectively. Title Pages will be prepared in manuscript.

Place	Date	Hour	Summary of Events and Information	Remarks and references to Appendices
nr BAILLEUL	21/8/16		Dry today and warmer. Regiment spent in the morning in Company training in bayonet work afternoon. Brigade mounted sports & other afternoon.	

JCMorrison
Lt Adjutant
1st Batt Gordon Highrs

SPMacDonald LtCol
O.C. 1/1st Gordon Highrs

6787
SB

1/4 1st Battalion London Regiment

VOL 19

Volume 20

War Diary

D/Headquarters 1st Inf Bgde

September 1-30 1916

6794
SB

1/10/16

No 20 VOLUME. 4 The Gordon High[landers] Army Form C. 2118

WAR DIARY
or
INTELLIGENCE SUMMARY
(Erase heading not required.)

6804

Place	Date	Hour	Summary of Events and Information	Remarks and references to Appendices
BAILLEUL	1/9/16		Bn today. Various Company parades during day.	
	2/9/16		Bn moved Bath. Bn arranged for this afternoon but orders received from Brigade to move in afternoon. Bn moved off by (6d.S.L.) Companies at ½ ʰᵒᵘʳ and marched to SOYER FARM area (6d.S.L.) Headquarters to Coy there. A Coy in billeting points. B & C Coy in from and D at THIEUZ all quite close to SOYER FME. About 8 ᵖᵐ received gas alert message at 11.15 ᵖᵐ a S.O.S. gas message was received and stand to. They were heard of our left. All ranks went at once awakened and stand to by wh gas helmets ready to put on. No gas could be smelt and a bit later message was received from Bde that alarm was off. Although Church services held in afternoon. D Coy took over trty train at GUNNERS FME and MAISON 1675 from 10ᵗʰ N Fus., and A Coy took over PATERNOSTER ROW and FUSILIER TCE from some Coy. Battn. Very quiet during day and night	
SOYER FARM	3/9/16		Bn today. Hdqr. S Coy B & C Coy drilling in small parties near BILLET	
	4/9/16		Wet today. B Coy find 2 parties of 44 working or NICHOLSON trench at GUNNERS FME. Balance of B C & S Coys drilling in Avenue trench. 1 MO men to Bath. at PONT NIEPPE	

WAR DIARY or INTELLIGENCE SUMMARY

Army Form C. 2118

4th Battalion Royal Welsh Fusiliers

Place	Date	Hour	Summary of Events and Information	Remarks and references to Appendices
SOYER FARM	6/9/16	Dry	Same parties from B Coy working on NICHOLSON AVENUE and 2 parties of 10 men C. Coy working on BURDER AV. also party of 10 men from C. Coy carrying T.M. Bombs. 100 men to Bath at POINT NEPTUNE Bathing. Coys carrying on usual Coy Officers & NCO's drill overnight. Same working parties from B & C Coy	687
	7/9/16	Dry warm	In addition 'S' Coy sent a working party of 10 to report to RE Officers at junction from C.O. went to Turmothy re making over shortly to him. 153rd Bn. which will recomplete left of their held to 153rd Bn. The C.O. and Coy Officer of 9th Royal Welsh Fusiliers sire this morning re complimentary those company they are to take over from our companies. Major Morgan also are tonight into over from us tomorrow.	
	8/9/16	Dry warm	Relieved by 9th Royal Welsh Fusiliers. Bath. marched by Steenwerck to billets in ARMENTIERES previously occupied this. All in by 7 pm. Men allowed out on leave during afternoon evening.	
ARMENTIERES	9/9/16	Dry warm	Bath relieved 6th Black Watch in Trenches	

WAR DIARY or INTELLIGENCE SUMMARY

4th Bn Norfolk Regt Army Form C. 2118

682X

Place	Date	Hour	Summary of Events and Information	Remarks and references to Appendices
Trenches S4&9	Feb		S4&9 in afternoon. A small mine was exploded by our mines under our own in front of enemy trench opposite our trench S8 at 5.30pm. At same time our artillery bombarded enemy trenches in vicinity for a few minutes. Four of our mines fell but landing in my trench just doing no damage. Enemy did not reply. Later on enemy sent over about ten 7" Mortar bombs nr HOBBS FARM.	
	Feb 10/9/16		Warm very quiet. Traffic stopped in various trenches from 8am to 5pm and again from 8pm till midnight whilst empty gas cylinders were being removed.	
	Feb 11/9/16		Very quiet. A Right of C. Coy shot through to head by an enemy sniper this forenoon. At 7.30pm enemy sent across 3 large T.M. bombs which landed near old Coy H.Qrs. of C. Coy in CAMBRIDGE AVENUE. One of the bombs landed right on the top of a shelter there killing Pte WISELY and L/C KING and 2 other ranks of C. Coy. Some more T.M. Bombs overnight otherwise quiet.	

WAR DIARY
INTELLIGENCE SUMMARY
(Erase heading not required.)

F Bull/Worker 7th Bn Fus
Army Form C. 2118

6834

Place	Date	Hour	Summary of Events and Information	Remarks and references to Appendices
Trenches Sept '09	11/9/16		Quiet. A few T.Mortar Bombs landed near top of Cambridge Avenue during evening.	
	13/9/16		Quiet not today. Tarzans shoot by Artillery + T.M. of own division on enemy's line in front of right Batt and our front. Enemy sent over at intervals number of T.M. Bombs in the course of the day damaging trenches & the craters of four Scotts. Gas cylinders brought up tonight.	
	14/9/16		Cooler today. About 9.30 am several hr. shells fell in the vicinity of Bn HQrs. The Subaltern of "A" Coy on his way to Orderly room killed, the Brigadier Liaison rad in front of HQrs hit by same shell and one man severely injured, two slightly wounded. Quiet rest of day.	
	15/9/16		Relieved this forenoon by 4 Camerons B-D Coy billets in HOOPLINES, remainder in factory in ARMENTIERES. Bn HQ at 7 Rue de Lesack ARMENTIERES.	

Army Form C. 2118

WAR DIARY or INTELLIGENCE SUMMARY

& Staff Work of 2nd Wimborne Regt

(Erase heading not required.)

684x

Place	Date	Hour	Summary of Events and Information	Remarks and references to Appendices
ARMENTIERES	16/9/16		Cleaning of 400 men sent to help at PONT NIEPPE. Rest of Bn. Trophinists carried attended functioning.	
	17/9/16		Church services by General. Touching receipts for Trophinists & Officers. 2nd MR employed in carrying gas cylinders to front line during the night.	
	18/9/16		Very wet. Balance of Bn. at Sets this forenoon. Carrying on with fisches of Sor Highlands. 230 OR employed or various RE fatigues & Skill wk. Enemy'sworks with some fatigues. L. addition 100 men worked at 6.30pm to carry T.M. Bombs up to trenches.	
	19/9/16		Not well. About 200 OR sent to Baths today. Morning open recurring that Bde is to be relieved on 22nd by 8th Aust. Infantry Bde.	
	20/9/16		Chill cold. Met open order received that Baths in the Battn. of 8th Infantry Bde. relieved tomorrow by Baths. of 8 Infantry Bde.	

4 Bn Wilshire Regt

Army Form C. 2118

WAR DIARY
or
INTELLIGENCE SUMMARY
(Erase heading not required.)

Instructions regarding War Diaries and Intelligence Summaries are contained in F.S. Regs., Part II. and the Staff Manual respectively. Title Pages will be prepared in manuscript.

Place	Date	Hour	Summary of Events and Information	Remarks and references to Appendices
ARMENTIERES	27/9/16		Relieved by 29th Inf Batt A.I.F. This forenoon and marched by Platoons to FORT ROMPU to billets there	
FORT ROMPU	28/9/16		Morn Physical and attack of the Coy marches to ARMENTIERES this forenoon to test the Footprints of B Coy at Batt at PONT NIEPPE. Parade in forenoon afternoon.	
	29/9/16		Church service in forenoon. Drill for b[attalion] & Coy and short route march in afternoon. Brigadier saw all the officers in forenoon.	
	30/9/16		Left FORT ROMPU this morning at 9.15 and marched with rest of Brigade to billets in ESTAIRES. Then mostly in old houses and lofts - officers all in houses.	
ESTAIRES	1/10/16		Brigade went for route march to NEUF BERQUIN this forenoon and were inspected by Army Commander (Gen. Munro) on route. Coy parade in afternoon.	6854

1875 W¹. W593/826 1,000,000 4/15 I.B.C. & A. A.D.S.S./Forms/C.2118.

Army Form C. 2118

4 R[oyal] Ir[ish] Fus[iliers]

WAR DIARY
or
INTELLIGENCE SUMMARY
(Erase heading not required.)

Place	Date	Hour	Summary of Events and Information	Remarks and references to Appendices
ESTAIRES	27/9/16		By turns in forenoon & afternoon. 2 officers & 200 men took part in scheme with contact aeroplane this afternoon - practicing sending & receiving messages to & from M.G. by aeroplane working very well. The rendezvous and whole scheme worked very well. 2 Cpls & 26 N.C.O.s proceeded to ABBEVILLE to join 5th Battalion party.	686x
			D. Coy RT. ZN PLINTHEV adjn. 66 arrived adjn.	
ESTAIRES	28/9/16		Drill today but warm. Coys paraded in forenoon & for route march in afternoon.	
	29/9/16		Bn. Coy organised in forenoon much marched. In afternoon new regimental arms dealt, were tested with new regimental today. Lt Col McClintock Last night and early day went to ambulance together and for last 2 days infection improved entraining at BAILLEUL this afternoon. Regt infect[ion] improved at	
	30/9/16		Short march in forenoon. Bn. rec[eived] orders to left Rest at 5 pm for MERVILLE in afternoon & both entrained at MERVILLE about 7 pm.	

[signed] Lt Col Comm[an]d[in]g 4 R[oyal] Ir[ish] Fus[iliers]

CONFIDENTIAL
No 21/A
HIGHLAND
DIVISION.

1/4th Battalion The Gordon Highlanders

Vol 20
Volume 21

War Diary

October 1916

To Headquarters
153rd Inf Brigade
1/11/16

No 21 Volume   4 Batt Forder Highrs

Army Form C. 2118

WAR DIARY
or
INTELLIGENCE SUMMARY
(Erase heading not required.)

Place	Date	Hour	Summary of Events and Information	Remarks and references to Appendices
AUTHEUX	1/10/15		Reached CANDAS Station at 1.10 am marched off alongside transport at that hour. Arrived at AUTHEUX at 5 am. Billets to men only two; empty old farm and houses. Men given tea and sent to bed. 10:30 am Cleaning up. aft. got inspection in afternoon. Physical drill in afternoon.	
	2/10/15		Not today. Short parade still in forenoon. Lecture in afternoon. Received orders from Bde at midnight that we were to move to SARTON from C/D early 3am	
	3/10/15		Very wet. Battalion marched off at 5.15 am. met 7th Argl. Highrs at TIENVILLERS and marched behind them to SARTON via CANDAS 9th R Scots & 4 Tenyths joined at CANDAS. The whole Bde marched as a Brigade to SARTON. 2nd Line transport was brigaded at CANDAS. Reached SARTON at 2 p.m. Men billeted very comfy and very crowded.	
SARTON	4/10/15		Battalion marched off at 11.25 am. Mh Hqs & 1 Ble at THIEVRES and therefore marched to Brigade to BUS LES ARTOIS. Road very wet and heavy.	

WAR DIARY
or
INTELLIGENCE SUMMARY
(Erase heading not required.)

Army Form C. 2118

4 Batt/Gordon Highrs

Place	Date	Hour	Summary of Events and Information	Remarks and references to Appendices
	4/10/16		Reached BUS LES ARTOIS about 2 p.m. Billets again very poor, only one billet available for C.O.; arrived all of this afternoon; ultimately got most of them into the School room.	
BUS LES ARTOIS	5/10/16		Dry this morning. Officers voyage sent up to work near HEBUTERNE at 9 a.m. Rest of Batt. on fatigue under Bay. engagements during forenoon and for 1 hour in afternoon.	
	6/10/16		Received orders at 11 a.m. that Batt. had to move to COURCELLES by 3 p.m. Billeting party sent in forenoon. Batt. arrived in COURCELLES at 3 p.m. Billets for men fairly good. Most of Batt. out working in trenches near HEBUTERNE over night.	
COURCELLES	7/10/16		Very wet. 5/9 Yrs on fatigue. Co. ore Coys went up to our line occupied by 6 & 7 a.t.s. H. which Batt. take over tomorrow.	
	8/10/16		Still wet. Had dinner at noon marched off by Platoons commencing at 1.30 p.m. Relief completed by 5.30 p.m. Trenches K.19.d & 15 Coy in front D Coy in support. A.Y.C.G. back in Fort Gr???venor K.H O.7.6.	

Army Form C. 2118

1 Bedfordshire Regt

WAR DIARY
or
INTELLIGENCE SUMMARY

(Erase heading not required.)

Instructions regarding War Diaries and Intelligence Summaries are contained in F.S. Regs., Part II. and the Staff Manual respectively. Title Pages will be prepared in manuscript.

Place	Date	Hour	Summary of Events and Information	Remarks and references to Appendices
Trenches	8/10/16		Night quiet, working parties from A Co. 90 men from D Co. working in front line & new trench.	
In the trenches	9/10/16		Dull. Enemy quiet. Our artillery registering.	
	10/10/16		Dull. I am still to am enemy sent over a contact. Steam of gas shell in direction of Battery in K 20 TK27. Our artillery active during day. Enemy quiet. D Coy changed over with B Coy.	
	11/10/16		From midnight till I am got chilly again sent over by enemy about some direction — last night. Our artillery very active during day. A raid was arranged for tonight under 2/Lt Henderson & 2/Lt J.R. Anderson but owing to the bright moonlight had to be postponed, as hopefully could not be placed in position, smaller enemy was.	
	12/10/16		Dull cold. Were instructed to carry out a smoke barrage commencing at 2.30am but a smoke bomb only commenced to arrive at 3am we could not proceed without part of the programme. Our artillery shelled enemy's wire from now to about 3am. and smoke was let off on battalion on both our flanks. Very little retaliation by enemy. Were relieved	

1875. Wt. W593/826 1,000,000 4/15 J.B.C. & A. A.D.S.S./Forms/C. 2118.

4 Batt Gordon Highrs
Army Form C. 2118

WAR DIARY
or
INTELLIGENCE SUMMARY
(Erase heading not required.)

Place	Date	Hour	Summary of Events and Information	Remarks and references to Appendices
	11/7/16		6th Black Watch (sic) BHQ conveying at 490 tr "B" finishing at 7am. Marched back by platoons to bivouacs in trenches COLINCAMPS. 390 O.R. out on various fatigues in trenches during most of night.	
COLINCAMPS	13/7/16		Day open rather sunny. Forenoon who had been out till early morning. Remainder digging trenches near bivouacs. Back and carrying ammunition. Stone for bivouacs too. Men out tonight carrying bombs. Made another attempt at sent movement on it aid but enemy to alert in observing totals what tanks force and to move the enemy working parties, the send had again to be postponed. Whole Battn on fatigue at night carrying ammunition stores to dumps in trenches.	
	14/7/16		Dry cold. Whole Battn again detailed for carrying fatigue tonight again. As we are not engaged by Div. that carrying party was not all the Bombs and equipment was instructed that all the Bombs and empty back from dumps Bomb Bucket has to be brought back from dumps	

WAR DIARY or INTELLIGENCE SUMMARY

Army Form C. 2118.

4 South Regt.

Place	Date	Hour	Summary of Events and Information	Remarks and references to Appendices
	13/4/16		At once 2 Officers and 115 sent off at 8hrs & finished burying by 5/30 am. At this hour we advised that the Butts had to move at noon	
COUINCAMPS	14/4/16		March burial turnout at 8 hrs marched off by Lt Col Pinches to Bertrancourt and marched by Coy to Louvencourt arriving here [illegible] somewhat again shortly afterwards with trenches. Heavy guns pitched by 4 Coms. The mining party having been left behind at Beauvois.	
LOUVENCOURT	14/4/16		Burying party marched to trenches about 2 am & buried 2 en engaged in entering [illegible] trench. They latter [illegible] ?? somebody killed and wounded [illegible] to bombing dugouts. We had [illegible] casualties in entering or returning from trenches except Lt Smedley who was slightly wounded. The Enemy was however killed by a machine gun bullet just as he was firing the rocket or trenches to signal to artillery that someone had entered.	

WAR DIARY
or
INTELLIGENCE SUMMARY

(Erase heading not required.)

Army Form C. 2118.

4th Bn Worc. Regt

Place	Date	Hour	Summary of Events and Information	Remarks and references to Appendices
	17/11/16		Pte J. Symons was also wounded in skull whilst asleep in front of our trenches (Coy report found attacker hands) Batt marched off at 9.45 am and reached FORCEVILLE about noon. Men reflected in billets.	
FORCEVILLE	18/11/16	10am	Left at 11 am and marched on a Batth to LEALVILLERS arriving there about noon. all in billets. Brigadier accompanied the Batth.	
LEALVILLERS	19/11/16		Very wet overnight during forenoon CDs cry at Batto during the day. Men engaged in carrying in & 4 cleaning their the lost or Sleves of equipment until the rain training of recruits of 4 bombing continued Coys on parade for 1hr in afternoon. Officers left by bus at 9am to reconnoitre trenches from D17.a.4.4 to Q.4.t.6.0. +3+ H Corps to Bath. & remainder on parade.	
	20/11/16		Dry and cold. Eight officers left by bus at 9am to reconnoitre trenches but returned about 11am not having been able to find bus owing to attack being a	

WAR DIARY
or
INTELLIGENCE SUMMARY

4 Battalion Fusiliers

Army Form C. 2118.

(Erase heading not required.)

Instructions regarding War Diaries and Intelligence Summaries are contained in F. S. Regs, Part II. and the Staff Manual respectively. Title Pages will be prepared in manuscript.

Place	Date	Hour	Summary of Events and Information	Remarks and references to Appendices
	21/10/16		Bombardment by our artillery heavy on enemy. Battn. practising attack formation by Coys in forenoon. In afternoon to attack Battalion was instructed that our B.W. worked 3 instruments. 3 officers joined Battery. Lieut. 152nd Bn. Horsman.	
LEALVILLERS	23/10/16		Left at 10am and marched as a Battalion to FORCEVILLE entering over billets. Men from 7th and 9th Batts attending Church Service in School. Army Service in afternoon and was addressed by Dr BROWN Moderator of the Church of Scotland and Dr Principal St. ADAM SMITH Moderator of the United Free Church of Scotland. Major General Sirs Stephens General was also present 370 O/R on various fatigues.	
FORCEVILLE	24/10/16		Dry cold.	
	24/10/16		Very wet. Getting ready to move up tonight to D or a as attack operation cancelled tonight owing to unfavourable weather conditions	
	25/10/16		Chill wet. 300 O/R on fatigue during afternoon carrying T.M. Bombs. Seven new officers joined early this morning.	

Army Form C. 2118.

WAR DIARY or INTELLIGENCE SUMMARY

(Erase heading not required.)

4 Bn M Hyland
Hylos

Instructions regarding War Diaries and Intelligence Summaries are contained in F.S. Regs., Part II. and the Staff Manual respectively. Title Pages will be prepared in manuscript.

Place	Date	Hour	Summary of Events and Information	Remarks and references to Appendices
FORCEVILLE	26/10/16		Day in morning. L/25/R. on review fatigue during day. Word that the 7 Officers who joined y'day had been sent in error and misdirected; had to go to 3 Armour or to 8 Armour; they proceeded in afternoon.	
	27/10/16		Bn. in fatigue today. Remain here for a short time and engaged in repairing and improving existing billets.	
	28/10/16		Bn. this morning. Remainder during forenoon & afternoon. On the in fatigue at night.	
	29/10/16		Bn. today. Church service in South's Churches. Tent at 11.15 am. 150 men on fatigue. Warned that Bn. had to return to trenches tomorrow and companies sent up to reconnoitre.	
	30/10/16		Bn. in morning. Instructions to proceed to trenches cancelled by Brigade early in the morning. Later on received instructions that Bn. was to proceed to	

WAR DIARY
or
INTELLIGENCE SUMMARY

Army Form C. 2118.

1st Gordon Highrs

Place	Date	Hour	Summary of Events and Information	Remarks and references to Appendices
RAINCHEVAL	31/1/16 Feb		Battn. marched off by Companies at 20 yds interval commencing with B Coy at 11am, men carrying their own blankets. Arrived at RAINCHEVAL about 3 pm. Every man owing to whole of the march and every one previously coated. Billets for men fair. Got bivouac going as soon as possible to try & dry clothes.	
RAINCHEVAL	2/11/16		Dry fresh day. Men put on fatigue drawing firewood & coal for about home in afternoon.	

SRMcc Ede Lt Col
Comdg 1st Batt Gordon Highrs

OPERATION ORDER NO.1
by
Lt.Col. S.R.McCLINTOCK, Commanding 1/4th Gordon Highrs.

****

For raid on enemy trenches on night of 16th-17th October 1916.

Reference :- Trench Map PUISIEUX-AU-MONT. Scale 1/5,000.

1.   A party of the 4th Bn. Gordon Highlanders consisting of 2/Lieuts. J.M.HENDERSON and J.B.ANDERSON and 30 other ranks will make a raid on the German front line opposite this Battalion front on the night of the 16th-17th October. 2/Lieut. J.M.HENDERSON will be in command.

2.   The object of the raid is twofold.
       (1) To obtain indentification of the troops opposite.
       (2) To ascertain the construction of the German front line.
The raiding party will not stay any longer in the enemy trench than is necessary to secure these results.

3.   The men will wear shorts, carry no equipment, rifle with bayonet fixed and dulled, 10 rounds S.A.A. in magazine, 15 in pocket and 15 Mills Bombs detonated in carriers each with exception of 4 men who will carry nothing save 2 stretchers, 15 rifle wire cutters will be carried, 10 ordinary pairs wire cutters and 8 electric torches distributed among the party. No title badges, identity discs, pay books, letters or any means of identifying our unit will be carried by any of the raiding party. Raiding party will blacken their faces.

4.   The wire will be cut by 2" Trench Mortars at K 23 d 77.45 between dusk and 7 p.m. The raiding party will be in position 50 yards or thereby short of the enemy's wire by 7 p.m. At 7 p.m. Trench Mortar Batteries will fire on point of entry. At 7.5 p.m. artillery will put barrage on trenches as arranged with R.A. The raiding party except the stretcher bearers, and a covering party of 3 men and an N.C.O. will make the raid, 4 men of the raiding party will be detached to deal with the sap at K 23 d 63.35.

5.   On return of party to our trenches 2 gold and silver rain rockets will be sent up for artillery to cease fire.

6.   Any prisoners will be sent to Battalion Headquarters under escort.

7.   2/Lieut. TENNANT and 12 men will be standing by in our front line in new cut behind hedge running into JOHN COPSE to send up the rockets and assist the raiding party to bring back wounded if required. They will also have no means of identification on them.

                              (Sgd) S.R.McCLINTOCK, Lt.Col.,
                                         Commanding,
                                    1/4th Bn. GORDON HIGHRS.
                                       16th October 1916.

Copy No. 1 4th Gordon Highrs.
         2 6th Black Watch.
         3 153rd Infantry Brigade.
         4 51st Division "G"
         5 File.
         6 War Diary.

Ref. Map. Trench Map France Sheet 57 D N.E. Edition 2 D

Report on Raid by 4th Bn Gordon H⁰ˢ on enemy trenches at
K.23.d.75.50.   16/17th Oct, 1916.

At 7.25 pm the raiding party was in position in shell holes about 60 yards short of the German wire. At 7.30 pm the 2" Trench Mortars opened and a good deal of small shrapnel and earth was thrown all round us though no one was injured. All the men had been instructed to watch the point bombarded so as to go straight to the gap. Immediately the trench mortars ceased fire, the barrage opened and we went forward. There was practically no trace of wire cut and for a minute or two we searched a little to left and right. I then decided to go through the entanglement which was about 12 yards in depth 2 feet high and moderately thick. The ground was more uneven than we had anticipated and there was a good deal of concealed wire in dips in the ground and one large shell-hole had been thoroughly wired all round. When half way through the wire we came on a path, about a foot broad and followed it into the trench. It was impossible to keep closed up and we went in in single file at intervals of 2 to 3 yards. Some men tripped badly in the wire. Meantime there was no fire directed towards us even though we must have been visible by the light of the flares. In looking for a path through I found my torch extremely useful.

We halted for a few seconds on the parapet and threw bombs into the fire bays on right and left and into the C.T. on the right.

At the trench the party divided into 2 squads. I worked to the left and 2/Lt. J.B Anderson to the right. I had four altogether in my party

party and 2/Lt Anderson had three. It was impossible to wait till the whole party had got through the wire as it would have taken up too much time and given the enemy a chance of inflicting casualties. We decided that each party would clear 3 fire bays.

<u>No 1 Squad.</u> As we entered the trench a man disappeared round the corner of a traverse. One of my Lance Corporals bayonetted and shot him and he fell in the third bay. We passed a lighted dug-out whence shots were being fired. I fired a shot into it from my revolver and ordered the man immediately behind me to throw bombs down, which he did. In the third bay I shot a sentry with my revolver as he was about to jump down from the firestep. We then turned back and on our way threw more bombs into the dug-outs. My party then returned crawling or leaping from shell hole to shell hole as there was continuous rifle and Machine Gun fire from the flanks.

<u>No 2 Squad.</u> turned to the right and after looking down the C.T. bombed the first dug-out. A German rushed out of it and we threw bombs after him and several more into the dug-out. We then went to the next bay and bombed a second dug-out. In the third bay was another dug-out from which a German came. As he ran along the trench 2/Lieut Anderson jumped on him and brought him down. He put up his hands but refused to get up and was bayonetted and shot. We then bombed the third dug-out.

We judged it best to remain no longer in the trench, as our parties were so small that we could have been very easily cut off and to get our parties made up quickly was out of

3

of the question as we had so much wire to come through. Again, had we had any casualties I am doubtful if we could have brought them back. In the actual raid there were no casualties save one man slightly scratched.

<u>Enemy trenches</u>. They are about 9 feet deep, are slightly wider than our own and have slightly longer fire bays. They were excellently constructed, revetted with wood and had a double wooden firestep. They are dry and well trench-boarded. They showed no trace of being damaged by shell fire. The dugouts are dug forward into the parapet, have a single stair and appeared to be about 12 feet down. They were very well lighted. The communication trench was narrow. The wire entanglement was close up to the trench and was quite low.

<u>Retaliation</u>. Our batteries were shelled and a barrage of shrapnel put up in no mans land immediately in front of the stepping off trench to the left of JOHN COPSE. An officer who was in charge of a small reserve party standing by in the advanced trench was mortally wounded, and a Lewis gunner lying in a shell hole in front was also wounded.

J.M.Henderson 2/Lieut.
O.C. Raiding Party
4th Gordon Hdrs.

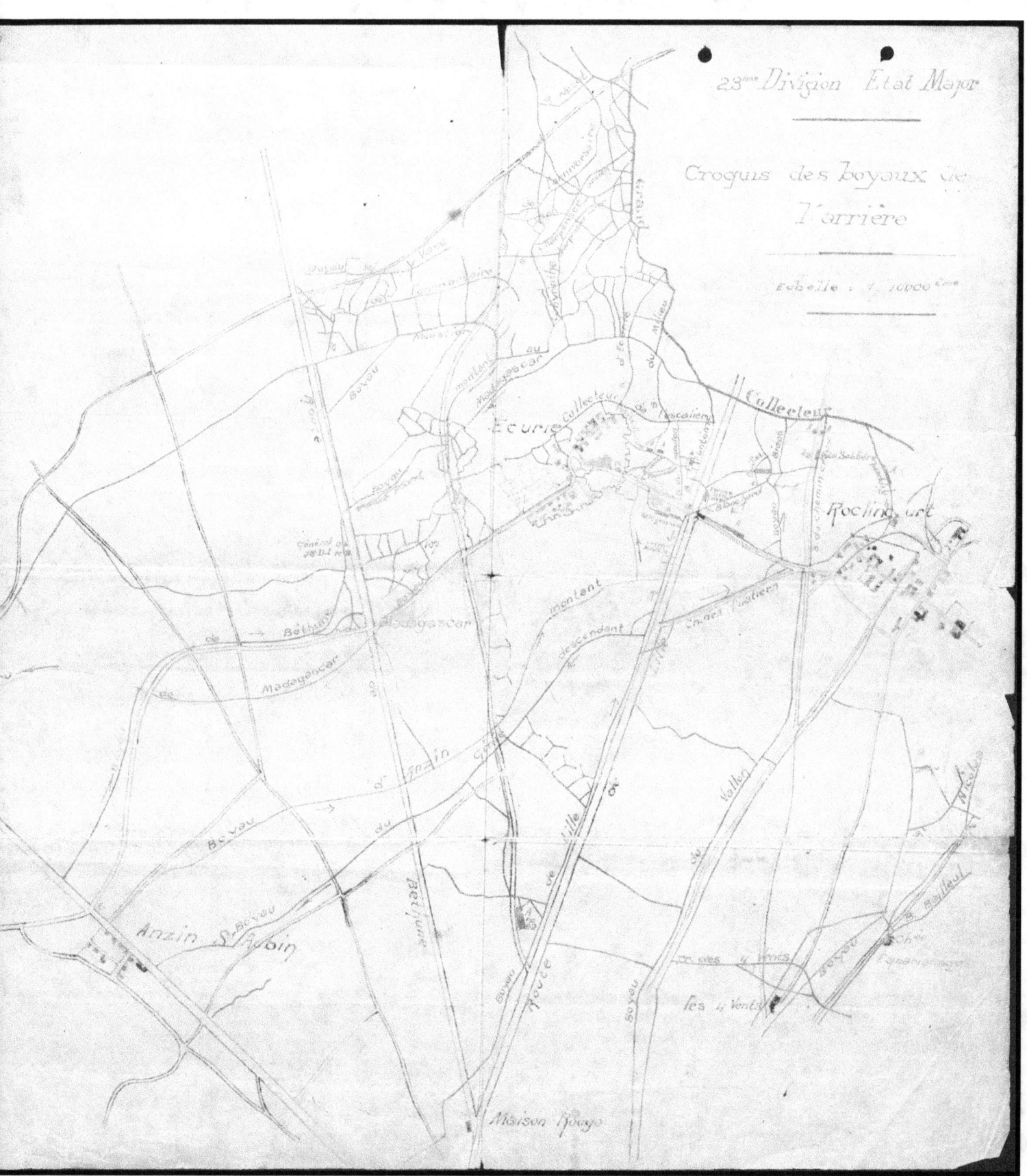

Buenos Aires

Defence Scheme for No 1. Subsector
1. Left Company in Front Line

S.24 and its Supporting Point

Should the bombers in the saphead be driven back they should fall back on the supporting point from which an immediate bombing counter attack should be launched. To enable this to be done a post has been established and a block built at the junction of BOYAU des MORTIERS, and supporting point and about 100 grenades are now kept there. This post is held by the company bombers of the half platoon who occupy the supporting point. A very effective covering rifle fire for this attack can be obtained from the left half of the supporting point. Should it be necessary to retake the supporting point this can be done by an immediate counter attack down the BOYAU MORTIERS.

This can be effectively covered by rifle and rifle grenade fire from the new front line. A block has been made a short distance up the BOYAU des MORTIERS from the new front line and a post of company bombers established there.

S.26 A and B

Should the bombers in the sapheads be driven back they should fall back on the new block forward of the main front line. If only those in 26 "A" are driven back they will fall back on the block in 26 "B". At the first hint of trouble a rifleman will be stationed at the cut which overlooks the junction of S.26 A & B and he should be able to to effectively deal with any of the enemy coming past the junction of the saps 26A and 26B. An immediate bombing counter attack should be launched from the main fire trench. Covering fire will be used from Trench Mortars and Rifle Grenades.

New Main Front Line - Left Sector.

Should this be taken and not the right sector an immediate bombing counter attack will be launched from the right sector and also down Avenue MORTIER CHEMIN CREUX and BIDOT and if necessary old FANTOME.

Defence Scheme for No 1. Subsector.
2. Right Company in Front Line

S.20 and its Supporting Point

Should the bombers in the saphead be driven back they should fall back on the supporting point from which an immediate bombing attack should be launched. If the supporting point were taken an immediate counter attack with bombers (six company bombers will be centralised at L.21 under a company bombing N.C.O). This counter attack will be supported by rifle grenade fire from L.20. It will be properly organized in bombing squads. There are two good blocks between supporting point S.20 and L.20/1 and at the first hint of trouble in the supporting point they should be garrisoned by a bayonet man (to fire through loophole) and a bomber.

L.21 and 22 and their Supporting Points.

Similar procedure will be carried out in the case of the sapheads.

Two additional blocks have been constructed, one at the fourth overhead traverse from L.21 in BOYAU "C" and the other before coming to the wire down from L.22 in BOYAU "D".

S.23 and its Supporting Point.

In case of the bombers being driven out of the sapheads an immediate bombing attack should be made from the supporting point. This should be helped by rifle grenade fire and the west spring gun from the right of the supporting point and from Trench X (see sketch). Note - A new T head should be be built here) If driven out of the supporting point a stand should be made at the junction of CHEMIN CREUX and Trench X. Trench X should be made into a T. head and a post established there. A counter attack can then be started from Trench X assisted by rifle grenades and bomb throwers. If Trench X were taken a counter attack would have to be made from the new front line. This could be assisted by rifle grenades.

Note:- There should be a post at junction of C.T. and front line here, but at present there is no place where a good block can be made as the C.T. is deep and winding.

Should these attacks fail artillery preparation will be called for through Battalion Headquarters.

New Main front line - Right Sector

Should this be taken and not the left sector an immediate bombing counter attack will be launched from the left sector and also down Avenues "A" and "C"

N.B. With regard to the system of holding the line by observation posts in front of the firing line it is to be distinctly understood by all ranks that the observation line must be held to the last by its garrison.

In the event of a heavy bombardment or mine explosions the sentries in the observation line will remain at their posts and keep a particularly sharp look-out.

In nearly all cases of German raids, small parties are sent forward first, and if the sentries in the observation line are withdrawn or are not on the lookout no warning of the raid will be received.

reported. On the other hand one determined sentry may succeed in preventing the raiding party from reaching our trenches.

Action in Case of Hostile Mine Explosion.

Should the mine damage any part of our observation line or sap the rear lip must be occupied and consolidated.

This probably will best be done by a bombing squad and a covering party making their way to the lip of the crater while other men with shovels etc going up C.T. or sap and then working out to the lip of the crater. Rifle grenades, Lewis guns and 3" Trench mortars could probably co-operate and support.

Should the crater be close to one of our saps or observation line, a sap should at once be dug out to the lip, or an old French disused sap could possibly be used. This could only be done at night. A bombing squad and covering party should occupy the lip during the night while sapping is in progress.

During the day the enemy could be prevented from occupying the crater by Rifle grenades, West spring gun and Trench mortars.

Should a mine be reported actually under an observation post the post is to be moved a short distance to a safe position and the sap watched by constant patrols.

Platoon commanders in the front line are to be prepared to occupy as soon as possible any mine crater which would overlook our line. They should have a definite scheme known to all concerned as to how this would be done.

done.

Company commanders will arrange beforehand for dumps of sandbags, wire, screw pickets, tools etc, being handy for the supporting platoons, who are told off to consolidate any craters. Companies in the front line will also have reserve dumps available.

<u>Action in Case the Enemy take our Main Front Line</u>

It is the duty of the troops occupying the COLLECTEUR trench to resist and prevent the enemy advancing beyond the main front line and as soon as possible to organize a counter attack to drive them back.

The COLLECTEUR will be reinforced by a company from ABRI CENTRALE

A bombing squad will be at once sent down each of the main C.T's forward to prevent enemy bombers bombing up them. That is down Avenues BIDOT MORTIER, CHEMIN CREUX and "A" and "G" and if necessary old FANTOME. Blocks will have to be made in these trenches to assist bombers in these duties, and small dug outs for Battalion Bombers to live in.

This counter attack will be made up the various Avenues and disused C.T's also over the open

2 platoons from between BIDOT - MORTIER on L24 and L25.
1 " " " CHARLES. BIDOT. on L. 27.
2 " " " CHEMIN CREUX and RIPPERT with left on L 23
1 " " " RIPPERT and Avenue "G" with right on Avenue G
1 " " " Avenues "A" and "C" on L 22, with right on Avenue "A"

These parties will have company bombers on flanks and will on reaching these points bomb outwards until they join up.

Reserve for garrison of COLLECTEUR one company of Battalion from ABRI CENTRALE and one platoon 4th

Vol 21

War Diary

1/4th Battalion Gordon Highlanders

November 1916

Volume No 22.

2/ Headquarters
1st Infantry Brigade

1/11/16

WAR DIARY or INTELLIGENCE SUMMARY

Army Form C. 2118.

No 22 Volume 4 Gmr High[rs]

Place	Date	Hour	Summary of Events and Information	Remarks and references to Appendices
RAINCHEVAL	1/11/16		Div. holiday. Men out on parade from 8.30 am to noon. Football in afternoon. Recvd order to proceed to French trenches tomorrow.	
	2/11/16		Very wet. Batt. turned out & marched off on morning with C.Os at 9 am. but heavy rain & mud outside village when marching was rec'd from Brigade that the move was cancelled. Returned to Billet. Men out for 1/2 hr in afternoon on terrain. Batt. ordered out again about 7pm at 9.30 for more route march att. att. at 11.30pm Bttn ordered that move was on. & that Batt had 60 hrs to trenches tomorrow.	
	3/11/16		Bn. Batt. left Raincheval at 8 am and marched to field near MAILLY where dinner was served by cooks to field kitchens sent with from the cooker. Men pushed with blankets on there their own kit at Raincheval and were brought on that evening by lorries when they were dumped to [?] Batt. dinner over from 7 to Black Watch to Highwood front over from 7th Black Watch and took over trenches very soon after built. Quiet night.	

Army Form C. 2118.

WAR DIARY
or
INTELLIGENCE SUMMARY
(Erase heading not required.)

4 Batt/Yorks Regt

Place	Date	Hour	Summary of Events and Information	Remarks and references to Appendices
Trenches	4/11/16		Wet. Quiet morning. Enemy artillery fairly active about 1pm. An intensive bombardment by our artillery took place from 4.30 to 4.35 p.m. Enemy sent up S.O.S. signal and C.T.'s hopidly went all ranges of hill from 7.7 to 5.9 for nearly an hour. Capt. Cutts was killed & 2 O/R killed and 6 O/R wounded. A few heavy shells sent over by enemy about 11 pm.	
	5/11/16		Intermittent shelling during early morning by enemy, one man wounded, an intensive bombardment by our artillery took place from 6.30 to 6.35 am — no retaliation by enemy.	
	6/11/16		Quiet overnight. Another intensive bombardment by our artillery from 12.45 pm to 1.15 pm. Enemy replied on our front support lines with a few 7.7 & 4.2 shell. Our casualties O/R 2 killed, 3 wounded & 1 shell shock.	
	7/11/16		Relieved by 5" Suffolks the forenoon and marched by platoon to Rents track in MAILLY.	

4th Yorkshire Regt Entries

WAR DIARY or INTELLIGENCE SUMMARY

Army Form C. 2118.

4th Batt Gordon Highlanders

Place	Date	Hour	Summary of Events and Information	Remarks and references to Appendices
MAILLY MAILLET	8/11/16		Wet. 230 O/Rs on various fatigues return to trenches during day. Arrangements to get the whole Batt. bathed out shortly afterward after fatigues.	
	9/11/16		Dry today. 300 O/Rs on fatigues, rest received in Bgd. improvement. Brigade warned that Bn. move to FORCEVILLE tomorrow morning & men warned accordingly.	
	10/11/16		At 10 a.m. Bn. cancelled movement to FORCEVILLE. 180 O/Rs on various fatigues. Rest cleaning up camp & equipment.	
	11/11/16		Dry but very cold. 470 O/Rs on fatigues during afternoon and evening.	
	12/11/16		Dull. Preparing for the attack. 2 officers 700 O/Rs detailed by Brigade as a carrying party. 1 officer & 16 O/Rs as a Scout control party.	
	13/11/16		Very misty. Breakfast 6 am and first showed up 6.40 a.m. then bread filled field kitchens and little after noon.	

WAR DIARY or INTELLIGENCE SUMMARY

Army Form C. 2118.

4 Bn/Works Regt.

Place	Date	Hour	Summary of Events and Information	Remarks and references to Appendices
MATELY WOOD	13/11/16		and inspected, then fallen out with orders to be ready to move at a moments notice. Message received from Brigade at 9.8 am to send up 2 Coys. to reinforce 153rd Bde, and to march orders on St JOHNS ROAD Brigade C.O. Corps with Seynelden Henri-jean marched off under Capt. Gillies. At 9 h 9 another message received from Brigade to send off other 2 Coys to report to 153rd Bde. A Cy marched off at 10.5 am and W/Yr immediately thereafter. B Coy left at 10.25 am. Headquarters started to G.H.Q. 153rd Bde in SEYMARD St at 11.15 am and Bn W/Yr was established there. There were some reports that the German Forces had shell fell some of the enemy fire. Very heavy combat enemy through in from Pere Bombing troops to GOC 153rd Bn. instructed M. Jean Pier Bombing troops to Cent out of line, ought, then this 3 Bombing troops to be out of line, ought, then on turnings from A. of helpful to send their objective on turning from N.G. pres. The other 2 parties from C.G. went right forward and on their appearance the Germans advised thin.	

2449. Wt. W14957/M90. 750,000. 1/16. J.B.C. & A. Forms/C.2118/12.

WAR DIARY
or
INTELLIGENCE SUMMARY
(Erase heading not required.)

4 Gordon High.

Army Form C. 2118.

Place	Date	Hour	Summary of Events and Information	Remarks and references to Appendices
In the trenches	10/11/16		Capt (tmp) Gillies was shot through the heart by a sniper whilst leaning over parapet of our own trench. At 5 am G.O.C. 153 Bde ordered that the Bath should advance to the preceding enemy north of they were then light would meet in front or might be light. Bath had then to send forward 2 Coys. and capture YELLOW LINE. The latter task was however cancelled. At 8.15 am the Bath advanced in 4 Bn Coys forming 1st 2nd 3rd Line and 5 Coy together forming the third line. The Bath reached their objective without opposition and at once proceeded to consolidate. The Sigs under Lt TRUP had at once sent out wires and within an hour of the advance the Bath was in touch with Bde. HQrs. FETHARD ST. The night was spent in consolidating the New trench.	

WAR DIARY or INTELLIGENCE SUMMARY

Army Form C. 2118.

4. Bull(?) Water High(?)

Place	Date	Hour	Summary of Events and Information	Remarks and references to Appendices
Trenches	14/11/16 6.45am		Very misty. The 152 Bdl attacked this morning at 6.45am on our left, but the attack failed. Spasmodic shelling during day by enemy. Bull bombing officer severely wounded by shell at entrance to Mgr. dugout. Still very quiet. Fire from artillery very weak.	
	15/11/16 pm		153rd Bdl relieved by the 154th Bdl this afternoon. Hqrs. of Regt established in same Dug Out in FETHARD St as our own Mgr. Snell overnight.	
	16/11/16 pm		Very cold overnight. Our artillery active, enemy shelling intermittently. Bath was relieved & then sent by 2 Corps Hqrs. & Scots and came back to Dugouts in vicinity of FETHARD St soon very tired. Very cold.	
	17/11/16 pm		Hard frost overnight. Very clear. Quiet on its whole throughout the day. Bath engaged in storing material — first German Zaries(?).	
	18/11/16 pm		Cold snowing early morning. At 1.30pm 13Ll were not that Bath had to go up to LEAVE AVENUE	

WAR DIARY
or
INTELLIGENCE SUMMARY

Army Form C. 2118.

4 Batt [illegible] Regt [illegible]

(Erase heading not required.)

Place	Date	Hour	Summary of Events and Information	Remarks and references to Appendices
Trenches	18/11/16		and got in North [illegible] 19.4.L.1. in NEW MONICA TRENCH and got under cover of 17th Bttn. Bath moved off by Coys at 2.30 pm Coy + pioneers proceeded to the MP 67g by tramway line after considerable difficulty found the line (no guides very awkward) to ensure their front that the R & 90c 97th Bde had just left to establish no Mans that the [illegible] Coys went back to White City and reported to 97 Bde HQrs. There and after communication found that the Batt were up after all regained HCo. more than [illegible] at MAGGON ROAD Frank Bank near there was at once sent it took 4 [illegible] in FETHARD ST. Bath & mend then about 3 am. as [illegible]	
	19/11/16		Men very tired. Return by 6 [illegible] in the afternoon marched back to camp in MAILLY WOOD WEST. Total casualties from 13th to 19th incl. Officers 1 killed 16 wounded O/R 24 killed 9x6 wounded 1 missing	

2449 Wt. W14957/M90 750,000 1/16 J.B.C. & A. Forms/C.2118/12.

WAR DIARY or INTELLIGENCE SUMMARY

Army Form C. 2118.

4 Gordon Highlanders

Place	Date	Hour	Summary of Events and Information	Remarks and references to Appendices
MAILLY WOOD WEST	26/11/16	—	Cleaning up & cleaning Camp. Very dull.	
	27/11/16	9.30 am	Cleaning Camp. Shelled this forenoon from 11.15 to 12 with 5.9 Shell. One landed at door of C.O.'s tent. B Coy & H.Qrs. having some slight damage.	
	29/11/16	9.00	Cold but clear today. 4 Officers + 200 O/Rs engaged on salvage work in 1st & 2nd German lines.	
	30/11/16	9.00	Marched by Coy to HEDAUVILLE this forenoon. Found Camp (huts) very dirty.	
HEDAUVILLE	1/12/16	8.45	C.O.S. & Adj left at 8.45 and marched by Coys to PUCHVILLE Rd arriving there about 11am. Huts for Officers & men.	
PUCHVILLERS	2/12/16	—	Very wet and many of the huts leaking very badly. Had to shift about 70 men to 2 empty Barns.	

2449 Wt. W14957/M90 750,000 1/16 J.B.C. & A. Forms/C.2118/12.

WAR DIARY or INTELLIGENCE SUMMARY

Army Form C. 2118.

4th Batt. Gordon Highrs

Place	Date	Hour	Summary of Events and Information	Remarks and references to Appendices
PUCHVILLERS	27/11/16		Left by Corps at 10.30 a.m & marched to OVILLERS POST via TOUTENCOURT, SENLIS & BOUZINCOURT. Reached huts at OVILLERS POST at 6 p.m. Very crowded. C.O. and all officers in one hut. Very cold.	
OVILLERS POST	28/11/16		Very misty cold. 2 officers + 100 O/R on fatigue during day.	
	29/11/16		Very misty. Cold overnight. Ordered to move to huts at OVILLERS this morning but move cancelled at last moment as the huts had not been vacated by Canadians. 8 officers + 200 O/Rs on fatigue nr POZIERES tonight.	
	30/11/16		Moved about 800 yds further up to OVILLERS HUTS this forenoon. Accommodation better. 4 officers + 200 M.R. on fatigue at night.	
OVILLERS HUTS	30/11/16		Very cold. 3 officers + 150 O/R on fatigue during day.	

J. MacPherson Major
and Lt/Col Comdg 4/G

Volume No 23

Vol 22

1/4th The Gordon Highlanders
period 1st to 31st Dec 1916

War Diary

23 Volume   1/4 Batt Gordon Highrs   Army Form C. 2118.

WAR DIARY
or
INTELLIGENCE SUMMARY
(Erase heading not required.)

Place	Date	Hour	Summary of Events and Information	Remarks and references to Appendices
OVILLERS HUTS	1/10/16	9pm	Very cold night. 5 officers 300 o/r on fatigue today. Men getting in bad condition on fatigues of that day for last 8 days sent to 7 ambulance. Principally owing to bad felt slips.	
	2/10/16	8am	Still very cold. 2 officers 100 o/r on fatigue. 10 train from ambulance went up to R Stuyche in relief of 5th Gordons this afternoon.	
	3/10/16	5pm	Still cold last night. 4.5 o/r reinforcements arrived this morning, transfer all arrived with them. Heather joining also recovd from Batty. Left huts at 5pm by platoons changing to Bazentin Trent Huts at 7.0.21.c.8.5 and thence to trenches relieving 5 Gordons their majority completely safely by 9pm. The whole thing complete safely with exception of 1 platoon of D Coy, in support on right of Batt. Sector Bush in front line with exception of 1 platoon of D Coy. Enemy shelling 74, 74a and shelling our right sting, trenches very bad. Knee deep in mud in middle of many places.	

WAR DIARY or INTELLIGENCE SUMMARY

4 Bn/London Regt. Army Form C. 2118.

Place	Date	Hour	Summary of Events and Information	Remarks and references to Appendices
Trenches	5/11/16		Informant of raid trenches during daylight hours by enemy sniper. Quiet during day except for intermittent shelling. One sniper hit & German seen.	
	6/11/16 day		Very intermittent shelling during day. Smoke enveloping men, many dry mornings and foot having been completed.	
	6/11/16 night		Quiet and foggy. Our troops got over the 6th German Lines & Supports. They enemy casualties - 3 Germans & 5 prisoners, 1 killed & 7 wounded. For the first days in trenches to August and shelter out our hits behind casualties. Marched back in platoons to August Comparidom. Very very few remained during relief. Very very few or Stretcher men allowed and any were kept during the day.	
August	7/11/16		Very windy. About 150 on sick parade, principally with sore feet. Strength 375 OR called for.	

WAR DIARY or INTELLIGENCE SUMMARY

Army Form C. 2118

4 Field / ... Hy C

Place	Date	Hour	Summary of Events and Information	Remarks and references to Appendices
August	7/11/16		Engaged for remounts &c &c; only able to supply mounts for SM. Sgt + two of shelling near Chilts.	
	8/11/16		Dull wet. HQ & C on fatigue in afternoon and evening. Chill very large civil funeral.	
	9/11/16		Dull wet. Relieved by 6 Yorkshires, tonight to trenches near the knoll H B. Gronelier our in support + 7 wounded.	
Bouce Huts	10/11/16		Cold. Men changed into full service marched off to Oy at 12.15 pm Brett's party SENLIS coming in forward + two Brett's party ... Dear D ... spent in Clement. gun.	
SENLIS	11/11/16		Dry cold. 170 the ... mostly at HVELUY. Cleaning up, inspection	

WAR DIARY
or
INTELLIGENCE SUMMARY

Army Form C. 2118.

4 Batt [Troops?] Higher

Place	Date	Hour	Summary of Events and Information	Remarks and references to Appendices
SENLIS	12/7/16		Dry. 2nd i/c on fatigue, of remainder of Batt. inspected kit inspection of platoons who were on fatigue yesterday. Bath in [river?].	
	13/7/16		Dry. Drill. Bath attacks of companies. 2nd i/c drill find on of open rifle butt.	
	14/7/16		Dry. Not many fact parties. Batt on parade for 2 hrs. in forenoon & 1 hr in afternoon. First draft unit sent to [Bouzincourt?] to have their But [Equipment?] tested.	
	15/7/16		Drill in forenoon. Bath in [Ancre?] by Coys during forenoon for 1 hr in afternoon.	
	16/7/16		Dry. Drill. Batt. marched off to Conference commencing at 11 am and arrived at BRUCE H.O.T.s about an hour later. About 150 m fatigue brought	

WAR DIARY or INTELLIGENCE SUMMARY

Army Form C. 2118

4 Bn M[?]tyr[?]

Place	Date	Hour	Summary of Events and Information	Remarks and references to Appendices
BRUCE HUTS	17/12/16		Still. Practically whole Battn. on fatigue either among dug out night	
	18/12/16		The whole of D Coy sent away for work on enemy's dug out 200 on fatigue when about 11 am shell began to drop near the huts. One of them scattered huts was blown just as Batt. got out & the men a the Battalion. A Coy hut and knocked it out. Three men were found dead inside tent, then seven found men wounded. Shelling continued only ½ an slightly wounded. Shelling continued for about half an hour. The rest of the shells landing some distance beyond our huts.	
	19/12/16		Foggy morning but commenced raining about 10 o/c on fatigue at night.	
	20/12/16		Dull wet. Blanket men kill and small kit packed in camp bag, sent to company at AVELUY in afternoon. Marched off for Warloy commencing	

WAR DIARY or INTELLIGENCE SUMMARY

Army Form C. 2118

4th Bn? [unclear] Regt.

Place	Date	Hour	Summary of Events and Information	Remarks and references to Appendices
	20/4/16	at 3 pm	at 3 pm returned 3 platoons to trenches. A & B Coys in front line and C Coy in support at P4 & SE of 70 S.T. Trenches in very bad condition. Two men killed during relief.	
	21/4/16		Met their machine guns quiet overnight. Good deal of M. gun fire on right. Intermittent shelling. C Coy no casualties. Patrols	
	22/4/16		Very wet. Some shelling. Gunners relieved by 4 Suffolks at night.	
	23/4/16	night	Wet. Very quiet. Relieved by 4 Suffolks at night. Heavy shelling during relief. Killed + 3 wounded. Marched to WOLFE HUTS arriving at Enfilade. Being 2 hrs late relief was much delayed and men had not all reach hut until after 3 am men very tired. All their hut under fire rubbed with whale oil they each given a hot bottle before they were allowed to sleep.	

WAR DIARY
or
INTELLIGENCE SUMMARY

Army Form C. 2118

(Erase heading not required.)

Instructions regarding War Diaries and Intelligence Summaries are contained in F.S. Regs., Part II. and the Staff Manual respectively. Title Pages will be prepared in manuscript.

Place	Date	Hour	Summary of Events and Information	Remarks and references to Appendices
WILFE AUTS	28/1/16		Bn. resting and cleaning up.	
			50 men on fatigue on huts here. Rest cleaning up and salving material in vicinity of huts.	
	27/1/16		Bn. resting and cleaning up.	
			Army Battn. marched off by Coys at 10 a.m. to BOUZINCOURT. Arrived there about midday. Billets fairly good. Rest of day spent in cleaning. A & B Coys at Baths. C Coy were relieved today by and marched to AVELUY.	
BOUZINCOURT	29/1/16		Battn. on parade for 2 hours in forenoon. Cleaning up and inspection. 'C' Coy marched here today. No fatigues.	
			'C' & 'S' Coys at Baths. 2 hrs drill but in before afternoon. Remainder of Batt. on parade. 40 O.R. on fatigue at AVELUY. Draft of 66 O.R. arrived.	
	30/1/16		Batt. on parade by Coys for 2 hours in forenoon. 40 O.R. on fatigue at AVELUY. Cleaning up & whitewashing billets. News	

WAR DIARY
INTELLIGENCE SUMMARY

4th Battn. Gordon Highrs.

Army Form C. 2118

Place	Date	Hour	Summary of Events and Information	Remarks and references to Appendices
BOUZINCOURT	31/12/16		Army Church service in Church Army Hut in forenoon. Billet inspection by C.O. 50 O.R. on fatigue at AVELUY.	Spencer take over O.C. 4th Gordon 1st Jan 1917

4th Gordons

It will depend on circumstances and losses if it is possible to make a further counter attack to regain the supporting points and saps.

Two platoons of company from ABRI CENTRALE and one platoon 4th Gordons are available as reinforcements if company commanders require them after attack on main firing line. They should bring a supply of bombs up with them.

Flank Defences.

Should the enemy attack and take the trenches in K.2 Subsector, Boyau "B" and Avenue RIPPERT should at once be manned by two platoons.

The Battalion commanders must be kept fully informed of everything of importance that is taking place, or otherwise action taken cannot be concerted. If telephones break down this must be done by orderlies.

In addition to bombing duties in the defence scheme for the battalion, four squads of Battalion bombers are permanently held in reserve, one squad in Avenue CHARLES, one squad in B. RIPPERT and two squads near Battalion Headquarters.

Should an attack occur or mine go up, the Bombing Officer will at once report at Battalion Headquarters for any orders. The squads opposite where the above occurs will at once advance up the C.T's to the threatened point, taking as many bombs and rifle grenades as possible with them.

One N.C.O. will proceed to the Battalion Bomb Store at LA SABLIERE and supervise the issue of further bombs as required.

O.C. coys in COLLECTEUR trench will have carrying parties ready detailed for this duty, and the company at ABRI CENTRALE will also carry up a supply of bombs if called upon to supply the COLLECTEUR line, or if asked to supply carrying parties.

The following are "DOWN" Trenches:—

Avenue "A"
" Mortier   ⎫ – In No 1. Subsector.
" Blanchard ⎭

" Bidot   As far as Collecteur Trench and thence ⎫ – In No 1. Subsector.
          via Charles and Blanchard   ⎭

" Fantome   ⎫ – In No 2 Subsector.
" du Labyrinth ⎭

" du Genie
" de Madagascar

The "UP" trench for ECURIE will be Avenue D'Anzin and Avenue de ROCADE (left branch.)

The "UP" trench for Brigade Battle Headquarters will be Avenue de LILLE or Avenue D'Anzin and Avenue de ROCADE, (right branch.)

8. Communications.

In the event of telephone wires being broken Visual Signal Station will be established at Brigade Battle Headquarters, at LA SABLIERE and at ECURIE

LA SABLIERE communicates direct with right artillery group and Brigade Battle Headquarters.

ECURIE will communicate with Brigade Battle Headquarters

Otherwise communication will be by orderly.

9. Grenades.

Brigade stores are situated as follows:—

<u>Rear Store</u> in ANZIN, 150 yards S.E of Church.

<u>Advanced Store</u>. (a) In ROCLINCOURT at old R.E. dump. (This store is to be moved to a dug out under the LILLE ROAD. S of FERMES des CAVES). (B) In SUNKEN ROAD at junction of MINOTAURY and VASE Avenues

From Battalion Headquarters forward the supply will be organized by Battalions.

In the event of an attack, the company of "C" Battalion

1/4th Bn Gordon Hrs

Provisional Defence Scheme.

Right sector is held by two Battalions. Each subsector is held by one Battalion (called "A" and "B" Battalions).

1. One Battalion (called C Battalion) less three companies, forms the permanent garrison of ECURIE, the remaining three companies (which form the Brigade Reserve) being in ABRI CENTRALE, ABRI MOUTON and SUNKEN ROAD respectively. Six Lewis guns of the battalion are in ECURIE one at SUNKEN ROAD and one at ABRI CENTRALE. One battalion (called "D" Battalion) is in Divisional Reserve in ETRUN.

2. Preparation of Scheme of Defence.

It is of great importance that Battalion and Company Commanders should work out plans of defence in detail and should put in writing the movements of reserves, machine guns, grenadiers, etc.

These plans should be known to all subordinate commanders.

Schemes should be framed to meet possible attacks against our right, left, centres, or whole front, or attacks on either flank.

In all schemes for counter attack in this complicated system of trenches, the importance of co-operation between bombers, rifle grenadiers, and Lewis guns must be borne in mind.

It must be remembered that, in this area where the ground is strewn with wire in every direction, a counter attack over the open will be impossible unless the ground has been prepared beforehand by cutting passages and marking them so that they can be found even at night. This applies mainly to the ground between GRAND COLLECTEUR and BONNAL trench.

trench.

A counter attack in front of the firing line would almost necessarily be confined to trenches.

It must be clearly understood that the efficiency of a counter attack depends more on the rapidity and certainty with which it is delivered than on the number of troops employed.

3. Gas Flame Attacks.

All ranks are to be taught the folly of falling back before hostile Gas or Flammenwerfer.

4. Warning of Attack.

A PRIORITY message ATTACK QUARTERS will be sent to all concerned, to give notice of a hostile attack.

5. Gas Alarm.

On receipt of a G.A.S. message the action will be identical with that laid down for ATTACK QUARTERS.

6. Notice.

Troops in ETRUN will be at one hours notice, excepting one company which will be at half an hours notice.

7. Communication Trenches.

Main trenches will be kept detailed for "UP" and "DOWN" traffic and will be marked by notice boards.

The following are "UP" trenches:—

Avenue D'Anjou
  " de Lille
  " des Filatiers
  " Bidot (As far as Grand Collecteur Trench).
Chemin Creux } – In No 1. Subsector.
Avenue "G" }
  " du Mouton }
  " Milieu } – In No 2. Subsector.
  " Fantome }

Battalion in Brigade Reserve will each send ten men under an N.C.O. to the Advanced Brigade Stores. Their duty will be to carry grenades without further orders up to Battalion Headquarters Stores, excepting the company in ABRI du MOUTON which will carry to company Headquarters in GRAND COLLECTEUR trench.

The supply from Rear Brigade Store in ANZIN will be carried out by reserves coming up from ETRUN.

Every company which passes ANZIN will draw from Rear Brigade Store 1000 MILLS grenades and 200 rifle grenades which they will carry up with them. These will either be sent up to Advanced Brigade Store or will be taken up to the Battalion Store of the Subsector which the company reinforces. An officer will report at Brigade Battle Headquarters for instructions on this point.

10. S.A.A.

35,000 rounds are kept in the Advanced Brigade Store.

Every man coming up from reserve will be issued with 100 rounds from regimental reserve. (S.A.A) carts before moving off.

11. The Main Line of Resistance.

Is the firing line ie. BONNAL trench and old M. intermediate line as far as point M.31 and then trenches M.31. 32. and 33. This will be fought to the last.

Nevertheless it must be understood that no ground in advance of the firing line is to be given up without stubborn fighting, and that the obstinate resistance of every advanced post is an essential factor in breaking down an attack.

12. The Method of Holding the Line of Observation.

Is on the outpost system: listening posts, supports and patrols.

The listening posts may be outside the saps, but are to be as far forward as the sapends, if not beyond them.

them.

Their role is one of resistance, and they will in case of an attack remain where they are fighting in order to gain time for the advances to be manned, and also if possible to break up the attack before it is launched in full strength.

It is essential that the ground in front (especially disused trenches) and both sides of saps be thoroughly entangled and open trenches well patrolled.

13. Protection.

The dug-outs in the fire trench are only for the use of the garrison in case of bombardment, when others in rear are completed.

Those in rear of the fire trench are to be used by the reliefs of the garrison when resting.

Strong sentry posts will be constructed for the protection of sentries who are to recognise that not even the powers of HELL are to make a British sentry quit his post.

14. Defensive Flanks.

In order to be prepared for the possible penetration by the enemy of the front of one of the Brigades adjoining the Right Sector, defensive flanks firestepped and protected by wire will be established as follows:—

(a) Along Avenue RIPPERT and Avenue "A". This is flanked by the machine gun in front of FERMES des CAVES.

(b) Along Avenue FANTOME

(c) "   "   MILIEU.

(d) Along SPOONER and MINOTAUR Avenues.

Emplacements for trench mortars and machine guns will be made within these flanks to which guns might be withdrawn if required.

Certain troops are to be told off to man these defences should the need for their occupation occur.

15. **Permanent Garrisons**

One platoon per company in the COLLECTEUR trench will be always told off by O.C. Coys occupying it as permanent garrison. These two platoons will on no account be used for a counter attack or to reinforce the firing line. They must know their exact positions to occupy in case of attack, after the remaining platoons have left.

These positions will be marked.

16. **Action in case of attack.**

In the event of a serious attack, actual or threatened on our front (or on receipt of a message ATTACK QUARTERS, or G.A.S) the following action will be taken:—

(a). The company of "C" Battalion in Brigade Reserve comes under orders O.C. Subsectors if required.

One N.C.O. and ten men will be sent at once by each company to Advanced Brigade Grenade Store (see para 9).

(B). All troops in ETRUN will stand to arms on their Alarm Posts.

"D" Battalion (in Divisional Reserve) will send one company at once to Avenue de ROCADE N. of Avenue D'ANZIN, to await orders. An officer will be sent to Brigade Battle Headquarters to report on arrival.

"D" Battalion less one company will move to Corps line N. of St. AUBIN and await orders from Division. Battle Headquarters will be in house on ANZIN ROAD at L.11.a.10-8.

(c) **Working Parties**

In the event of an infantry attack, working parties in the firing line will man the parapet. Working parties behind the front line will be collected in the nearest support trench by the Officer in charge, who will at once send an orderly to report his position and the strength of his party to the Battalion Commander.

In the event of a heavy bombardment, working parties will take cover in the nearest shelter, and will be withdrawn from the front line trenches as soon as an opportunity offers.

offers.

In the event of an infantry attack and as soon as the bombardment lifts, men of Tunnelling Company and Mining fatigues will first of all man portions of fire trench in vicinity of shaftheads under orders of O.C. Subsector. As soon as feasible they will be moved via "DOWN" trenches only, with places shown in the table

Unit	Accommodated at	Where Working	Position in Case of Attack	Junction	Under orders of.
185th Tunnelling Company R.E.	LA SABLIERE and CHEMIN CREUX.	Old Left Sector.	LA SABLIERE and CHEMIN CREUX.	Reserve for No. 1. Subsector.	O.C. No 1. Subsector.
Do.	ARIANE.	Old M. 1. Subsector	ARIANE.	Brigade Reserve.	G.O.C. 154th Infantry Brigade.
Mining fatigue party.	ABRI CENTRALE. (or men from ANZIN actually in trenches at time of the attack).	Old Left Sector.	ABRI CENTRALE	Brigade Reserve.	G.O.C. 154th Infantry Brigade.
Do.	ANZIN. (Only men actually in trenches at the time of the attack).	Old. M. 1. Subsector.	Firestepped portion of LABYRINTH Avenue E. of BETHUNE ROAD) A.26.b & O.25.	Flank defences and if necessary reserve for ECURIE defences.	O.C. ECURIE Defences.

(D). <u>Detached Men.</u>

All men undergoing courses, employed men etc, whose duties are not directly concerned with the fighting efficiency of units will fall in on Battalion or Brigade Alarm posts and await orders.

(E) Transport.

Echelon "A" first line Transport will accompany units in reserve to their Alarm Posts.

Echelon "B" will remain in their present position.

(F). Should the attack take the form of a heavy bombardment, the firing line will not be reinforced. All troops will stand to arms in their appointed positions which will be pointed out to them on their arrival in the trenches.

The garrison of the firing line will at once stand to arms, but will remain in dug-outs prepared for them in the fire trench, ready to occupy the positions allotted to them, at a moments notice. Every section must be detailed to a dug-out and to a definite fire position, and these

8

these must be known to every man.

Sentries and the next relief will remain in the fire trench and will not go into dug-outs.

Should the enemy's infantry attack the trenches will at once be manned.

WM 23

1/4th Gordon Highlanders.

War Diary for Month of
January 1917

Volume No. 24

**CONFIDENTIAL.
No 21 (A)
HIGHLAND
DIVISION.**

CONFIDENTIAL

No 21(a) **HIGHLAND DIVISION**

2nd Volume

WAR DIARY or INTELLIGENCE SUMMARY

1/4th Battn Gordon Highrs.

Army Form C. 2118.

(Erase heading not required.)

Instructions regarding War Diaries and Intelligence Summaries are contained in F. S. Regs., Part II. and the Staff Manual respectively. Title Pages will be prepared in manuscript.

Place	Date	Hour	Summary of Events and Information	Remarks and references to Appendices
BOUZINCOURT	1/1/17		Dry & cold. No parade. 16 offr. + 406 other ranks went to AVELUY SIDING as a working party. Men had plum puddings, wine, cigarettes and tobacco sent by ladies of ABERDEEN.	
BRUCE HUTS	2/1/17		Dull. Battn marched to BRUCE HUTS and took over from 4th Gordon Highrs. Men very comfortable with plenty of accommodation. No fatigues today.	
	3/1/17		Cold, some rain. 110 other ranks on fatigue today. Remainder did 2 hours parade in forenoon.	
	4/1/17		4 offrs. + 200 other ranks on fatigue this morning to POZIERES burying cable. Remainder cleaning up round huts.	
	5/1/17		Very cold. Same fatigue as yesterday. Details cleaning up and generally improving condition of huts.	
	6/1/17		Cold. Same fatigue as yesterday. Details employed as yesterday.	

Army Form C. 2118.

WAR DIARY or INTELLIGENCE SUMMARY

1/4th Battn. Gordon Highrs.

(Erase heading not required.)

Instructions regarding War Diaries and Intelligence Summaries are contained in F. S. Regs., Part II. and the Staff Manual respectively. Title Pages will be prepared in manuscript.

Place	Date	Hour	Summary of Events and Information	Remarks and references to Appendices
BRUCE HUTS	7/1/17		Army. Same fatigue as yesterday. Remainder attended Church service held in one of the huts.	
WOLFE HUTS	8/1/17		Fine day. Battn. marched to WOLFE HUTS in forenoon and took over from 5th Gordon Highrs. Men very crowded. In the afternoon "C" Coy. marched to FRASER POST.	
	9/1/17		Rain today. Day spent in cleaning up round huts. Parties sent out salving.	
TRENCHES	10/1/17		Army. Clear. Battn. marched to trenches in afternoon and relieved 9th ROYAL SCOTS. Relief completed very quickly. No casualties. Trenches in a very bad state.	
	11/1/17		Snowing slightly today. Very quiet. 8 offrs. + 138 other ranks reinforcements arrived today.	

2449 Wt. W14957/M90 750,000 1/16 J.B.C. & A. Forms/C.2118/12.

WAR DIARY or INTELLIGENCE SUMMARY

1/4th Batt. Gordon Highrs.

Army Form C. 2118.

Place	Date	Hour	Summary of Events and Information	Remarks and references to Appendices
TRENCHES	12/1/17		Day very cold. Batt. relieved tonight by 24th ROYAL FUSILIERS. Very quiet during relief. No casualties. 1 man 1st Lewis Gun team left till tomorrow night. Batt. marched back to WOLFE HUTS where they changed into kilt. Dry socks were issued to each man and hot soup & tea provided. Each man then issued with a blanket before going on leave which were waiting for Batt. Not sufficient leaves. 60 men left behind.	
RUBEMPRE	13/1/17		Buses arrived at RUBEMPRE at 8 a.m. Very cold with sleet showers during journey. Men in fairly good billets with plenty of accommodation. Details left behind joined tonight. 3 Offrs. reinforcements arrived today.	
CANDAS	14/1/17		Fine day. Batt. marched this forenoon to CANDAS. Men had dinners on the way. Men in quite good billets.	
MAISON ROLLAND	15/1/17		Very cold. Batt. marched to MAISON ROLLAND. Dinners on the way. A few men fell out but generally doing very well. Good billets.	

WAR DIARY or INTELLIGENCE SUMMARY

1/4th Battn. Gordon Highrs.

Army Form C. 2118.

Place	Date	Hour	Summary of Events and Information	Remarks and references to Appendices
SAILLY BRAY	16/1/17		Hard frost. Fine day for marching. Battn. marched to SAILLY BRAY. Dinners on the way. Men beginning to feel the strain. A good many fell out. Accomodation very poor. 'C' Coy. billeted at BONNELLE, 'D' Coy. Kenis Gunners at PONTHOILE. Billets very bad. 'D' Coy. joined Battn. here, coming by train.	
	17/1/17		Snowing slightly. Day spent in cleaning up.	
BONNELLE HUTS	18/1/17		Dry. Battn. marched to BONNELLE HUTS. Accomodation plentiful.	
	19/1/17		Hard frost. Day spent cleaning up.	
	20/1/17		Hard frost. Very cold. Parade from 9-30 a.m. to 12-45 p.m. Afternoon devoted to football. 15% of Battn. allowed leave to ABBEVILLE.	

Army Form C. 2118.

WAR DIARY
or
INTELLIGENCE SUMMARY

1/4th Batt. Gordon Highrs.

(Erase heading not required.)

Instructions regarding War Diaries and Intelligence Summaries are contained in F. S. Regs., Part II. and the Staff Manual respectively. Title Pages will be prepared in manuscript.

Place	Date	Hour	Summary of Events and Information	Remarks and references to Appendices
BONNELLE HUTS	21/1/17		Hard frost. Very cold. Church service in forenoon. Football in afternoon. 1 Offr. & 138 Other ranks reinforcements arrived today.	
	22/1/17		Still hard frost and very cold. Parades from 9-30 a.m. to 12-45 p.m. afternoon devoted to football. 2 Offrs. reinforcement arrived.	
	23/1/17		Very hard frost very cold. Battn. was inspected by Corps today by Brig. General Hamilton at 7-30 a.m. Parades till 12-45 p.m. G.O.C. Division (Harper) inspected the Battn. at training this forenoon. Afternoon devoted to football, cross country running, bomb throwing & bayonet training.	
	24/1/17 25/1/17 26/1/17 27/1/17		Very hard frost very cold. Training in forenoon and recreation in afternoon.	

Army Form C. 2118

WAR DIARY
or
INTELLIGENCE SUMMARY

1/4th Battn Gordon Highrs.

(Erase heading not required.)

Instructions regarding War Diaries and Intelligence Summaries are contained in F. S. Regs., Part II. and the Staff Manual respectively. Title Pages will be prepared in manuscript.

Place	Date	Hour	Summary of Events and Information	Remarks and references to Appendices
BONNELLE HUTS	28/1/17		Hard frost, very cold. Church service in forenoon. Kit inspection by coys. Hut inspection by C.O.	
	29/1/17		Hard frost very cold. Training in forenoon. Inter company competitions in Bomb & Bayonet fighting in afternoon. Won respectively by D + B Coys.	
NOUVION	30/1/17		Hard frost, very cold. Training in forenoon. Battn. marched to NOUVION and took over billets there in afternoon. Billets fairly good.	
	31/1/17		Hard frost. Some snow. Training in forenoon. Battn. played 1/4th Seaforth Highrs. at football in afternoon, resulting in a win for the Seaforth Highrs. by one to nil.	

1.2.17

SRmere[?] Lt R Peal
Capt A/ Gordon Highrs

Secret No 25

War Diary

Volume No 25

1/4th Bn The Gordon Hrs.

February 1917

25th VOLUME   1/4 Batt Gordon Highrs   Army Form C. 2118

WAR DIARY
or
INTELLIGENCE SUMMARY
(Erase heading not required.)

Place	Date	Hour	Summary of Events and Information	Remarks and references to Appendices
NOUVION	1/2/17	—	Hard frost, very cold. Training in forenoon. Football vs in afternoon.	
	2/2/17	—	Hard frost. Training during forenoon. Inter Coy. cross country race run in afternoon won by S Coy. A Coy being second. 2/Lt Smith A Coy finished first.	
	3/2/17	—	Hard frost. Training in forenoon. Bayonet fighting and Bombing competitions in afternoon. Battn. Bombing team 2nd losing 1st place by 1 point. In 3 individual competitions Batt. was 2nd in each. Bayonet fighting team was 3rd. In 2 individual contests Batt. gained one and got third place in the other.	
	4/2/17	—	Hard frost. Church service in forenoon. 300 men at Baths in afternoon.	
	5/2/17	—	Snowing this morning. Batt. marched to CANCHY in afternoon roads very slippy. Billets fairly good. Officers + 39 NCOs Reinforcements arrived.	
CANCHY	6/2/17	—	Hard frost. Batt. marched to GUESCHART. Billets fair but not very content.	

WAR DIARY or INTELLIGENCE SUMMARY

Army Form C. 2118.

1/4 Batt Gordon Highrs.

Place	Date	Hour	Summary of Events and Information	Remarks and references to Appendices
GUESCHART	7/11/17	9.08	Hard frost. Batt. marched to BACHIMONT and RUGEFAY.	
BACHIMONT	8/11/17	9.08	Chill hard frost. Batt. marched to HERICOURT and GUINECOURT.	
HERICOURT	9/11/17	9.08	Hard frost. Batt. marched to CHELERS. Billets fair.	
CHELERS	10/11/17	9.08	Resting.	
	11/11/17	9.08	Batt. marched to BETHONSART in afternoon and Billet fair at BETHONSART and good at CAUCOURT. A and S Coys at battn HQrs at CAUCOURT.	
BETHONSART	12/11/17		Training in forenoon and cleaning and improving billets in afternoon. Hard frost.	
	13/11/17		Hard frost. 1 Officer & 30 ORs to AUBIGNY Station in morning to unload ammunition. Batt. training in forenoon & cleaning up billets and villages in afternoon. 1 Officer and 129 ORs unloading coal at AUBIGNY Station for training in evening.	

WAR DIARY or **INTELLIGENCE SUMMARY**

Army Form C. 2118.

1/4 Batt Gordon Highrs

(Erase heading not required.)

Place	Date	Hour	Summary of Events and Information	Remarks and references to Appendices
BETHONSART	14/5/17		Rest day. Training in forenoon returning billets & village in afternoon. Officers and some of O.R's sent to SAVY in afternoon, on a permanent working party. 5" Coy shifted over from CAUCOURT in huts afternoon.	
	15/5/17		Training in forenoon cleaning up in afternoon. Coy 1 officer & 50 O.R's sent to AUBIGNY early in morning to unload store at Canteen. Went first.	
	16/5/17		Bn. 1st tpt. motor lorry. Morning cleaning up etc. Bn. Hdqrs. 2 officers and 250 O.R. staff for work at ANZIN under Capt Henry arrived. Coy brought over from CAUCOURT in afternoon.	
	17/5/17		With today. Training cleaning up as before and Gas drawing water off roads and around billets. Training of Grenades continued.	
	18/5/17		Wet today. Carry up on training	

1/4 Bn London Regt

Army Form C. 2118.

WAR DIARY
or
INTELLIGENCE SUMMARY.
(Erase heading not required.)

Place	Date	Hour	Summary of Events and Information	Remarks and references to Appendices
BETHONSART	19/3/17		Dull. Carrying on training	
	20/3/17		Dull. Carrying on training	
	21/3/17		Well. Marched to billets in TREULLERS this morning. Training continued in afternoon. Officers & 40 O.R. to AUBIGNY on fatigue at 1pm. returned to TREULLER about 6 pm	
TREULLERS	22/3/17		Dull. Continued training.	
	23/3/17		Training and cleaning up billets	
	24/3/17		" " " "	
	25/3/17		Draft of 20 N.C.O.s arrived. 11 am Church Service in afternoon. Training for 12 hours	
	26/3/17		Very mild bright. Training continued & improving of billets	

Army Form C. 2118.

1/1c Ayrshire (?) Bty

WAR DIARY
or
INTELLIGENCE SUMMARY.
(Erase heading not required.)

Instructions regarding War Diaries and Intelligence Summaries are contained in F. S. Regs., Part II. and the Staff Manual respectively. Title pages will be prepared in manuscript.

Place	Date	Hour	Summary of Events and Information	Remarks and references to Appendices
FREVILLERS	30/1/17	9am	Left at 9 am and marched to tents in BOIS DE MAROEUIL arriving there at 1.15 pm. The trunks of 2 officers ~250 yds which had been working at ANZIN reported Bath. This afternoon. 220 yds or Infantry near Railway near Dumt tonight. Bulk of L.S. arriving tonight. Bull & 8 officer ~ 4.10 y.Rs on Fatigue today at	
BOIS DE MAROEUIL	18/1/17		ECURIE & MADAGASCAR Burying Cables for comd. Signals.	

1.3.17

Spencer de Hoche (?)
O.C. 1/4 Gordon Hyrs (?)

Volume 26

1/4 Batt Gordon Highrs Vol 2

WAR DIARY
or
INTELLIGENCE SUMMARY.

Army Form C. 2118.

Place	Date	Hour	Summary of Events and Information	Remarks and references to Appendices
BOIS DE MARIEUX	1/3/17	a.m.	Batt. Officers + 210 Other ranks working daily burying dead and clearing	
	2/3/17	a.m.	A.T.D.N. + GENIE trenches	
	3/3/17	a.m.		
	4/3/17	a.m.		
	5/3/17	a.m.	Relieved 6/Seaforth Relieved 9/Royal Scots in trenches this afternoon. Very quiet day, but from about 10 a.m. to 11.30 a.m. enemy shelled our front support trenches. B.D. in McCrombie a.r.c. Cup in front line and Buckhurst.	
TRENCHES 6/3/17	6/3/17	a.m.	Bright today but quiet. Northern trenches in very bad state. right flank received hit and thought of water supply in front lint Retained very little shelling by enemy	
	7/3/17	a.m.	front first today	

WAR DIARY
or
INTELLIGENCE SUMMARY.

(Erase heading not required.)

Army Form C. 2118.

1/4 Batt. Gordon Highrs.

Place	Date	Hour	Summary of Events and Information	Remarks and references to Appendices
TRENCHES	8/3/17		Frosty. Quiet day. Lympanis changed over this afternoon.	
	9/3/17	8.00	Cold. Snowing in morning. Enemy aircraft activity today. One Enemy forced our aeroplane to descend and also another. Trench action in afternoon. Enemy artillery active.	
	10/3/17	4.00	Mild. Many aeroplanes active. Enemy artillery front & support lines during forenoon. Afternoon	
	11/3/17		Mild today. Enemy artillery fairly busy. Fourteen 8 inch Big Trench Mortar fired this evening. Thirteen went in a.m. Relieved by 4 Seaforth in afternoon. Marched back to Halloon & billets in MARUEVIL.	
MARUEUIL	12/3/17		Mild. 1 officer & 250 O.R. on working parties. Remainder at Bath and training. Improving.	

A.534 Wt. W4973/M687 750,000 8/16 D. D. & L. Ltd. Form/C.2118/13.

Army Form C. 2118.

WAR DIARY
or
INTELLIGENCE SUMMARY.

(Erase heading not required.)

14 Ath Lewis Dy ???

Instructions regarding War Diaries and Intelligence Summaries are contained in F. S. Regs., Part II. and the Staff Manual respectively. Title pages will be prepared in manuscript.

Place	Date	Hour	Summary of Events and Information	Remarks and references to Appendices
MARŒUIL	14/8/17		Batt. left at 2 am. for Enguinegatte and arrived at billets at HERNIN arriving there at 7 am. Roads very bad. Billets fair.	
HERNIN	15/8/17		Mill. turning up and kit inspection in forenoon. Training in afternoon.	
	16/8/17		Training in forenoon. afternoon.	
	17/8/17		" " "	
	18/8/17		Church Service in forenoon. Inter Company at Bath. C.O. went to Hospital at ST POL today. Major Sherbrooke commenced Battalion training on MONCHY BRETON area.	
	19/8/17			
	20/8/17		Batt. training. Batt. training on MONCHY BRETON area.	
	21/8/17		" " "	
	22/8/17		Batt. training. Brigade training on MUNCHY BRETON area.	

WAR DIARY
or
INTELLIGENCE SUMMARY.

(Erase heading not required.)

Army Form C. 2118.

1/4 Bn [?] Highrs

Place	Date	Hour	Summary of Events and Information	Remarks and references to Appendices
HERMIN	24/2/17		Batt. paraded along with 9th and 7th Highrs near TREVILLERS in forenoon & afterwards presented to various officers & men of the Division including the Corps Commander. Training carried on for 2 hours in afternoon.	
	25/2/17		Church service in forenoon, and training carried on thereafter.	
	26/2/17		Wet & stormy. Training carried on under cover in the forenoon and outside in the afternoon.	
	27/2/17		Dry cold. Batt. marched out to training area at 9.15 practised attack. Broken out. Back to billets about 6 p.m.	
	28/2/17		Cold. Out at training area in forenoon. Practised attack along with 9th and 7th Highrs and 2 Companies of 7th Black Watch. Contact aeroplane cooperating.	
	29/3/17		Wet. Training carried on under cover.	

WAR DIARY or INTELLIGENCE SUMMARY

Army Form C. 2118.

1 Bath Forden High

(Erase heading not required.)

Place	Date	Hour	Summary of Events and Information	Remarks and references to Appendices
HERMIN	30/7/17	9:05	Battalion practised attack on training area in forenoon. Training carried on for 14 hrs in afternoon.	
	31/7/17	9:05	Battalion training during forenoon and afternoon. Raining part of day.	

C.B. Peterkin, Major
Comdg 1/4 Batt Gordon High
31/7/17

1/4th Battalion
The Gordon Highrs.

War Diary

Volume No. 24.   April 1917.

Volume 27   1/4 Batt'n Gordon High'rs
                                             Army Form C. 2118

WAR DIARY
or
INTELLIGENCE SUMMARY
(Erase heading not required.)

Place	Date	Hour	Summary of Events and Information	Remarks and references to Appendices
HERNIN	1/4/17		Civil. Church Service in Afternoon. Training Troops at Billets at CAUCOURT in afternoon.	
	2/4/17	9am	Training continued near Billet. Host Reminder of Battalion at Billets at CAUCOURT during day.	
	3/4/17	8am	Very stormy, heavy snow in morning. Forenoon started for MONCHY BRETON AREA, but cancelled on Regiment moving to number. Training continued in Billet.	
	4/4/17	9am	Very stormy. Men practicing attack during forenoon. Training in vicinity of billet in afternoon.	
	5/4/17	9am	Left HERNIN at 6.30 am and marched to BRAY arriving there about 1.30pm to Billet.	
BRAY	6/4/17		Men getting cleaned up and institution of gas arrangement. 2/Lieut WADDELL and C.S.M. Thom recruiting trench 78th cable from Sgt IRENE seventy grounded all D Coy.	

WAR DIARY
or
INTELLIGENCE SUMMARY.

4 Rl/Forder Highrs Army Form C.

(Erase heading not required.)

Instructions regarding War Diaries and Intelligence Summaries are contained in F. S. Regs., Part II. and the Staff Manual respectively. Title pages will be prepared in manuscript.

Place	Date	Hour	Summary of Events and Information	Remarks and references to Appendices
BRAY	7/4/17	9a.m.	Reporting for the attack. Lt Col McClintock returned from Hospital today and took over command.	
	8/9/17		Jeffery & Blundell. Church Service in afternoon. Packs and Blundell for the morning, got rations, sent to M & R.E.VII during afternoon. Bombs & so rough to Zavaham afternoon. Lt Col McClintock went to Zavaham Division for Zavah with, when Maj. C.O. fetching the Bath marched off from BRAY commencing with B Coy at 8 pm movement was very slow, frequent stops being over very little hostile shelling on route. Considerable congestion in and around the BARRICADE TUNNEL. reaching in assembly in army in delay in arrival at position in assembly trenches B, D Coys were in BUNYAK from Sap 22 & Sap 16 and A C Coys in left COLLECTEUR from Chevin Cent to Billet Avenue	
	9/4/17	5a.m.	At Zero 5.30 am Barrage commenced. Reply by enemy artillery was feeble. At 5.30 am B & D Coys moved forward to capture the BLUE LINE. Found casualties in B Coy	

WAR DIARY
or
INTELLIGENCE SUMMARY.

4 Batt Norfolk Reg^t Army Form C. 2118

Place	Date	Hour	Summary of Events and Information	Remarks and references to Appendices
	9/4/17		at once owing to hostile shelling. After considerable opposition from M.G. and Snipers first of B Coy reached first objective in BLUE LINE and got in touch with Canadians on left. D Coy was held up by M.G. fire about 1000 yards from BONNEVAL. At 9.35 am instructions were sent to A + C Coy to advance at once to reinforce D + D Coy and then to push on to their own objective. A + C Coy moved up at 11am then covering advance of D Coy to enable D Coy to reach objective of the BLUE LINE which they at once proceeded to consolidate. By this time the enemy who was slightly counter attacking. With the only officer left in D Coy and all the left were casualties. Left platoon of D Coy not change of D Coy and sent this enemy down & and took of D Coy (with platoon of returning of A Coy) took direction and went the far to the right. The platoon of A Coy referred to managed to reach direction however and reaches the gaulf reached objective in BROWN LINE and established connection with Canadians on left.	

WAR DIARY or INTELLIGENCE SUMMARY

Army Form C. 2118
1/4 Batt:[?] Northum[berland] Fusiliers

Place	Date	Hour	Summary of Events and Information	Remarks and references to Appendices
	9/4/17 9:00		The 7th Argylls on our right were responsible for mopping up lost division between ZEHNER WEG & ZEHNER WEG 5 (ie 152 Bde area) C Coy & D platoon of A Coy following	
	10/4/17 9:00		Each Coy having got Coys indzib[?] that they were not in their proper position and along with some of the 5" Gordons bombed along ZEHNER WEG and other post men to the jm with southly point O.5 GIN TRENCH to complete. About noon Capt Henderson was sent forward to ascertain position and arranged with O.C. 7 Argylls to withdraw A&C Coy from ZEHNER WEG, GIN TRENCH with exception of half a Company left to reinforce 152nd Bde in the jm with West companies were moved into ALLGAUER WEG SUNKEN ROAD until about 80 men were brought up from the BLUE LINE & TOAST TIRED in order to bomb to form the left flank of both objectives of B R W N LINE. This kind to be abandoned about 11.30 pm owing to continued fire from own guns on B & D Coys men were relieved	

WAR DIARY
or
INTELLIGENCE SUMMARY.
(Erase heading not required.)

Army Form C. 2118.

1/1 Batt Gordon H[ighlanders]

Place	Date	Hour	Summary of Events and Information	Remarks and references to Appendices
	10/5/17		Relieved by 2 Coy of 6 H.L.I. Batt and moved back to dugouts in Chemin'Cint.	
	11/5/17		During forenoon arrangements were made for A & C Coys to pass round a bombing party along each flank of TIRED trench whilst 3 platoons of 9th R. Scots attacked regained the BROWN LINE. These parties moved off about 2.30 hrs but about 5.30 hrs it was ascertained that enemy had evacuated that portion of BROWN LINE and A & C Coys moved into trench forward to occupy their front. They most BROWN LINE. This was done and trench was gaining. They left with Grenadiers and on right with R.F. trench. Sgt B.J. Coy. 7 Little "B" LARESSFT. About 1am A & C Coys were relieved by 24 R Fusiliers and moved back to dugouts in Chemin'Crent. Later we returned and regained men were rested till 10am. Other boys were fortunate.	
	12/5/17			

WAR DIARY

INTELLIGENCE SUMMARY

1/4 Batt'n Northumberland Fus[iliers]
Army Form C. 2118.

Place	Date	Hour	Summary of Events and Information	Remarks and references to Appendices
LARFESSE	11/4/17	a.m.	Batt'n marched back to billets in LARFESSE having their about 3 am. Casualties amongst officers & other ranks fairly incurred Capt R Fuller 2/Lt Mitchell 2/Lt ? missing ? wounded.	
	12/4/17		Having rest. Reorganizing Companies	
	13/4/17	a.m.		
	14/4/17	a.m.	2/Lt Ingleton rejoining up. Warning order received in evening that Battalion had to move to ATHIES (in support) tomorrow.	
	15/4/17	a.m.	Rain all day. Commanding Officer and 4 Coy Officers went to reconnoitre new line in the morning. Battalion marched off at 2 p.m. Transport, Quartermaster's stores notable deferred. Roads very crowded, progress very slow especially in outskirts of ARRAS. arrived at area between BLANGY and ATHIES about 6 p.m. Very few dugouts. Men dug into railway cutting embankment and made bivouacs. Headquarters in old German anti-Aircraft Gun pit. Very cold overnight.	
BLANGY	16/4/17		Fine clear day. Considerable aerial activity. Cookers came up in forenoon. Sgt Anderson (Transport) wounded slightly on road near camp. Commanding Officer and Coy Officers reconnoitred ground in front. Very wet in evening. 15 men on fatigue at Divisional Headquarters.	

Army Form C. 2118.

WAR DIARY 1/4th Battn. Gordon Highrs.
or
INTELLIGENCE SUMMARY

(Erase heading not required.)

Instructions regarding War Diaries and Intelligence Summaries are contained in F.S. Regs, Part II. and the Staff Manual respectively. Title pages will be prepared in manuscript.

Place	Date	Hour	Summary of Events and Information	Remarks and references to Appendices
BLANGY	17/4/17 WGB		Mist and cold. Snow in evening. Some corrugated iron received from R.E's for shelters. Bombs and Sandbags issued to Coys. 15 men on fatigue at Divisional Headquarters. 2 8" guns were put in position at Headquarters street.	
	18/4/17 WGB		Raining all day. 15 men on fatigue at Divisional Headquarters. 1 Officer + 25 men on fatigue with C.R.E. in evening. Considerable artillery activity on both sides.	
	19/4/17 WGB		Dry and clear. Two 2.8" guns were put in position near Battn. Headquarters. Draft of 129 other ranks arrived. 5 Officers + 300 other ranks on fatigue carrying gas cylinders. Casualties 2 killed 18 wounded.	
	20/4/17 WGB		Dry and bright. S Coy at Battle of St Nicholas. 50 other ranks on fatigue with R.E.s. 15 men on fatigue at Divisional Headquarters. 5 Officers + 300 other ranks on fatigue digging assembly trench overnight in agreement. Aeroplane activity during day. Enemy guns commenced firing today.	
	21/4/17 WGB		Fine day. Ground drying up very quickly.	
TRENCHES	22/4/17 WGB		Fine day. Battalion left for assembly positions at 9 p.m. Rear platoon of A Coy and S + H Coys. were heavily shelled going up. Casualties 2 killed 4 wounded. Battalion arrived in assembly positions at 10 p.m.	

WAR DIARY
or
INTELLIGENCE SUMMARY

Army Form C. 2118.

1/4th Battn Gordon Highrs.

Place	Date	Hour	Summary of Events and Information	Remarks and references to Appendices
TRENCHES	23/4/17		B & C Coys. left assembly trench in front of sunken road at Zero hour i.e. 4-45 a.m. They got into parts of the German front line, but in the parts the Germans still held out particularly on the left near Railway in front of Chemical Works where a party of 50 or 60 Germans with a machine gun held out until much later. A & D Coys. left the assembly position in sunken road at Zero plus 10 mins. On the left they were completely held up before reaching the Black line, but the Coy. on the right (D Coy) appears to have lost direction, discovering no enemy in the Black line. One platoon of this Coy. went right through Roeux towards the right and gone right through ROEUX village. This platoon remained through ROEUX somewhere in I.19.d. for at least 15 mins. No one appeared on the right or left of this platoon the commander decided to withdraw as he was being heavily fired on by machine guns & snipers from all sides. He withdrew along the front of MOUNT PLEASANT WOOD & the Black line. Just west of MOUNT PLEASANT WOOD this platoon took 25 prisoners. About 6-30 a.m. part of this Coy. appears to have accompanied a tank into ROEUX village where it remained for some time, holding the line of the tramway track. On the left of the attack the two Coys held up appear to have been enabled to get into the Black line by the action of the 4th Seaforth Highrs. Who came up about 8-30 a.m. working along the railway. 60 to 90 Germans were captured more along with one machine gun. A small bombing squad from the right two Coys. appears to have worked its way forward along a communication trench as far as the Chemical Works Road, where it held on for some time.	

WAR DIARY
or
INTELLIGENCE SUMMARY

1/4th Batt. Gordon Highrs.

Army Form C. 2118.

Place	Date	Hour	Summary of Events and Information	Remarks and references to Appendices
TRENCHES	23/4/17		The barrage appears to have been very light, and the German front line seems to have been very little damaged when the companies entered it. The enemy appears to have been very quick in getting machine guns into action as soon as the barrage lifted, and also appears to have held up the advance by machine gun fire through the barrage. Telephone communication was never established. Casualties in Officers and N.C.O.s were very heavy, and nearly all commanders were casualties very early in the attack. Companies positions thus became very much disorganised early in the operation. The Battalion attack on a small frontage appear to have penetrated easily as far as the Eastern edge of the group of buildings near the Chemical Works. But there were unsupported and isolated and had little effect on the operations generally. The bulk of two platoons of the night Blue line company appear to have gone right through towards their objective but have not returned. The remains of all 4 companies were in the Beach line holding it in conjunction with a company of the 4th Seaforth Highrs. They remained there until about 9 p.m. when they were withdrawn to the assembly positions by order of the O.C. 4th Seaforth Highrs.	
	24/4/17		The Battalion remained in the assembly positions, carrying on, until relieved tonight. Casualties – Officers Capt. Smirn, Lieut S.F. Ross, Lieut R. Anderson, 2/Lt J.F. Anderson, 2/Lt W.J. Henderson, 2/Lt A.V. Stewart – Killed, Commanding Officer, Adjutant and 8 others wounded. Other ranks 4 & 8 killed 197 wounded 64 missing.	

Army Form C. 2118.

WAR DIARY 1/4th Batt. Gordon Highrs.
or
INTELLIGENCE SUMMARY
(Erase heading not required.)

Instructions regarding War Diaries and Intelligence Summaries are contained in F. S. Regs., Part II. and the Staff Manual respectively. Title pages will be prepared in manuscript.

Place	Date	Hour	Summary of Events and Information	Remarks and references to Appendices
ARRAS	25/4/17 WGB		Battalion reached ARRAS about 4 a.m. and remained there till 12-30 when they marched to Station entrained. Train left about 5-30 pm reached LIGNY ST FLOCHEL about 9 p.m. where Battn detrained and marched to GOUY EN TERNOIS arriving there about midnight. The details who had been at A.C.Q joined the Battalion here having marched from there in the afternoon. Billets very good and men comfortable.	
GOUY EN TERNOIS	26/4/17 WGB		Fine sunny day. Men cleaning up. Kit inspections were held.	
	27/4/17 WGB		Good day but a little cold. Men on parade forenoon & afternoon. Lt Col. Lyon A.S.O. arrived and took over command of Battalion. 8 officers and 380 other ranks reinforcements arrived.	
TINQUES	28/4/17 WGB		Fine day, warm. Battalion marched to TINQUES. Billets fairly good.	
	29/4/17 WGB		Fine day. Battalion at Batta in forenoon. Church Service was held in the afternoon. 1 Officer reinforcement arrived today.	

Army Form C. 2118.

WAR DIARY 1/4th Battn. Gordon Highrs.
or
INTELLIGENCE SUMMARY.
(Erase heading not required.)

Place	Date	Hour	Summary of Events and Information	Remarks and references to Appendices
TINQUES	30/4/17		This day, warm. Battalion on parade for an hour before breakfast and during forenoon. Afternoon devoted to games. Draft of 159 other ranks reinforcements arrived today.	

Alexander Lyon Lt.Col.
Comdg. 1/4 Battn. the Gordon Highlanders

30/4/17.

Operation Order No 1. by Lt Col S R McClintock
Comdg 1/4 Gordon Highrs.

Ref Maps 51 B. N.W. 1/20000 ED 6A.
  Trench Maps 51 B NW (Part of)
  T.S. No. M, 8, 13.

1. The enemy is holding trenches in squares H 12, H 18, I 13, west of MT PLEASANT WOOD also CHEMICAL WORKS and ROEUX with a support line in I 14 and I 19

2. Intention. To capture these trenches, CHEMICAL WORKS ROEUX & Support line.

3. PLAN OF ATTACK. The 154th Bde will attack south of the Railway with two Battalions each supported by two Coys.
(a) 4th Gordon Highrs plus two Coys 9th Royal Scots on the left.
(b) 7th A&SH plus two Coys 9th Royal Scots on the right.

The Battalion will assemble in SUNKEN ROAD through H·24·b & trench in front on a two Coy front — Companies on a two platoon front.

Boundaries. On the left the line of the Railway exclusive as far as level crossing I.13.c.9.8. Then due East.

On the right about H.24.6.6.3 to I.19.a.7.6 Thence due East.

The advance will be in three waves. B & C Coys will form the first two waves, B on the left C on the right; and will assemble in trench in front of sunken road.

A & D Coys each less two platoons will form the third wave. A on left D on right & will assemble in SUNKEN ROAD.

Division between Coys:-
BLACK LINE. I.13.c.60.15.
Road through CHEMICAL WORKS I.13.d.13.30
Thence due East to BLUE LINE.

The first wave will capture the BLACK LINE
The Second wave the Road through CHEMICAL WORKS to ROEUX & all buildings on Eastern edge of Road.
The Third wave the BLUE LINE.

The two platoons of A & D Coys will be in Battalion Reserve & will assemble in Sunken Road & follow Third wave as far as the Road through CHEMICAL WORKS. They will assist any part of the attack which is held up & after the BLUE LINE is taken will assemble in & consolidate BLACK LINE.

The two Coys, 9th Royal Scots will assemble in the Sunken Road & will leave there at Zero + 70 minutes. They will follow the Third wave & consolidate the BLUE LINE.

On reaching objectives Coys will at once proceed to consolidate position won.

The Companies capturing the BLUE LINE will push out patrols & Lewis Guns to cover the works of consolidation by the 9th Royal Scots.

The Os C 'C' & 'D' Coys will watch for opportunities to assist with fire or otherwise the 7th A & S.H. attacking ROEUX.

4. Battalion Headquarters will be in SUNKEN ROAD about H 24 B 6.3.

5. After attack O.C. Coys will at once reorganise their Coys who may be required as carrying parties to BLUE & RED LINES.

6. O.C. Coys will notify Battalion Headquarters as soon as their Coys are in Assembly Positions.

7. The attack on BLACK LINE will take place at ZERO + 19 mins & on BLUE LINE at ZERO + 100 mins.

8. ZERO hour will be notified later.

(Signed) J.R. Thomson Lt.
Adj. 4th Gordon Highrs.

22/4/17.
Issued at 12.30 p.m.
Copy No 1 Retained.
      2. War Diary.
      3. O.C. A Coy.
      4. O.C. B. Coy.
      5. O.C. C Coy.
      6. O.C. D Coy.
      7. File.

SECRET   Vol 27

War Diary
May 1917
1/4th Gordon Hrs

WAR DIARY
INTELLIGENCE SUMMARY

Army Form C. 2118.

Volume 28

1/4th Batt. Gordon Highrs.

Place	Date	Hour	Summary of Events and Information	Remarks and references to Appendices
TINQUES	1/5/17		Fine day. Battalion on parade in early morning and forenoon, afternoon devoted to games. Company Commanders:- A Coy. Captn. W.B. Williamson; B Coy. Captn. J.M. Henderson; C Coy. Lieut. J.McK. Calder; D Coy. 2/Lieut. H.P. Stockle. Strength :- Officers 33, other ranks 712. Ration Strength :- Officers 26, other ranks 626. Extra Regimentally Employed do. 7 do. 86.	
	2/5/17		Very warm. Parades as yesterday. Transport inspected by G.O.C. Division (Harper). Battalion concert in evening at which 'Balmorals' (Divisional Pierrot Troupe) performed.	
	3/5/17		Beautiful day, very warm. Training as before. 39 other ranks reinforcements arrived.	
	4/5/17		Fine weather. Training carried on. A & B Coys. on rifle range	
	5/5/17		Weather still continues fine. C & D Coys. were on range today. Battalion sports in afternoon.	
	6/5/17		Cooler today. Inspection of billets by Commanding Officer. Church service held in afternoon.	
	7/5/17		Weather continues good except for a little rain on morning of 7th. 9 other ranks reinforcements arrived on 7th. Training continues.	
	8/5/17			

Army Form C. 2118.

WAR DIARY
or
INTELLIGENCE SUMMARY.

1/4th Battn. Gordon Highrs.

(Erase heading not required.)

Instructions regarding War Diaries and Intelligence Summaries are contained in F. S. Regs., Part II. and the Staff Manual respectively. Title pages will be prepared in manuscript.

Place	Date	Hour	Summary of Events and Information	Remarks and references to Appendices
TINQUES	9/5/17 WSB		Fine day. Training continues. G.O.C. Division (Harper) inspected A & B Coys doing a practice attack. D Coy. out on range today.	
	10/5/17 11/5/17 WSB		Fine weather. Carrying on with training. 216th men reinforcements arrived on 10th. 1 Officer (Lieut. J.F. Mackintosh) reinforcement arrived on 11th.	
Y Huts ETRUN	12/5/17 WSB		Fine day, very warm. Battalion marched to Y Huts near ETRUN. Accommodation plentiful.	
	13/5/17 WSB		Very warm - showers in afternoon. Church service in open with 9th Royal Scots, 154 Trench Mortar Battery & Machine Gun Coy.	
ARRAS	14/5/17 WSB		Very warm - some showers. Battalion marched to ARRAS today. Billets dirty but plenty of accommodation.	
	15/5/17 WSB		Fine day. Forenoon spent in training on ground near St. Catherine.	
RAILWAY CUTTING H 23 c 9.9	16/5/17 WSB		Dry in forenoon, wet in afternoon. On receipt of message that the enemy were attacking in force, the Battn. marched to the railway embankment between BLANGY and ATHIES in support. Day spent there. At midnight the Battn. moved into close support - A & B Coys under Captn Williamson and Lieut. J.F. McPartick, being in CRUMP TRENCH (H24 b 6.8 & 4.2) and C and D Coys.	

A 5834 Wt.W4973 M687. 750,000 8/16 D.D. & L. Ltd. Forms/C.2118/13.

Army Form C. 2118.

WAR DIARY
or
INTELLIGENCE SUMMARY.

1/4th Battn. Gordon Highrs.

(Erase heading not required.)

Place	Date	Hour	Summary of Events and Information	Remarks and references to Appendices
RAILWAY CUTTING H23 c 9.9			under 2 Lieut. H.A. Sinclair & Captain Skakle, in Railway Cutting at H23 c 9.9. (Ref. Map. Sh. 51B N.W.). Echelon B remained in ARRAS under Major Petrhin.	
	17/5/17 W.O.P		Good day. Men busy making shelters. Two working parties out tonight – one of 2 Offrs + 60 other ranks, and the other 1 Offr + 35 other ranks. Casualties 2 o.r. wounded.	
	18/5/17 W.O.P		Fine weather. Two working parties out tonight – 1 Off. 2 Offrs + 65 o.rs. and the other of 1 Offr + 35 o.rs. A Coy. had parties engaged in salving material which was lying about in great quantity. B Coy. were engaged collecting & burying the dead. Echelon B went to Divisional Depot Battn. SAVY today.	
	19/5/17 W.B.		Fine day. Clear. Enemy shelled railway cutting heavily today – casualties 1 killed + 4 wounded other ranks. Companies were moved from cutting to steep bank on road about H23 c.2.9. Working party of 2 Offrs + 60 other ranks digging trenches tonight.	
TRENCHES H14 c 2.1 to H20 c 7.8	20/5/17 W.O.P		Good day. Some hostile shelling of CRUMP TRENCH. 2Lt. F.N. Robertson was wounded, and 1 killed + 3 wounded other ranks. Battn. relieved 4th Seaforth Highrs. in line tonight. Quiet relief, no casualties. A Coy. were in front line.	

Army Form C. 2118.

WAR DIARY
or
INTELLIGENCE SUMMARY. 1/4th Batt. Gordon Highrs.
(Erase heading not required.)

Place	Date	Hour	Summary of Events and Information	Remarks and references to Appendices
TRENCHES	21/5/17. WGB.		Warm, clear. Situation quiet except for intermittent hostile shelling of ROEUX and CHEMICAL WORKS. Battalion Hdqrs. in CRUMP TRENCH (H 24 b 7.1) was shelled in afternoon. There was considerable aerial activity. Early this morning the sunken road at H 14 c 5.1 was patrolled, and finding it unoccupied, 2 posts were established there. These posts were called Currie and Sheriff's posts after the N.C.Os in charge.	
	22/5/17. WGB.		Very heavy rain in early morning. Patrols were sent out in the early morning to ascertain if enemy was withdrawing but were held up by enemy snipers. Battalion continues sapping & improving trenches. D Coy. relieved A Coy in front line tonight.	
	23/5/17. WGB.		Fine day. Considerable hostile shelling of support line. Enemy got a direct hit on one of our posts in ROEUX; casualties 2 killed & 2 wounded other ranks. Patrols out again but ran up against enemy.	
	24/5/17. WGB.		Beautiful day. Enemy put down barrage in front of our front line this morning. There was considerable hostile shelling during the night, and in the forenoon. One of the bridges over the Scarpe at H 24 d 8.9 was blown up. Battalion was relieved tonight by 9th Royal Scots. There was a little shelling, and the relief for one of the posts in ROEUX was scattered, the guide being wounded. This delayed the relief considerably as another relief had to be sent for this post. Casualties 1 other rank wounded.	

Army Form C. 2118.

WAR DIARY
or
INTELLIGENCE SUMMARY.

1/4th Battn Gordon Highrs.

(Erase heading not required.)

Place	Date	Hour	Summary of Events and Information	Remarks and references to Appendices
RAILWAY EMBANKMENT H13d.9.9 (map Ref: Sh.51B N.W.)	25/5/17. WGB		Fine day. Battalion arrived back in the early morning. Men accomodated in shelters. Day spent in resting and cleaning up.	
	26/5/17. WGB		Beautiful day. 2 hours training in forenoon. The following Officers reinforcements reported here today:- Captn. R.I. Mackinnon, 2/Lieuts. Troup, Inlah, Kynoch, Williamson, and Hunt.	
	27/5/17. WGB		Fine day - very warm. 2 hours training in forenoon. Battn. was shelled a little today. Casualties 16 other ranks wounded.	
	28/5/17. WGB		Still very warm. 2 hours training in forenoon.	
	29/5/17. WGB		Dull today. 2 hours training in forenoon. All available men were out on a working party at night bringing cable.	
	30/5/17. WGB		Dull today. Heavy showers in afternoon. Men resting.	

Army Form C. 2118.

WAR DIARY 1/4th Batt. Gordon Highrs.
or
INTELLIGENCE SUMMARY.

Place	Date	Hour	Summary of Events and Information	Remarks and references to Appendices
ARRAS	31/5/17		Fine day. Battalion was relieved in forenoon by 5th Batt. Cameron Highlanders marched back to ARRAS, where it was billeted in the Citadel. Billets good.	

Alexander Lyon Lt.Col.
Comdg. 1/4 Gordon Hrs.

31/5/17

Volume 29.

Vol 28

WAR DIARY

of

1/4th Battn. The Gordon Highlanders.

JUNE 1917

WAR DIARY
INTELLIGENCE SUMMARY

Army Form C. 2118.

1/4 Bn. Gordon Hgrs.

(Erase heading not required.)

Place	Date	Hour	Summary of Events and Information	Remarks and references to Appendices
TOURNEHEM	20.6.17	9am	At TOURNEHEM. Battalion day outpost scheme on in Training area.	
	21.6.17	9am	Do. Companies parading under Coy arrangements. 30 yard range etc. Aquatic sports held with great success in the afternoon.	
			Draft of 50 O.R. arrived.	
LEDERZEELE	22.6.17	9am	Battalion left TOURNEHEM (regretfully) and marched to LEDERZEELE. Billets very fair, but very scattered. Some trouble over	
			their allocation owing to this being a new billet area. A pouring wet day on the march, as far as WATTEN.	
	23.6.17	9am	AT LEDERZEELE Companies parading under company arrangements. Difficulty in getting ground for training. Draft of 500 R (2/6 A&SH) arrived.	
	24.6.17	9am	Do. Church parade in the forenoon. Draft of 500 R (2/6 A&S Hgrs) arrived.	
	25.6.17	9am	Do. Companies parading under Coy arrangements.	
	26.6.17	9am	Do.	
	27.6.17	9am	Do.	
	28.6.17	9am	Do. Company Training on the VOLKERINCKHOVE training area. Very wet afternoon. Dinners at Training Area.	
	29.6.17	9am	Do. Companies parading under Coy arrangements. Draft of 25 O.R. arrived. Draft of 110 R arrived.	
	30.6.17	9am	Do. Marched to VOLKERINCKHOVE training area, and carried out a Battalion attack. Rain all the time.	
			A demonstration with projectors throwing drums of burning oil, which was to have taken place at 11.30 A.M. was cancelled.	

Ration Strength 41 officers - 781 O.R.
30.6.17.

Co. Commanders.
"A" Coy   Capt W. B. Williamson
"B" "   Lieut (act capt) J. F. McIntosh
"C" "   2/Lieut (act capt) H. A. Sinclair
"D" "   Lieut (act capt) H. P. Shak &c.

Alexander Lyon Lt. Col.
Cmdg 1/4 Gordon Highrs.

Army Form C. 2118.

WAR DIARY
or
INTELLIGENCE SUMMARY.
(Erase heading not required.)

VOLUME 29   1/4 Bn Gordon Hgrs

Place	Date	Hour	Summary of Events and Information	Remarks and references to Appendices
ARRAS.	1.6.17	9 am	Battalion entrained at ARRAS, detrained at TINCQUES and marched to MAGNICOURT. Billets good.	
MAGNICOURT	2.6.17	8 am	At MAGNICOURT - Interior economy + kitting. Draft of 9 officers & 117 o.R. arrived. Lieut G. Howay, 2/Lieut (H. Brown, 2/Lieut Kind, 2/Lieut G. Lindsay, 2/Lieut J. Strachan, 2/Lieut F. Jaulson, 2/Lieut G. T. Mitchell, 2/Lieut J. Morgan, 2/Lieut A. Bell	
	3.6.17	9 am	At MAGNICOURT. Church parade in forenoon.	
MAREST	4.6.17	8 am	Battalion moved from MAGNICOURT to MAREST. Warm marching. 2/Lieut F. a. Melone in flank position.	
	5.6.17	8 am	Battalion marched from MAREST to MATRINGHEM. Very stiff march, heat terrific. Billets quite good.	
MATRINGHEM	6.6.17	9 am	At MATRINGHEM - resting. Transport moved to WITTERNES.	
	7.6.17	9 am	Battalion moved by bus from MATRINGHEM to TOURNEHEM. Billets very good. Transport rejoined Bn in the evening.	
TOURNEHEM	8.6.17	9 am	At TOURNEHEM. Companies parading under Coy arrangements. Draft of 200 o.R. arrived.	
	9.6.17	9 am	Do. Company training at "W" training area. " 32 "	
	10.6.17	9 am	Do. Bn practised the attack at "W" training area. Church parade in the afternoon.	
	11.6.17	9 am	Do. Do. Draft of 17 o.R. arrived	
	12.6.17	9 am	Do. Bn took part in Brigade attack at "W" training area.	
	13.6.17	9 am	Do. Companies parading under Coy arrangements - 30 yards range, practising attack, musketry &c. Band and -----	
	14.6.17	9 am	Party of 30 o.R. under the brevery officer at service held in memory of a fallen french soldier in church	
	14.6.17	9 am	At TOURNEHEM. Battalion at "A" range. Dinners at range.	
	15.6.17	9 am	Do. Companies parading under Coy arrangements. 30 yard range - hat nets - artillery formations, &c. Companies set "night patrolling" 10-11.30 pm	
	16.6.17	9 am	At TOURNEHEM. Companies parading under Coy arrangements. 30 yard range, musketry, gas drill &c.	
	17.6.17	9 am	Do. Church parade in the afternoon. 100 o.R. left for 14 days musketry course at 1st Army School of Musketry.	
	18.6.17	9 am	Do. Advanced guard scheme on the way to and at "w" training area.	
	19.4.17	9 am	Do. Battalion at "B" range. Firing very fair. Dinners at range. Divisional Horseshow.	

Cover for Documents.

No 31 (A) Highland Division.

Vol 29

154/51

Nature of Enclosures.

WAR DIARY
for
JULY 1917
of
1/4th GORDON HRS.

Notes, or Letters written.

WAR DIARY
or
INTELLIGENCE SUMMARY. 4th Batt. The Gordon Highrs.

(Erase heading not required.)

Army Form C. 2118.

Place	Date	Hour	Summary of Events and Information	Remarks and references to Appendices
LEDERZEELE	1.7.17	A.M.	Church Service with 4th Seaforths in forenoon. 9.50 A.M. joined from course at 2nd Army School of Musketry. Lt Jewatt to F Ambulance sick.	
"	2.7.17	A.M.	Training in ST MOMELIN area under Coy arrangements. Offs Shake & Macintosh & Lts Watts & Henry to Coy commanders course at VOLKERINCKHOVE.	
"	3.7.17	A.M.	Training in ST MOMELIN area under Coy arrangements. Battalion sports in field beside A' Coys billet in afternoon.	
"	4.7.17	A.M.	Do. A, B & C Coys at baths at LE BEAUSTACKE	
"	5.7.17	A.M.	Bn practised attack on green line on ST MOMELIN area. F moel frontage somewhat small. D, S, & H Coys at baths at LE BEAUSTACKE. 2/Lieut Anderson to O.C.	
"	6.7.17	A.M.	Training in ST MOMELIN area under Coy arrangements. Proceeded to 5th Army Rest Camp.	
"	7.7.17	A.M.	Bn practised attack to green line on ST MOMELIN area. Bn frontage finished very well. 2/Lieut Human & 160 O.R.s proceeded to 19th Tunnelling Coy R.E.	
"	8.7.17	A.M.	Wet. No church parade owing to rain.	
A.30 Central Camp	9.7.17	A.M.	Bn left LEDERZEELE & marched to ST OMER entraining there for POPERINGHE. Bn in tents at A.30 Central. Very crowded. Capt. Wilkinson proceeded on leave.	
"	10.7.17	A.M.	Dry & dull. Some shots fell near camp during the night. 1 offr & 100 O.R.s on working party under C.R.E. at 8 P.M.	
"	11.7.17	A.M.	2 offrs & 100 O.R.s on working party under C.R.E. at 8 P.M.	
TRENCHES	12.7.17	A.M.	Battalion relieved 1/4 Seaforths in trenches. Bn H.Q. LANCASHIRE FARM, with dessert/Lt.H. front dug-out. 2 Coys in front line and 2 Coys A & B in Canal Bank. Gas shells on the way up. A quiet night. 10 O.R. wounded by rifle & anti-aircraft shell in camp.	
Do	13.7.17	W.LB	Enemy's artillery somewhat aggressive. About 1120 rounds from his Heavies sent Bn H.Q. from 10:15 A.M. to 11:30 P.M. but no casualties. Number of working parties supplied from Canal Bank Companies, & also from B & D Coys. Casualties 10 O.R.	

Casualties:

WAR DIARY or INTELLIGENCE SUMMARY

Army Form C. 2118.

1/4 Batt. The Gordon Highrs.

Place	Date	Hour	Summary of Events and Information	Remarks and references to Appendices
TRENCHES	13.7.17	9 P.M.	0 R killed, 3 wounded. Enemy shelled C.T.'s from support to front line during the night. 2/Lieut J.F. Cumming rejoined ECHELON 'B' from Cavé. Party of 1 officer & 100 o.R's under C.R.E. at 8 P.M. from ECHELON 'B'.	
"	14.7.17	9 P.M.	Enemy's artillery active, especially in the vicinity of 'LANCASHIRE FARM' & EALING TRENCH. Steady shelling of these points from his heavies from about 10 A.M. - 2 P.M. Our heavies woke up in the afternoon. About 9 P.M. the enemy started a fierce shelling of all our C.T's and put on a double barrage (1) between FRONT & GOTT line (2) in rear of support line. He stopped about 9.30 P.M. but began again some 20 minutes later; eventually he became quiet about 10.30 P.M. Our guns replied heartily. The remainder of the night was moderately quiet. Working parties as usual. Casualties 2 o.R's killed 6 o.R's wounded. Echelon 'B' provided working party of 1 officer & 100 o.R's under C.R.E. at 8 P.M. Draft of 20 o.R's arrived.	
"	15.7.17	9 A.M.	Our artillery very active and the enemy's very quiet. He shelled our right support line with what was thought to be a 6" gun about 8 P.M. Battalion was relieved by 1/9 Sherwood Foresters - the relief passed off very quietly and the Bn. got back to tents in A30 Central between 2 A.M. and 4 A.M. Casualties 1 o.R killed, 4 o.R's wounded. Echelon 'B' provided working party of 1 officer & 100 o.R's under C.R.E at 8 P.M.	
A30 Central	16.7.17	9 A.M.	Bn. resting, cleaning up. "Standing by" from 12 noon - 12 noon.	
"	17.7.17	9 P.M.	Bn. provided working parties of (1) H.Q. o.R's 250 o.R's under C.R.E. (A) 2 officers 150 o.R's under Divisional "G". They went by train to AUSTRALIA FARM, Coy. RAILWAY TRIANGLE at 8 P.M. 'C' Coy. proceeded to Canal Bank. Casualties 2 o.R's wounded (both 'C' Coy). Capt FALCONER rejoined from leave.	
"	18.7.17	9 P.M.	Bn. standing to from 12 noon - 12 noon 19.7.17. 2/Lt Cumming & 500 o.R's proceeded to Canal Bank for work under Cdr. M.G. Coy. Casualties 3 o.R's (all 'C' Coy) wounded.	

Army Form C. 2118.

WAR DIARY
or
INTELLIGENCE SUMMARY. 1/4th Batt. The London Highrs

(Erase heading not required)

Instructions regarding War Diaries and Intelligence Summaries are contained in F.S. Regs., Part II. and the Staff Manual respectively. Title pages will be prepared in manuscript.

Place	Date	Hour	Summary of Events and Information	Remarks and references to Appendices
A30 Central	19.7.17	P.M.	400 o.R.s out as working party & 60 offrs & officers. 200 under C.R.E. & 100 under "J." 5 O.R. reinforcements arrived. Casualties 3 o.R. wounded	
"	20.7.17	P.M.	Bn. Standing by from 12 noon – 12 noon 21.7.17. 'B' Coy relieved 'C' Coy in the Canal Bank. Casualties 1 O.R. wounded.	
"	21.7.17	P.M.	4 offrs & 150 o.R's out as working party under C.R.E. Shelling round camp in evening – H.V. pretty close to H.Q. officers. Lt. E.R. Watts to F.A. Capt Williamson returned from leave.	
"	22.7.17	P.M.	Bn. Standing by from 12 noon – 12 noon 23.7.17. 2/Lieut Diack & party of 500 o.R's relieved 2/Lieut Cumming & party at Canal Bank. Capt J.R. Hay reported. Casualties 3 o.R's wounded	
"	23.7.17	P.M.	'A' Coy relieved 'B' Coy at Canal Bank – rtly carried out in districts of Lt. Col. Hogues & 50 o.R's out as working party under C.R.E. 2/Lt T.H. Abbot proceeded on leave. Casualties 2 o.R. wounded. 1 O.R. gassed	
"	24.7.17	P.M.	Bn. Standing by from 12 noon – 12 noon 25.7.17. 2 offrs & 500 o.R's out as carrying party at 6 A.M. 2/Lt (?) Morgan to Field Ambulance. Casualties 1 O.R. wounded (suspected S.I.) 1 O.R. gassed.	
"	25.7.17	P.M.	4 offrs & 140 o.R's out as working party under C.R.E. Casualties 1 O.R. wounded.	
"	26.7.17	A.M.	Bn. Standing by from 12 noon – 12 noon 25.7.17. 2/Lt Diack & party returned to camp from Canal Bank.	
"	27.7.17	P.M.	"Echelon B" under Capt J.R. Hay proceeded to HOOTKERQUE.	
"	28.7.17	P.M.	'A' Coy left Canal Bank & returned to camp at 5.30 A.M. Bn. Standing by from 12 noon – 12 noon 29.7.17.	
"	29.7.17	P.M.	Deluge of rain from 9.30 A.M – noon. Service of Holy Communion in the afternoon.	
"	30.7.17	P.M.	2/Lt Lunan proceeded on leave. 1 Platoon of 'A' Coy & 1 Platoon of 'C' Coy, 1 Field Co. R.E. Mitchell attached to 400th Field Co. R.E. Bn. Standing by, the detachment commanded by 2/Lt A.T.H.	

WAR DIARY or INTELLIGENCE SUMMARY.

1/4th Batt. Gordon Highrs.

Army Form C. 2118.

Place	Date	Hour	Summary of Events and Information	Remarks and references to Appendices
A30 Central Camp Ref. Sh. 28NW.	31/7/17		Battn standing by. 2nd Lieut. A.M.W. Keith was wounded today. 51st Division attacked enemy positions North of YPRES. 154th Brigade in Reserve. Battalion in camp at A 30 Central. Raid did not move.	

C B Colerton Major for Lt Col.
Comdg. 1/4 Bn. The Gordon Highlanders.

WAR DIARY

OF

4TH GORDON HDRS.

FOR AUG 1917

Vol 30

VOL. 31

Headquarters
154th Infantry Brigade.

Enclosed herewith
War Diary, Volume No. 31
for month of August. 1917.

W.G. Rosenberg? Lt
Capt & Adj'

for O.C. 1/4th B. Gordon Heights
1.9.17

Army Form C. 2118.

VOLUME 31

WAR DIARY
or
INTELLIGENCE SUMMARY.   1/4 Bn. Gordon H'flrs

(Erase heading not required.)

Instructions regarding War Diaries and Intelligence Summaries are contained in F. S. Regs., Part II. and the Staff Manual respectively. Title pages will be prepared in manuscript.

Place	Date	Hour	Summary of Events and Information	Remarks and references to Appendices
A.30 Central	1.8.17.	9AM	Bn. moved up the line leaving camp at 10AM. Bn H.Q. Tunnel, LANCASHIRE FARM. 'A' & 'B' Coys Blue line, 'D' Coy MAFIELD TRENCH & POTTS Tunnel. 'A' & 'C' Coys Canal Bank. Very wet day and mud very bad. Casualties 2 other ranks wounded.	
Support Line	2.8.17.	9AM	Bn. in positions as on 1st inst. Continuous rain and mud very bad. Casualties 5 O.R. wounded.	
	3.8.17.	9AM	Bn. in same position. Slight abatement of rain, but weather conditions still very bad. Casualties 10 O.R. killed 30 O.R. wounded.	
Front Line	4.8.17.	9AM	Bn. moved up to the front line. Bn H.Q. GOURNIER FARM – 'A' & 'C' Coys in front holding the post line across the STEENBEEK, & also supporting points, with joint Bn H.Q. at FRANCOIS FARM. Bd D Coys in Reach Line – 'B' Coy H.Q. MACDONALDS FARM, 'D' Coy H.Q. HOSPITAL FARM. Bn relieved 4th Seaforths, the relief went smoothly & quickly being complete before midnight. Weather faired up, but the ground was in a very bad state. Casualties 30 O.R. wounded.	
	5.8.17.	9AM	Considerable artillery activity on both sides. Bn H.Q. coming in for a very fair share of the enemy's attention. Shortly before midnight military road bridge, just in rear of Allient Mestons posts across the STEENBEEK, went in the air. Some doubt at first existed as to whether or not the Germans had succeeded in carrying down to the bridge but there is little room now to doubt that the bridge was blown up by means of a land mine placed there by the Germans before they retired, & wiped from a considerable distance off. The weather continued fresh, fair & the ground to improve. Echelon 'A' Transport Lines near HOSPITAL FARM were bombed about 12. noon. 2 O.R.s being killed 7 wounded, and 13 horses killed 16 wounded. Total casualties 2 O.R.s killed 17 wounded over & 1 Lieut J.B. Anderson went on leave	
	6.8.17.	9AM	Artillery continued active on both sides. Weather continued good, & the ground became more or less passable. Casualties 8 O.R. wounded. 1 O.R. killed.	

Army Form C. 2118.

WAR DIARY
or
INTELLIGENCE SUMMARY. 1/4 Bn Gordon Hghrs
(Erase heading not required.)

Instructions regarding War Diaries and Intelligence Summaries are contained in F. S. Regs., Part II. and the Staff Manual respectively. Title pages will be prepared in manuscript.

Place	Date	Hour	Summary of Events and Information	Remarks and references to Appendices
	7.8.17	Front Line 6 am	About 6 a.m. the S.O.S. signal was put up on the front. It was relayed at Coy H.Q. again from Bn H.Q. 18½ minutes later the artillery put on a thin barrage. Machine gun fire was heard on the front, but no shelling at all. It eventually transpired that there had been a slight scrap on the left, & the S.O.S. having gone up, the infection had been caught on our front, the remainder of the day was fairly quiet until the relief hour. 8th Bn Duke of Wellington regiment relieved us, just as things were starting the S.O.S. went up again on the left, followed by a terrific barrage from our left, the infection was again caught, & matters were hotting up for another hour when everything died down. The relief however went quite well, & with very few casualties to ourselves, though the Wellingtons were not quite so lucky. During the day the front posts claimed 25 Germans sniped at Curr's gunner. A British plane was brought down east of FRANCOIS FARM at 4pm, & the pilot killed. Casualties 10 OR killed 50 OR wounded.	
ST. JANSTER BIEZEN	8.8.17	8am	Bn moved down to CANAL BANK in the early morning, leaving again at 9am. We entrained at VLAMERTINGHE & detrained ½ mile short of POPERINGHE, marching from this point to Tunnelling Camp, ST JANSTER BIEZEN, & arriving here at 12.M. Echelon 'B' rejoined from HOUTKERQUE in the afternoon along with a draft of 6 ORS. Resting & refitting. Capt H.P.S.RAE proceeded to 5th Army Infantry School, & Lieut F. MacIntosh Allieu to 5th Army Infantry School, & Lieut F. MacIntosh to PARIS for 1 week.	
POORTIEOULINGHEM	10.8.17	8 am	Bn moved to POORTIEOULINGHEM. Entrained at PROVEN at 8am, arriving WATTEN at 12M & marched from there to POORTIEOULINGHEM. A charming rustic village & billets quite good. Training ground appears excellent, & it is to be hoped that there will be no trouble in getting it. Transport left ST JANSTER BIEZEN at 10.15 am, but is taking two days to complete the trek. Capt McIntosh proceeded on leave to PARIS. Capt McMillan admitted hospital 11th & 15th August. Large numbers from base allied with from injuries.	

A 8334 Wt. W4973 M687 750,000 8/16 D.D. & L. Ltd. Forms/C.2118/13.

Army Form C. 2118.

WAR DIARY
or
INTELLIGENCE SUMMARY. 1/4 Bn Gordon Hghrs.
(Erase heading not required.)

Instructions regarding War Diaries and Intelligence Summaries are contained in F. S. Regs., Part II. and the Staff Manual respectively. Title pages will be prepared in manuscript.

Place	Date	Hour	Summary of Events and Information	Remarks and references to Appendices
OOHTLEOLOOF NORD	11.8.17	9 AM	Day set out to clean up H.S. refitting. Transport arrived. Draft of 160 O.R's arrived	
"	12.8.17	9 AM	Church parade in forenoon. 2/Lt Strachan to hospital.	
"	13.8.17	9 AM	Battalion proceeded to Northern Training Area, new and Company Training. Capt Sinclair proceeded to 2 on Course 2/Lt McInnes returned from course.	
"	14.8.17	9 AM	Coy training carried out on ground round WILLS	
"	15.8.17	9 AM	Brigade Field Day. 1/4 H ready to line firing in course at LE TOUQUET	
"	16.8.17	9 AM	Battn had baths at ETAPLES Coys had use of armies firing range	
"	17.8.17	9 AM	Coy training carried out in greater round WILLS. 2/Lt Keith proceeded on leave. 1/4 Bns proceeded to Base for a morning instructional duty. Capt McIntosh rejoined from PARIS. Capt 2/Lt Anderson from Course	
"	18.8.17	9 AM	Coy Training carried out in Southern Training Area. 1/Lt JB Grieve proceeded to BHQ as relieve observing officer 2/Lt 2/Lt Church Serjeant in Harrison. Capt R L Mackinnon went to PARIS on leave 2/Lt J Strachan rejoined from hospital	
"	19.8.17	9 AM	Battalion firing at 6" Range. Draft of 100 O.R. arrived.	
"	20.8.17	9 AM	Battalion proceeded to Southern Training Area, carried out attack practice by companies. 2/Lt McInnes proceeded on leave.	
"	21.8.17	9 AM	" Northern " carried out company training. Transport left for WORMHOUDT in	
"	22.8.17	9 AM	route for ST JANSTER BIELEN.	
"	23.8.17	9 AM	Battalion left OOHTLEOLOOFHEM. Entrained at WATTEN detrained at ABEELE & marched thence to N camp at 10.15 p.m.	
ST JANSTER BIELEN	24.8.17	9 AM	JANSTER BIELEN at 4.15 a.m. on 24-inst. Battalion resting in Camp. Lieut Hendry rejoined from course	
"	25.8.17	9 AM	Company Training carried out round camp. 2/Lt Rule went to course at XVIII Corps Infantry School. Captain Sinclair rejoined from course.	

WAR DIARY
or
INTELLIGENCE SUMMARY. 1/4 Bn Gordon Highrs

Army Form C. 2118.

Place	Date	Hour	Summary of Events and Information	Remarks and references to Appendices
ST JAMES's CAMP	26.8.17		Church Service in forenoon.	
"	27.8.17		2/Lts G.F. & St. J. HOSTER DIETED Company Training carried out round camp. Capt R.F. Mackinnon Transfd from B.E.F. His Co.	
"	28.8.17		Company Training carried out round camp. Draft of 130 O.Rs arrived. Major J. Rowbotham Kn 8th H.L.I. joined Battalion and took over command. 2/Lt D.W. Grice and 4 N.C.Os attached permanently to 401st Fd. Co. R.E. as schoolmates.	
"	A.M. 29.8.17		Battalion moved to MORAT CAMP and transfd to HOSPITAL FARM. Lt-Col Lyon proceeded on leave.	
MORAT CAMP	P.M. 30.8.17		Company Training in the vicinity of camp. 2/Lt W. Imlah went to Lewis gun course.	
"	A.M. 31.8.17		Companies practised attack on NIEUPORT town & rifd. 2/Lt A. Murray went on leave. 2/Lt J.F. Cumming proceeded to India office for interview re transfer to Indian Cavalry.	

31.8.17

J. Rowbotham
Major.
Commanding 1/4 Bn. the Gordon Highrs

WO 31

I 154/5-1

War Diary
of
4th Battn Gordon Hrs
for
September 1917.

Army Form C. 2118

Volume 32

WAR DIARY
or
INTELLIGENCE SUMMARY. 1/4 Bn. the Gordon Highs.
(Erase heading not required.)

Instructions regarding War Diaries and Intelligence Summaries are contained in F.S. Regs., Part II. and the Staff Manual respectively. Title pages will be prepared in manuscript.

Place	Date	Hour	Summary of Events and Information	Remarks and references to Appendices
MURAT CAMP.	1.9.17	9am	Battalion practised attack on Murat Training Area in the afternoon. Capt Beveridge R.A.M.C. went on leave, Capt Gillespie taking his place. 2/Lt Leith went to Brigade as Intelligence officer	
"	2.9.17	9am	Church Service in forenoon. Camp shelled about 10.45 a.m. – casualties 1 O.R. killed 3 O.R. wounded	
"	3.9.17	9am	Battalion practised attack on Murat Training Area in forenoon. 2/Lt Weston rejoined from Shu Yung Course	
DIRTY BUCKET CAMP	4.9.17	9am	Battalion moved to Dirty Bucket Camp	
"	5.9.17	9am	Attack done on Murat Training Area before G.O.C. Division	
CANAL BANK WEST	6.9.17	9am	Battalion relieved 6 Seaforths in Canal Bank W.S.I. Echelon B remained at Dirty Bucket Camp	
"	7.9.17	9am	4 Coys in turns Lewis Gun and Bombing gone on with whole Battalion bathed	
"	8.9.17	9am	"	
"	9.9.17	9am	" Coy Cmdrs reconnoitred the line.	
LINE	10.9.17	9am	Battalion relieved 4 Seaforth Highrs in the line. Bn. H.Q. at C5A1.9. 'B' Coy on right front, 'D' Coy on left front, 'A' in support and 'C' in reserve. A quiet night	
"	11.9.17	9am	Enemy quiet, but got our own field artillery rather active on out front posts. Our howrs fired into gap on PHEASANT TRENCH during the day. Shortly after the two "pill-boxes" in front of PHEASANT FARM. They did not appear to be damaged. One British plane brought down south east of Bn H.Q. Casualties thirteen and unusual was	
"	12.9.17	9am	Our own field officer again practised out front posts. PHEASANT TRENCH again shelled by 18 inchs 8 12 my but the pill-boxes did not appear to have been hit. Three British planes seen to be brought down, one falling between Pill-Coy H.9 and "DOG HOUSE", & a aviation was seen through our lines but were not seen again. Casualty 1 wound by	
"	13.9.17	9am	Enemy artillery fairly active, especially on points with the STEEMBEEK. Battalion was relieved at night by 1/6	

A5834 W+ W4973 M687 750,000 8/16 D. D. & L. Ltd. Forms/C.2118/13.

Army Form C. 2118.

WAR DIARY
or
INTELLIGENCE-SUMMARY. 1/4 Bn The Gordon Highrs

(Erase heading not required.)

Instructions regarding War Diaries and Intelligence Summaries are contained in F. S. Regs., Part II. and the Staff Manual respectively. Title pages will be prepared in manuscript.

Place	Date	Hour	Summary of Events and Information	Remarks and references to Appendices
LINE	9/9/17	12.9.17	Bn. Billet WORTH. Relief went very well. Bn. on relief went to SIEGE CAMP.	
SIEGE CAMP	9/9/17	13.9.17	Bn. resting and refitting	
"	9/9/17	14.9.17	Coys. practised attack and bayonet courses on BRIELEN Training Area	
"	9/9/17	15.9.17	Company & Battalion attack carried out on BRIELEN Training Area. Lewis Gun and Bombing Classes in the afternoon. Camp was bombed at 12.15 a.m. by hostile aircraft – 2 O.R.s (including R.S.M.) killed, 2/Lieut. Williamson & 23 O.R.s wounded.	
"	9/9/17	16.9.17	Battalion at SIEGE CAMP. Bath Division Parade. Church Parade at 12.30 P.M. Battalion attack on BRIELEN Training Area in afternoon.	
"	9/9/17	17.9.17	Brigade attack on BRIELEN Training Area in forenoon. Two Companies at SIEGE CAMP range in afternoon. Lewis gun and Bombing Class carried on with.	
"	9/9/17	18.9.17	Brigade attack at dawn on BRIELEN Training Area.	
"	9/9/17	19.9.17	Battalion moved up the line & got into assembly positions preparatory to attacking the enemy's positions south west of POELCAPPELLE.	
Line	9/9/17	20.9.17	154th Infantry Bde. attacked the enemy's positions at 5.40 a.m. 4th Seaforths taking 1st objective (dotted blue line) on left and 9th Royal Scots on right. Second objective (BLUE LINE) was allotted to 4th Gordons on left and 7th A & S Hrs. on right. The Seaforths on our front experienced a fair amount of trouble in taking their objective especially at PHEASANT FARM PILL BOXES where the Germans put up a stiff resistance. The remnants of German dead lying about here testified to the stiffness of fighting. The Battalion passed through the Seaforths, and reached their objective about 7.30 a.m. with the except on of the left "D" Company owing to the Division on our immediate left being held up by Germans who were not able to get into the place to the G. of E. N.W. but had to	

A5834 Wt. W4573 M687 750,000 8/16 D. D. & L. Ltd. Forms/C.2118/13.

Army Form C. 2118.

WAR DIARY
or
INTELLIGENCE SUMMARY. 1/4 R. Scots. Hughes
(Erase heading not required.)

Place	Date	Hour	Summary of Events and Information	Remarks and references to Appendices
LINE (cts)	20-9-19	9am	to swing round in a big curve to the left forming a defensive flank. The objective was taken without a great deal of opposition & our estimated casualties but at 2/Lieut Lomax, 2/Lieut Grey, Capt Williamson, 2/Lieut MITCHELL, 2/Lieut KRAUCH, 2/Lieut LAMBERT & 6 O.R.'s. More officers were sent for to come up & take their places. Just then the enemy counterattacked but was successfully driven back. From this time onwards our men speedily dug in the front line posts were very much thinned by our own artillery firing short & several casualties were caused by it. In several cases the front line had to be withdrawn 30 to 50 yds. At about 5.30 p.m the Germans attacked in considerable numbers , the units on without flanks were seen to be retiring. Our men putting up a stiff fight were presumably driven along the whole front, the Coy of 8-A&S Hgrs attached to us from the 157 Bde had also to withdraw. The retiral went back, as far as well behind the dotted green line. Battalion H.Q. turned out and observed forward to... Germans had put up a very strong barrage, each as far as Battalion H.Q, & especially along the front. Shortly the Pill boxLine. Shortly after this two companies of 8- A&S Hgrs came up and took up a position along CEMETERY ROAD. It was now dusk, and a reorganisation of the Battalion was made. 2/Lieut Meston with A' Company held the right flank & posts of collected from various stragglers were pushed out from PINEAPPLE ROAD the left under S/M Gordon, had taken up a fairly strong position W.E. of the CEMETERY with the 8- Argylls in rear. The position afterwards strongly held E very Company offset was set of action - 2/Lieuts Lomax, Dunn & Killen ||		

A 5834 W.W 4973 M 687 750,000 8/16 D. D. & L Ltd. Forms/C2118/13.

WAR DIARY or INTELLIGENCE SUMMARY.

Army Form C. 2118.

1/4th Bn Seaforth Highlanders

Place	Date	Hour	Summary of Events and Information	Remarks and references to Appendices
Hill 9	20.9.17	8 pm	Laurence wounded, 2/Lieut Kyrock Gp Shranck, affect Brown sick. 2/Lts Strachan MacNaughton, McInnes came up in the evening. Enemy shelling remained fairly constant & casualties to OR's estimated at 200.	
Hill 9	21.9.17	8 am	A comparatively quiet day. Our posts were again troubled by our own artillery firing short. Almost all that during the day, 3 three fresh posts under 2/Lieut MacNaughten pushed out to the N end of the cemetery. About 4 pm various reports were received at Bn H.Q. that the enemy was massing in considerable strength about 500 yds in front of PHEASANT FARM. The artillery were communicated with and a heavy barrage put on by the gunners at 6.30 pm. The enemy replied hotly and the duel went on for about an hour and a half. No enemy counter attack developed at all. The Battalion were relieved by the 5th Seaforth Hgrs and went into SIEGE CAMP. The total casualties for the action were Killed 2 officers & 37 other ranks. Wounded 6 officers & 131 other ranks. Unwounded missing 10 other ranks, missing 66 other ranks missing believed killed 2 officers, injured strs 2. officers, 11 other ranks. Total 12 officers 257 other ranks. One point which should be specially emphasised is that the men ran out almost entirely of S.A.A. It was all expended on good targets with good results. When the main Counter attack developed ammunition was actually being sent up but of course would not get to the men in time. Copy of operation order for the Attack is with War Diary also detailed account.	

WAR DIARY
or
INTELLIGENCE SUMMARY. 1/4 Bn. Gordon Highrs.

(Erase heading not required.)

Army Form C. 2118.

Instructions regarding War Diaries and Intelligence Summaries are contained in F. S. Regs., Part II. and the Staff Manual respectively. Title pages will be prepared in manuscript.

Place	Date	Hour	Summary of Events and Information	Remarks and references to Appendices
SIEGE CAMP	22-9-17	N.A.B	Battalion arrived in camp during the morning. Day spent resting and cleaning.	
	23-9-17	N.A.B	Fine day. Church service in forenoon. Baths in afternoon. Captn. R.L. MacKinnon proceeded on leave.	
POPERINGHE	24-9-17	N.A.B	Fine day. Battalion marched to POPERINGHE today. Billets fairly good.	
	25-9-17	N.A.B	Refitting being carried out. Echelon B and 4 Officers (Lt. B.C. BRODIE, 2/Lt. J.T. STEPHEN, 2/Lt. J.T. SUTHERLAND, 2/Lt. M.A. BOYD) and 115 O.Rs. ranks reinforcements joined today.	
	26-9-17	N.A.B	Training in forenoon. Advance party of 20 o/Rs ranks under 2/Lt. J.W. MESTON proceeded to COURCELLES AREA today. Captn. J.F.M. Gutosh rejoined from leave.	
	27-9-17	N.A.B	Training in forenoon.	

Army Form C. 2118.

WAR DIARY
or
INTELLIGENCE SUMMARY. — 1/4th Gordon Highrs.
(Erase heading not required.)

Instructions regarding War Diaries and Intelligence Summaries are contained in F. S. Regs., Part II. and the Staff Manual respectively. Title pages will be prepared in manuscript.

Place	Date	Hour	Summary of Events and Information	Remarks and references to Appendices
POPERINGHE	28-7-17	WB	Training in forenoon. Capt. SKAKLE proceeded on leave today. Battn. preparing for move.	
	29-9-17	WB	Battalion paraded at 1-30 a.m. marched to HOPOUTRE entraining there. Time of departure of train 3-20 a.m. arriving at BAPAUME MAIN STATION at 1-20 p.m. Battn. marched from there to huts at COURCELLES. accommodation good.	
COURCELLES	30-9-17	WB	Church service in forenoon.	

J. Rowbotham Lt. OC
Lindsay 1/4th Gordon H. dos.
1/4th Gordon H. dos.

REPORT ON ACTION FROM 20/9/17 to 22/9/17
ASTRIDE KEERSELARE - POELCAPPELLE Rd.

Reference Map... POELCAPPELLE. 1/10.000. Edition 3.

(1). OBJECTIVE:- U.24.d.8.2, ROSE HOUSE, DELTA HOUSE CHURCH TRENCH, MALTA HOUSE, U.25.2.8.1.

(2). ORDERS. Copy of orders issued are attached.

(3). ASSEMBLY...Completed by 1.30 a.m. 5 Casualties. Hot tea was issued.

(4). Advance at ZERO plus 10 to PHEASANT TRENCH completed with difficulty owing to M.G. and Rifle fire coming from parts where fighting was still in progress. German barrage opening behind the Battalion.

(5) The ADVANCE through the LEADING Battalion was completed up to time and PROTECTIVE BARRAGE was reached. Barrage was good and easy to distinguish. LEFT of Battalion was involved in fighting still in progress about WHITE HOUSE. Casualties to Officers..5.

(6) BARRAGE advanced again and battalion attacked and reached all objectives after very hard fighting. LEFT Company was not in touch on left. At least 7 Machine Guns were destroyed.
The Battalion was very weak and only 3 Officers remained in FRONT LINE which was being held by 6 platoons of approximately 10 men each.
RIGHT Company under command of 2/Lieut.DAWSON.
CENTRE Company " " 2/Lieut.KYNOCH.
LEFT Company " " Lieut. McDONALD.
Two more Officers were still available with the SUPPORT Company.
2/Lieut.ROSE with two platoons formed LEFT FLANK.
The remaining two platoons of the RESERVE Company had been drawn into the fighting and were in STROOM TRENCH.
The LINE was now re-organised and 1 Company 8th A. & S. Highlanders was sent forward to occupy a line 250 yards behind the BLUE LINE for immediate counter attack.
Only ONE line, the BLUE LINE was then being held by us.
Shelling by 6" and 4.5" guns of our front positions wounded LEFT Company Commander and caused RIGHT Company to withdraw from CHURCH to BEER TRENCH. DELTA and ROSE HOUSES were both held but Lewis Gun Team at DELTA HOUSE was destroyed by our GUN FIRE.
At this time, 11 a.m., the ENEMY were seen to be forming up and advancing in waves.
RIGHT Company Commander, who had occupied a Tank as his H.Q. sent up the TANK LEWIS GUNS and S.A.A.
At about 12.30 enemy came on and was driven off. Several smaller attempts were all driven off.
During the AFTERNOON Enemy massed heavily and advanced in waves to CHURCH TRENCH where many succeeding waves closed up. Our BARRAGE

BARRAGE was then behind them. The Company H.Q.
were in the Tank which was at Wx2X.V.25.a.15.65.
They fired all the S.A.A. left and most of the
rounds of 6lb shell. They were instructed in
the use of this weapon by the TANK Officer before
he left the TANK.
Over 300 rounds of S.A.A. per man had been issued
from the TANK.

The enemy attacked at about 5.30 p.m. between
DELTA HOUSE and the LEKKERBOTERBEEK and was
opposed very strongly till S.A.A. gave out. The
front posts then gave way and all posts in rear
also went back at the same time. There were no
Officers left by this time.
Machine Guns at MKXXX MALTA HOUSE and
1 platoon 8th A. & S. Highlanders retired.
Post at 82 also retired.
A general retiral then took place and about 300
men crossed PHEASANT TRENCH and ran back towards
Battalion Headquarters.
These men were rallied here and led forward and
launched forward from PHEASANT TRENCH.
The enemy had come down the V formed by the
POELCAPPELLE ROAD and LEKKERBOTERBEEK and were
xxxxxx past the DOTTED BLUE LINE.
6 platoons of 8th A. & S.Highrs. then arrived
and these were extended and launched from
PHEASANT TRENCH and occupied ROAD from U.30.b.30.65
to Road JUNCTION at U.30.b.75.15. The enemy fired
heavily during the advance.
The men were then re-organised and a line
established in front of the 8th A. & S. Highrs.

The situation was very obscure. ROSE HOUSE
seems to have held for dome time. The LEFT Company
fell back along KANGAROO TRENCH and during evening
got into touch with the LEFT but lost all touch with
Battalion. The Enemy were then 50 yards from EAST
END of CEMETERY.

Three Officers joined my battalion and during
night the situation was cleared and by daylight
posts had been collected and put in front of the
8th A. & S. Highrs. The part of the line from
U.30.b.30.60 to LEFTB BOUNDARY was taken over by
4th Seaforths..

On the afternoon of the 21st the enemy again
massed for COUNTER ATTACK.

BARRAGE Line was shortened and attack stopped.
Enemy put down a very heavy barrage.

(7) RELIEF   The 5th BN. SEAFORTH HIGHLANDERS relieved
on night 21st/22nd.
A line was handed over roughly through
U.24.d.30.45, U.30.b.55.90, U.30.b.78.15 and
U.30.d.90.90.

(8) 1. SUMMARY   The Battalion advanced well and captured
all objectives with moderate losses but heavy
Officer casualties
ii. First Counter attack was stopped but line
shaken and being fired on by our own 4.5" and 6"
shells.
Second Counter attack could not be met with S.A.A
available. Most men had none when they retired.
The retiral of FRONT POSTS caused complete retiral
of all men behind RIGHT and CENTRE Companies.
Loss of all Officers caused disorganisation.
Re-organisation was most difficult.
The enemy CONCRETE POSTS were captured without
much difficulty by method adopted, i.e. Section

Section rushes and attacking from flanks while all under fire and unable to move open fire on loopholes.

As the result of this action, I consider that, with the few Officers allowed for action, at least 4 should be kept in Battalion Headquarters ready to go up to their companies if necessary.

More stress should be placed on Rallying Posts for stragglers and men who get lost. They could then be organised and sent forward, otherwise, they are not under control and their value reduced.

More S.A.A. be carried and fewer No.33

Lieut.Colonel,

Commanding 1/4th Battalion The Gordon Highlanders

22nd September, 1917.

Copy No 3 War Diary.

SECRET.

OPERATION ORDER NO. 7
BY
Lieut.Colonel J.Rowbotham, M.C.,
Commanding 1/4th Battalion The Gordon Highlanders.

In the Field......17th Septr. 1917.

Reference :- (POELCAPPELLE, EDITION 3, 1/10.000
             (SKETCH "A".

1. OFFENSIVE.

   An offensive action will take place about the 20th inst. The main attack will be made South of our front on the PASCHENDALEV RIDGE by the IInd ANZAC CORPS.

2. OBJECTIVE.
   (a)   The 154th INFANTRY BRIGADE will attack on the whole Divisional Front.
   (b)   They will attack from U.30.a.10.80. to C.6.b.5.10. to the BLUE LINE, a depth of 1.000 yards.
         The boundary between Battalions will be the LEKKER.
   (c)   The enemy defences are divided into two stages by the DOTTED GREEN LINE.
   (d)   The DOTTED GREEN LINE will be captured and consolidated by the 9th ROYAL SCOTS on RIGHT, 4th SEAFORTH HIGHLANDERS on LEFT.
   (e)   The BLUE LINE by the
         7th ARGYLLE & SUTHERLAND HIGHLANDERS on RIGHT
         4th GORDON HIGHLANDERS on LEFT.
   (f)   Battalion on LEFT of 4th GORDON HIGHLANDERS is 13th BN. K. R. R.

3. ACTION.

   The Battalion will attack on a three Company Front in accordance with Scheme shewn on SKETCH "A".
   "C" Company will detail two Platoons for the RIGHT and two for the LEFT to follow the attacking waves and remain at KUMMENTER. U.24.d.2.3. (Approx.) and U.30.b.2.2. (Approx.) There will be an officer with each and they will, in the event of the enemy breaking through, counter attack on their own initiative. O. C. "C" Company will remain in Battalion H.Qrs. with necessary runners.

4. ASSEMBLY.

   Battalion will assemble along line of discs parallel to and about 70 yards in front of trees from DOG HOUSE to U.30.c.3.7.
   Assembly will be carried out in two lines with at least 25 yards between them and all available use made of shell holes for cover.
   "C" Company will assemble two Platoons in rear of RIGHT and two in rear of LEFT Company.
   Company Boundaries are shewn by a double round disc on Post.
   Disc 4 inches diameter - Post two feet long.

5. BOUNDARIES.

   All Boundaries are shewn on Map and Sketch "A".

-------- S H E E T 2. ---------

6. ARTILLERY BARRAGE.
   24 hours PRELIMINARY BOMBARDMENT.
   Barrage will start on PHEASANT TRENCH and advance at rate of 2 minutes for every 50 yards for first 200 yards. It will advance at rate of 3 minutes per 50 yards from here till DOTTED GREEN LINE and at rate of 4 minutes per 50 yards for remainder of attack.
   It will be protective from ZERO plus 26 minutes to ZERO plus 1 hour 33 minutes in front of 4th SEAFORTHS and will contain BLACK SMOKE there.
   For the last 8 minutes it will quicken up to intensive again preparatory to advancing.
   Covering Barrage will finally halt 250 yards in front of BLUE LINE.

7. TIME TABLE.
   ZERO   Barrage comes down
   ZERO plus 10 mins   Battalion advances about 300 yards and takes up a position just short of PHEASANT TRENCH and remains there. Reorganisation into waves will be carried out. Scouts will be put out for finding landmarks and compass bearings taken.
   ZERO plus 23 "   SEAFORTHS in Objective and Barrage comes to a standstill.
   ZERO plus
   1 hr. 8 mins   Two attacking waves advance in extended order and catch up Barrage.
   ZERO plus
   1 hr. 18 mins   "C" Company advances and proceeds to position.
   ZERO plus
   1 hr. 33 mins   Barrage advances followed by two leading waves.
   ZERO plus
   2 hrs. 1 min.   Barrage comes to a standstill in front of Objective.

8. Tanks will be used and carry S.A.A. for Infantry.

9. SIGNALS AND COMMUNICATION.
   (a) Two rocket signals per leading Company are issued.
   (b) Runners will be used.
   (c) Tank Signals are as follows :-
        1 RED DISC = POSITION CAPTURED
        1 RED)
        1 RED) " = Broken down tank.
        1 RED)

        1 RED)
        1 WHITE)" = Enemy is in Concrete Emplacement near
        1 RED)   tank.
   (d) 1 H.Q. Scout per Company will follow leading Companies and return with information.
   (e) VISUAL Signalling will be established as soon as possible
   (f) Telephones will also be established.
        Contact Aeroplanes will pass over position at
             ZERO plus 1 hour   )
             ZERO plus 2 hours 30 minutes)
             ZERO plus 4 hours   )
   If called for by dropping WHITE FLARES or using KLAXON HORN, Battalions will light red ground flares.

        Pigeons will be used.

SHEET 3.

10. **REPORTS.**
 Reports on situation must be sent in as early as possible.
 The rocket will nearly carry from objective to Battalion H.Q. where there will be a look out man.

11. **HANDSHAKING.**
 This will be carried out by detailed parties and will be reported as HAND COMPLETE or INCOMPLETE.

12. ZERO hour and Z day will be notified later.

13. **LOCALITIES.**
 BRIGADE H.Q.   at C 9 a 6.3   CANE POST
 BATTALION H.Q.   at U 29 d 67.50   Old "D" COY. H.Q.
 AID POST   at C 5 a 1.9   Old BATTALION H.Q.
 WATER   at AID POST   Old BATTALION H.Q.
 S.A.A., BOMBS)   at U 29 d 67.50)   BATTALION H.Q.)
 FLARES   )   and U.29 b 7.4)   DOG HOUSE.   )
 BN. on LEFT H.Q.   at U 29 b 60.98
 BN. in REAR H.Q.   at U 29 b.7.4   DOG HOUSE.

14. Acknowledge.

 (sgd) R.L.Mackinnon, Capt. & A/Adjt.,
 1/4th Battalion The Gordon Highlanders.

Copy No. 1 - 154th Infantry Brigade.   Copy No 7 - O.C. 'B' COMPANY
        2 - File   8 - " 'C' "
        3 - War Diary   9 - " 'D' "
        4 - Commanding Offr.   10 - " 'S' "
        5 - Second in Command   11 - MEDICAL
        6 - O.C. 'A' COMPANY.   12 - 7th A & S HIGHRS.
                                                    (for information)

ADDENDA No. 1 TO OPERATION ORDER No. 7
BY
Lieut. Colonel J. Rowbotham, M.C.,
Commanding 1/4th Battalion The Gordon Highlanders.
In the Field.....19th Septr.1917.

9. SIGNALS AND COMMUNICATION.

S.O.S. = 2 RED 2 GREEN Rockets, Flares or Grenades.
Special Aeroplanes are detailed to look for German Counter attacks. They will drop Parachute Flares giving BROWN column of smoke to indicate Counter attack developing. No attack of less than one Company will be signalled.
Signals will be dropped over part of Trench the enemy seems to be preparing to attack.
There will be a special party at DOG HOUSE detailed to pick up Aeroplane Messages. If message flares are fired in that direction (end of Trees) they will be picked up.
Messages must be carefully addressed.

15. MACHINE GUNS.

As soon as DOTTED GREEN LINE is captured two Machine Guns will be sent to U.30 b 8.2.
When BLUE LINE is captured two Machine Guns will be sent to ROSE HOUSE and two to MALTA HOUSE.
Acknowledge.

(sgd) R.L.Mackinnon, Capt. & A/Adjt.,
1/4th Battalion The Gordon Highlanders.

Copies to all recipients of O. O. No. 7.

CONFIDENTIAL.
No 21 (A)
HIGHLAND
DIVISION.

Vol 32

1/4th Battalion The Gordon Highrs.

War Diary. — Volume 33

October 1917.

Army Form C. 2118.

VOLUME 33

WAR DIARY
or
INTELLIGENCE SUMMARY.

1/4 Bn The Gordon Highrs.

(Erase heading not required.)

Instructions regarding War Diaries and Intelligence Summaries are contained in F.S. Regs., Part II. and the Staff Manual respectively. Title pages will be prepared in manuscript.

Place	Date	Hour	Summary of Events and Information	Remarks and references to Appendices
COUTURELLES	1-10-17	8am	Training under Company arrangements. A Coy at A range in the afternoon.	
"	2-10-17	8am	Do. B Coy at A range in the forenoon.	
"	3-10-17	8am	Do. C Coy at A range in the afternoon. 2/Lt R Imrie joined reinforcements arrived	
"	4-10-17	8am	Do. D Coy at A range in the forenoon	
NEUVILLE VITASSE	5-10-17	8am	Battalion moved by buses in the afternoon to a camp near NEUVILLE VITASSE, relieving 4th East Yorks R. Position 2½ miles behind front line. Following officers reinforcements arrived 2/Lts H.M.FRASER, A.W.ORR, W.A.ROSS, J.MCLEAN, W.J.DONEAN, A.M.LOE, W.D.PATEL, A.R.WATSON. Capt MacKinnon rejoined from leave.	
"	6-10-17	8am	Training under Company arrangements. Sports in afternoon.	
"	7-10-17	8am	Do. Voluntary church service in morning. Draft of 37 O.R. arriving	
"	8-10-17	8am	Do. 2/Lt E.W.G.Kinn rejoined from training cattle or Peter	
"	9-10-17	8am	Do. Sports in afternoon	
"	10-10-17	8am	Do.	
"	11-10-17	8am	Do. Draft of 75 O.R. arrived. 2/Lt A.J.G.Troup rejoined on duty	
"	12-10-17	8am	Do. Sports in afternoon. Bath mat NEUVILLE VITASSE	
LONE	13-10-17	8am	Battalion relieved 9th Royal Scots in the line, Bn HQ BOSK RESERVE Lofts Burry HQ at rt H.R.Said Front Coy APE SUPPORT Support Coy LION Reserve Coy PANTHER Relief passed off quietly and was complete by 12 noon. Casualties nil	Right Front Coy BISON RESERVE kept commanding officer
"	14-10-17	8am	O.C. & O.C. B, C & D Coys rejoined with draft carried out for successful daylight raid at 4:55 P.M. Gen. EDWARDS, G.O.C. 153rd Brigade on an official vicinity on our left. Carried out on an official invitation. Casualties 2 O.R. sick, 3 O.R. wounded. Commanding officer went to F.A. sick, Major Pet__ took over command.	

M 5834 Wt. W4973 M687 750,000 18/76 D.D. & L.Ltd. Forms/C.2118/13.

Army Form C. 2118.

WAR DIARY
or
INTELLIGENCE SUMMARY.
(Erase heading not required.)

Instructions regarding War Diaries and Intelligence Summaries are contained in F.S. Regs., Part II. and the Staff Manual respectively. Title pages will be prepared in manuscript.

Place	Date	Hour	Summary of Events and Information	Remarks and references to Appendices
LINE	15-10-17	am	Wiring, Works Patrolling proceeded with. Casualties 1 O.R. wounded	
"	16-10-17	am	Do. Casualties Nil	
"	17-10-17	am	C & D Coys relief. Relieved A & B Coys in the front line. Relief went off quietly and was completed by 11.30 pm	
"	18-10-17	am	Wiring Works Patrolling proceeded with. Casualties one O.R. wounded	
"	19-10-17	am	Wiring Works Patrolling proceeded with. Casualties Nil	
"			Do. Casualties one O.R. at tank, accidentally wounded while cleaning a	
"	20-10-17	am	Wiring Works Patrolling proceeded with. Casualties 1 other rank wounded.	
"			Rl of Scots relieving the Battalion in the line. Relief went very quietly and was completed by 12.30 pm	
			The C.O. was handed over to the O.C. Royal Scots with all the front line signposts. The front lines +	
			Completed wired, and considerable progress in rehauling. passing was assuming consistent form	
			the Battalion on relief proceeded to YORK LINES where very good accommodation by Jains	
YORK LINES	21-10-17	am	Day spent in cleaning and refitting. C & D Coys at baths at BEAURAINS in the afternoon. Following is	
			an extract from Battalion orders of the day: "Para 8. Under Authority granted by His Majesty the King	
			the Field Marshal Commanding in Chief has awarded decorations as stated to the undermanned for	
			gallantry displayed on 20 September 1917. The Fifth Army commands 18-orks commands and Divisional	
			Commanders congratulate the recipients:— The Distinguished Service Order—Captain (A/L+ Col) J Hector Ham	
			M.C.—Rgt: R. Mi. Staff Rgt. Allied (A/P) captain) H.Q. Sindaurnye — the Military Cross — Allied Lt Gen	

A5834 Wt.W4973 M687 750,000 8/16 D.D.&L.Ltd. Forms/C.2118/13.

WAR DIARY or INTELLIGENCE SUMMARY

Army Form C. 2118.

14th Bn. the Gordon Highrs.

Place	Date	Hour	Summary of Events and Information	Remarks and references to Appendices
YORK LINES	22.10.17 (Sat)	9.AM	200 11.5 C.S.M. A.J. Anderson (B Coy) - The Yistinguished Conduct Medal - 200011. C.S.Majr G Smith (a Coy). 207735 L-Cpl Dalton (ECoy) 240583 L-Cpl A Davidson (D Coy) 207446 Pte R Sweet (A Coy). Draft of 130 O.R. reinforcements arrived.	
"	23.10.17	9AM	Companies Training round camp; C&D Coys working on Range; Bayonet Assault Course; camp Improvements. Lecture in evening by Capt J.R. Gordon on "General Surrounding Country, Points of Interest, Enemy system of Defence." Also — Officers - NCOs Attended. Lieut S.H. Duncan went on leave.	
"	24.10.17	9AM	C Coy Training on Assault Course. D Coy Training inside Camp. A & B Coys working on Assault Course, Range and Camp Improvements. Patrick Duncan continued out by Squads of 1 NCO and men per Coy. 1st of October Reports N. & R. I. from leave.	
"	25.10.17	9AM	C & D Coys Training round camp. A & B Coys working on Range; Assault Course; Camp Improvements continued. Capt J.R. Gordon went on leave. Draft of 130 O.R. reinforcements arrived. Lecture in evening on organization of platoon etc by C.O. Placers & C.Os to Section-Leaders — Points 5:14-15:16-17, page 14b-	
"	26.10.17	9AM	A & D Coys Training round Camp. B & C Coys working on Assault Course, Range, Camp Improvements continued. Battalion was preparing to move to trenches the next day but the move was cancelled at 7:30PM	
"	27.10.17	9AM	A & B Coys Training round camp. C & D Coys working on Assault course, Range, Camp Improvements, Public Duties continued. 10 O.R. reinforcements arrived.	
"	28.10.17	9AM	Battalion relieved by 14th Essex and entrained at STONE SIDING, travelled to VANQUITIN by light railway. The railway ran on a narrow gauge line of about two tracks, and the trucks in which we were squashed	

Army Form C. 2118.

WAR DIARY
or
INTELLIGENCE SUMMARY.

1/4 Bn The Gordon Hgrs.

(Erase heading not required.)

Instructions regarding War Diaries and Intelligence Summaries are contained in F. S. Regs., Part II. and the Staff Manual respectively. Title pages will be prepared in manuscript.

Place	Date	Hour	Summary of Events and Information	Remarks and references to Appendices
LATTRE-ST-QUENTIN	28-10-17 (con)	9 AM	Squaded had a habit of inhaling smoke from the engines, the journey in consequence took about four hours but e. Coys train took two hours more than this. Train got wrong route to WANQUETIN the Battalion marched to LATTRE-ST-QUENTIN. Billets were fairly good.	
"	29-10-17	9 AM	All Coys training in ground round billets. Captain McLeod (2nd) & Lieut. W. Imlah returned from Coast.	
"	30-10-17	9 AM	All Coys training in ground round billets. "D" Coy at HAUTEVILLE range in the afternoon. Lecture in evening by Captain J.F.M. Mackintosh on "The Rifle Parts-Mechanism, Care, Sights, S.A.A. Points of Interest," 2/Lieut Meston on leave.	
"	31-10-17	9 AM	All Coys training in ground round billets.	

31-10-17

C.D. Coles Vain, Major.

Commanding 1/4 Bn The Gordon Hgrs.

CONFIDENTIAL
No 31(A)
HIGHLAND DIVISION.

Vol 33

1/4th The Gordon Highrs

War Diary —
Volume No. 34
November 1917

SECRET

Army Form C. 2118.

WAR DIARY
or
INTELLIGENCE SUMMARY.

(Erase heading not required.)

VOLUME 34

Instructions regarding War Diaries and Intelligence Summaries are contained in F. S. Regs., Part II. and the Staff Manual respectively. Title pages will be prepared in manuscript.

Place	Date	Hour	Summary of Events and Information	Remarks and references to Appendices
LATTRE ST. QUENTIN	1-11-17	9 A.M.	Companies training on ground round billets. B and C Companies at MOREUETTE miniature range. Lecture in evening by Lewis Gun officer on "The Lewis Gun - it's history and characteristics. Lt. W. R. J. Macnaughton went on leave	
Do	2-11-17	9 A.M.	Companies training on ground round billets. A & D Companies at MOREUETTE miniature range	
	3-11-17	9 A.M.	Companies training in ground round billets. B & C Companies at MOREUETTE miniature range. Lecture in evening by Major C. D. Peterkin on "Working Parties". Lt-Col. Bruce Thom rejoined from leave	
	4-11-17	9 A.M.	Church Parade in forenoon, followed by Billet Inspection	
	5-11-17	9 A.M.	Companies training on ground round billets. A & B Companies at MOREUETTE miniature range. Lecture in evening by the Commanding officer on the Compass & Map Reading. 250 R. went to join 401st Field Coy R.E. as Sappers/Miners	
	6-11-17	9 A.M.	Companies training on ground round billets. B & C Companies at MOREUETTE miniature range & also at baths in forenoon.	
	7-11-17	9 A.M.	B&C Companies practising attack etc. on ground round billets. A & D Coys at MOREUETTE miniature range, and also at baths in forenoon. Lecture by Commanding officer in evening on "Explosives" (demon.)	
	8-11-17	9 A.M.	Companies practising attack on taped out system. B & C Companies at MOREUETTE miniature range. Lt. Brown went to Brigade for course in Staff duties. Major Peterkin went on and Capt. Gordon rejoined from leave. Major Wigot A. & Q. team M.C. joined from 7th A.P.S.H.	

A5834 Wt.W4973 M687 750,000 8/16 D. D. & L. Ltd. Forms/C.2118/13.

WAR DIARY or INTELLIGENCE SUMMARY

Army Form C. 2118.

Place	Date	Hour	Summary of Events and Information	Remarks and references to Appendices
LATTRE-ST-QUENTIN	9-11-17	9.am	Companies practising the attack tapped out as at system. A & D Companies at Norquett range. Lecture by Capt. MacKinnon in the evening on "The History of the Battalion".	
	10-11-17	9.am	Companies practising the attack on tapes out system. B & C Companies at Norquett range. 2/Lts. J. Middleton, J.B. Gray & group reinforcement w. Philip Div. will. S.S. Devijanes. Battalion Bisley displayed 255. 2nd Lt. A.F.A. at ARHEUX in second round Div. Association championship & won 5-3.	
	11-11-17	9.am	Church service followed by G.O.C. Inspection. 2/Lts. Middleton, Gray, Redmynsen, Willis, Grove reposted and left for 2nd Battalion from hqrs. Capt. G.F. Grove went to course at 4th Army Infantry School. Capt. J.R. Hay went on leave to Paris. 2/Lt. L.H. Cunsisa went & joined.	
	12-11-17	9am	Brigade inspected by Corps Commander Genl Sir Chas. Ferguson Bt., and medals presented. Capt. G. Falcons went on and 2/Lt. F.W. Melton returned from leave. 2 O.R. reinforcements arrived.	
	13-11-17	9am	First anniversary of BEAUMONT HAMEL and general holiday in the division. Brigade sports in the forenoon and Battalion concert in the evening.	
	14-11-17	9am	A Company carried out musketry competition. B, C, & D Coys practising artillery formations, deploying etc. 2/Lt. J.F. Stephen went to 4th Army Musketry School. 45 O.R. reinforcements arrived.	
	15-11-17	9am	Companies carried out artillery formations, deploying & attacking under Platoon Commanders. Capt. J.M. Henderson M.C. went on leave.	
	16-11-17	9am	Companies practising artillery formations etc. and all attacks during the day. Battalion (minus 6th Black Watch detachment) entrained at TINQUES at 4.45 for MOREUVILLE at 10.15 p.m.	

WAR DIARY
or
INTELLIGENCE SUMMARY.
(Erase heading not required.)

Army Form C. 2118.

Place	Date	Hour	Summary of Events and Information	Remarks and references to Appendices
MH.H.H.Hatte St-Quentin	17-11-17	9am	Battalion left LATTRE-ST-QUENTIN and entrained at BEAUMETZ at 4 p.m., detraining at BAPAUME. Thence they marched to camp near BEAUREGARD. Echelon 'B' proceeded to YTRE-LE-HAMEAU.	
YTRES	18-11-17	9am	Battalion marched to LITTLEWOOD CAMP besides YTRES, arriving there at 11 p.m. Billetted in huts.	
Do	19-11-17	9am	Battalion remained in huts. Battle stores issued.	
YTRES	20-11-17	9am	Battalion left YTRES at 3 a.m. & proceeded to METZ where it went into billets, arriving there at 4.45 a.m. At 6.20 a.m. the 3rd Army attacked the German Hindenburg line. At 8.10 a.m. the Battalion moved to starting position just outside METZ and at 9.30 a.m. received orders to proceed to the old British front line. Here it stayed the whole day and night.	
CANTAING	21-11-17	9am	At 6.10 a.m. the attack was continued, and at this hour the Battalion left the old British front line with the 9th A&S Hrs on our left and the 9th Argyle Scots following in rear of us. The Battalion proceeded in column of route as far as the Railway Embankment S.W. of FLESQUIERES, where it halted after an hours wait. Word came through that FLESQUIERES had fallen. At 8.30 a.m. the Battalion moved forward again, this time in artillery formation. Good touch was kept with the 7th A&S Hrs on the left, and the advance continued till 300 yards short of sunken Road from GRAINCOURT to MARCOING where outposts of 5th Seaforths & 8th A&S Hrs were found to be holding a line. They reported that the village of CANTAING was held by the enemy. Reconnaissance was made & this was confirmed. The attack was ordered at 10.30 a.m. "C" Company on the right and "D" Company on the left, with "A" in rear of C, & "B" of D. The attack developed, but was held up by heavy rifle and machine gun fire. Two lines of trenches were dug in front of the village thinking to force a serious attack	

WAR DIARY
or
INTELLIGENCE SUMMARY.
(Erase heading not required.)

Army Form C. 2118.

Instructions regarding War Diaries and Intelligence Summaries are contained in F. S. Regs., Part II. and the Staff Manual respectively. Title pages will be prepared in manuscript.

Place	Date	Hour	Summary of Events and Information	Remarks and references to Appendices
CANTAING	21-11-17 (cont)	3.0.P.M.	Shortly after this nine Tanks appeared from the direction of PREMY CHAPEL and got into the east end of the village. The infantry followed with great dash and heavy fighting ensued in the streets, but the village was completely cleared of the enemy by 12.40 P.M. A strong hostile post N.W. of the village held out till about 3 P.M. but was eventually cleared by one of the Tanks. The Battalion took close on 300 prisoners including four officers, and 6 M.G. The Battalion pushed on through the village, but as the 7th A. & S. H'rs had not been able to come thro' with both flanks our left, a defensive line was hastily formed in front of the village. Our losses were eventually secured with. Killed Capt H.P. SHAKE Lieut N.J. GIBSON, 1 & 9 O.R. Wounded 7 & O.R. 2/Lt. J. GIBSON, 160 OR., Missing	
do.	22-11-17	3.0.A.M.	Battalion was relieved at 3 a.m. by 11th Royal Scots, but A Coy remained in support to 9th Royal Scots, and under their orders. Battalion moved back to Gun Pits, a mile and a half in rear of CANTAING. The day was spent in reorganizing & issuing of fresh battle stores. At 4.45 P.M. word came that the Battalion was to move at once to support. Battalion was in position by 5.30 P.M. two companies in old German trenches south of CANTAING and two companies in Sunken Road 800 yards in rear. Night was normal.	
do.	23-11-17	8.0 A.M.	Battalion came under orders of G.O.C. 152nd Inf. Bde., & was ordered to be ready to support an attack on FONTAINE-NOTRE-DAME, but did not become involved in the attack, & remained in support.	
do.	24-11-17	3.0.A.M.	Battalion was relieved by Guards Division at 3 A.M. and returned to METZ.	
METZ	25-11-17	9 A.M.	Left METZ at 9.30 P.M. and proceeded to YPRES. Remained five hours in the rain waiting for HUTTANT	

REPORT ON ACTION
20th to 24th NOVEMBER, 1917,
AND
CAPTURE OF CANTAING,
BY
1/4th BATTALION THE GORDON HIGHLANDERS.

Reference Map - NIERGNIES 1/20.000

NOVEMBER, 19th.
The Battalion was in huts at YTRES and was equipped for battle.
Night of 19/20th moved to METZ into cellars.
No shelling.

NOVEMBER, 20th.
ZERO was 6.20 a.m.
The Battalion moved to Starting Place clear of village of METZ and formed up there in column of route at ZERO plus two hours.
At 9.30 a.m. Battalion was ordered to FRONT BRITISH TRENCHES, Q. 5 c. and Q. 5 d.
Arrived in position at 10.30 a.m. in column of route.
No shelling. Weather was misty.
Progress of battle could not be ascertained.
Tanks could be seen on FLESQUIERES RIDGE. Slight shelling on left. Considerable movement of Cavalry visible. Prisoners coming in.
At 4 p.m. Battalion was ordered to take up position for night in BRITISH FRONT LINE TRENCHES. In position by 5 o'clock.
Rain had started to fall about 3 p.m. and continued nearly all night.
At 8.45 p.m. received warning Order to assemble at X Roads K.16 d.8.4 and attack FLESQUIERES from FLANK.
The necessary reconnaissance was carried out.
During night received orders to attend conference at 7th A. & S. Highrs. H.Qrs. and was ordered to assemble on RAILWAY LINE from RIBECOURT STATION to SUNKEN ROAD K.24 c.75.15.
7th A. & S. Highrs. were to be on LEFT FLANK with 4th Seaforth Highrs. in their SUPPORT, while 9th Royal Scots were in our SUPPORT.
General Scheme was to pass through 152nd and 153rd Infantry Brigades and capture final objective, CANTAING - FONTAINE LINE.
4th Gordon Highlanders. To cover Frontage of 152nd Inf. Brigade

NOVEMBER, 21st.
Assembled in position along RAILWAY LINE and remained there till 8 a.m. when information was received that FLESQUIERES had fallen and we could advance.
Arranged with O.C. 7th A. & S. Highrs. to start at 8.30 a.m.
Advance commenced in Artillery Formation of Platoons and was continued till 500 yards short of SUNKEN ROAD from GRAINCOURT to MARCOING where 5th Seaforth Highrs. and 8th A. & S. Highrs. were holding outposts.
Good touch was kept with 7th A. & S. Highrs. on left who had met opposition from ANNEUX and had extended. No troops advanced on our right. No opposition as yet on Battalion Front.
Outposts of 5th Seaforth Highrs. and 8th A. & S. Highrs. reported that enemy held CANTAING.
Heavy Rifle and Machine Gun Fire was going on on 7th A. & S. Highrs. Front and their line was not forward on the left.
Reconnaissance was made and reports confirmed that village of CANTAING was held/

Sheet.....3.

Held by the enemy who seemed reluctant to fire and allowed a good inspection to be made. Wire and trenches both were much more formidable than expected.
No casualties or no shelling up to this stage.
Battalion H.Qrs. was still marching between two REAR Coys.
Attack was ordered for 10.30 a.m. in accordance with scheme pre-arranged.
At 10.5 a.m. message arrived stating tanks would assist and arrive at 10 a.m. None were in sight at 10.15 a.m. Two guns of 'C' Battery, 79th Brigade, R.F.A. arrived and took up position at 10.15 a.m. at L.8 c.80.90 opened fire at 10.45 a.m. and did very good execution.
At 10.30 a.m. no tanks in sight and attack commenced.
Enemy withheld fire till waves were well on move and then opened with from 4 or 6 M.Gs. in trench and two in high buildings.
Fire was also opened from Light Trench Mortars.
A sharp encounter started.
'C' Company which was to work round RIGHT of village was the only Company to get any way ahead.
'D' Company was completely held up. Heavy casualties were incurred here. CAPTAIN SKAKLE and LIEUT. GIBSON were both killed.
'A' and 'B' Coys. were in support and ordered not to become involved in fight. Sniping from buildings was very accurate.
R.F.A. Guns worked splendidly. M.G.C. and T.M. Battery were kept in reserve.
Tanks appeared in sight from PREMY CHAPEL and entered EAST end of Village at 12.35 p.m. followed by Infantry. 'A' Coy. was ordered to follow the tanks.
Heavy fighting then took place in the streets but village was all cleared by 1 p.m. except a strong pocket from CANTAING ROAD to L.3 a.5.9 which held out till 3 p.m. They were in both systems of trenches and prevented any advance on NORTH OF ROAD CANTAING - FLESQUIERES. The road itself, being sunken, was passable to small parties.
Trench Mortars were then ordered up but did not manage to clear up the pocket. This was eventually done by a tank.
The three companies involved in the fight had, by the time the village was cleared, become disorganised. The advance was proceeded with but soon became disjointed, especially as the two LEFT Companies could not advance past pocket. Touch could not be established and in spite of there being little resistance, on RIGHT flank, the forward movement came to a standstill with two Coys. WEST of CANTAING VILLAGE and two Coys. holding line from NINE WOOD to F.28 d. 5.9. There was no touch with 7th A. & S. Highrs. and their progress was unknown.
Village was shelled immediately we occupied it.
Three Squadrons of Cavalry arrived which I took command of and posted round the village.
In all about 300 prisoners were captured.
I then saw the Commanding Officer of the 9th Royal Scots who said he was ordered not to go through my Battalion and as I could not hope to hold against any counter-attack I asked for relief. The Battalion was then re-organised and took up a line roughly from F.27 Central through F.28 a. 9.9 , F.28 d. Central to L.10 Central where touch was established with 39th Division.

NOVEMBER 22nd.
This line was handed over at 3 a.m. 22nd to 9th Royal Scots and Battalion, less 'A' Coy., which remained under Command of O.C. 9th Royal Scots in trenches at L.3 a. c and d., moved back into/

Sheet....3.

into gun pits in L.14 a. Night of 21/22nd was spent in these dug-outs and on 22nd Battalion was re-equipped for action by 12 noon. One platoon of 'B' Coy. sent forward with S.A.A. to 4th Seaforth Highrs. and became involved in fight. At 4.45 p.m. Battalion was ordered to move into Support and at 5 p.m. moved off. Battalion was in position by 5.30 p.m. the leading two Coys. in trenches from L.3 d. 4.5 to F.27 c. 1.4, and two Coys. in SUNKEN ROAD, L.8 b., where the Battalion remained till relieved by units of the Guards Division.
Night of 22/23rd was spent in positions as above.
Intermittent shelling and everything normal.

NOVEMBER, 23rd.
Battalion came under orders of G.O.C. 152nd Inf. Bde. and was ordered to be ready to support an attack on FONTAINE NOTRE DAME. ZERO 10.30 a.m.
Attack was launched. Moderate shelling.
CANTAING heavily shelled.
Battalion H.Qrs. at L.3 c. 2.2 and in touch with 152nd Inf.Bde. at L.1 d. 9.5.
Numerous wounded from attacking units passed through Aid Post. The Battalion was not involved in this action and remained in support.

NIGHT 23rd/24th NOVEMBER.
Relieved by units of GUARDS DIVISION. Complete at 3 a.m. and returned to METZ.
CASUALTIES TO DATE.....2 Officers killed,
         16 Other Ranks killed
         80 Other Ranks wounded.
         6 Other Ranks missing.

NOVEMBER 24th.
Arrived in Billets at METZ at 6.45 a.m.
Rested till 9 p.m. 9.30 p.m. marched to YTRES STATION by very muddy route.
Arrived Station 12.15 a.m. Remained in open till 5 a.m. on morning of 25th. Men very wet, having remained 5 hours in rain.

NOVEMBER 25th.
Arrived BUIRE 9 a.m. and billeted. Owing to failure in Motor Lorries only a few blankets had arrived and men were without Blankets on night of 25th / 26th .

  The following points which came under observation appear to be of interest :-

1. COMMUNICATION.
  The great necessity for better Communication and Intelligence in the Field.
  Brigade Signals to connect up to Battalions sooner.
  On November 23rd a wire was laid by the Battalion to 152nd Inf. Bde. Brigade should have laid to us.
  This wire was used by 9th Royal Scots also and proved of great value later.
  Better arrangements for obtaining wire and carrying it forward. Battalions cannot carry wire in excess of that required for Company work.
  Better planning of Visual Stations beforehand.
Section. Brigade Signal ~~Station~~ to co-operate more with Battalions in joining up.

2. TANKS.
  The/

REPORT ON
MEDICAL ARRANGEMENTS
IN THE RECENT ACTION",
20th to 24th NOVEMBER, 1917.

On 21st November, Regimental Aid Post was established in ruined house at cross roads outside CANTAING. Notice was sent by runner to Advanced Dressing Station, giving location and requesting bearers and stretchers. This was sent off at 10.45 a.m. A second message left at 12.30 p.m. by mounted orderly. No reply came to either message by 6 p.m. and I sent my Medical Corporal down with a very urgent message. At 10 p.m. five R.A.M.C. Bearers arrived with one stretcher. By this time all the stretchers taken into action by the Regtl. Stretcher Bearers had been used and I was in urgent need of more. A full complement of stretcher bearers did not arrive till 2 p.m. on 22nd, when Battalion was in reserve.

                               Hope M Gillespie
                                Captain, R.A.M.C.,

M.O. i/c 1/4th Battalion The Gordon Highlanders.

In the Field,
    27/11/17.

Sheet.....4.

The great value of Tanks was demonstrated.
The Battalion is certainly indebted to them for making opening into CANTAING. They can replace wirecutting and barrage. Better time table work in conjunction with them should be attempted, also a method of street fighting with them should be laid down.

3. Necessity of training Section Commanders.

4. Necessity for most careful mopping up.
Large parties of civilians and enemy remained in cellars which were difficult to find. Enemy very reluctant to surrender and made for own lines at night.

5. ENEMY DEFENCES.
The outstanding feature was their so called "imcomplete trench", F.26., F.27., and L.3. This was a very well sited trench which had been spit-locked out. Only short lengths were dug. M.G. Emplacements and Dug-outs were completed and wire was very strong indeed.
Enemy retired to this line and dug in hastily but was in a well selected position and capable of being re-organised easily. Pocket which held out was almost entirely dug by wnemy who had retired from FLESQUIERES.
The next remarkable feature was the immediate shelling of CANTAING as soon as it was captured also the prompt and accurate shelling xxxxxxxxxxxxxxxxxxxxxx of Tanks as they advanced, whereas Infantry was not much molested.

6. MEDICAL ARRANGEMENTS.
Medical Officer's Report is attached. I concur with it entirely.
(sgd) J. Rowbotham, Lieut. Colonel,

Commanding 1/4th Battalion The Gordon Highlanders.

26/11/17.

SECRET.   Copy No. 11

OPERATION ORDER No. 18
BY
Lieut. Col. J. Rowbotham, D.S.O., M.C.,
Commanding 1/4th Battalion The Gordon Highlanders.
In the Field...19th Novr., 1917.

Reference Maps - (51 c.
              (51 c. S.E.
              (NIERGNIES
              (SKETCH issued.

      In continuation of Instructions issued verbally to Company Commanders, the following information in available:-

BOUNDARIES.
    As shewn on Maps.
    RIGHT BOUNDARY does not include NOYELLES.

MOVES.
    The Battalion will be ready to move to Starting Position at 8.30 a.m. on 'Z' Day.
    Starting position....Q.20 b. 1.3.
    The Battalion will then follow up the attack and proceed along ROUTE as follows :-
        Parallel to and SOUTH of Road Q.20 b.3.6 to Q.21 b.6.4 thence to track running parallel with SHAFTESBURY AVENUE to CRATER on LANCASTER Road at K.36 c.0.1 thence via LANCASTER Road to GRAND RAVINE at K.30 c.7.8 and to CROSS ROADS at K.24 b. 7.3.
    Care must be taken to avoid all guns firing.
Cavalry will probably move with and across Battalion Front.
Company Commanders will have reconnaissance of Route made early on 'Z' Day.

ACTION.
    If the Cavalry Action is successful the Brigade is ordered to occupy FONTAINE. A line will be formed round it roughly as follows :-
    F.16 Central.   In Touth with Cavalry.
    F.16 a.25.35
    F. 9 c.70.20
    F. 9 c.40.10   In touch with 7th A. & S.Highrs.
    If the action of the Cavalry is not successful a line will be established roughly along unfinished Trench System from BOURLON WOOD to NINE WOOD.

SPEED.
    Speed is the Chief Factor in this operation. All Commanders must handly their men quickly past all obstacles.

SHELLING OF METZ.
    In the event of METZ being shelled while the Battalion is in Billets there, Company Commanders will march their Coys. out to Q.20 b.

SIGNALS.
    S.O.S. ....2 Red and 2 White   Very or Rockets.

    Lift Barrage   )
    or Start Rolling) White, Red, White.   Very in quick
    Barrage forward)   succession.

    Attention is drawn to Tank Signals.
All/

Sheet......2.

All signalling will be done by Visual till operation comes to a standstill when telephones will be installed.

SCOUTS.
   No formation is to move forward without being covered by Scouts.

LIGHTS AND FIRES.
   METZ is under observation and both must be screened during night in METZ.

                    (sgd) R.L. Mackinnon, Capt. & A/Adjt.,
                    1/4th Battalion The Gordon Highlanders.

   Copy No. 1 - File
            2   O.C. 'A' Company.
            3   'B'
            4   'C'
            5   'D'
            6   Commanding Officer.
            7   Second in Command
            8   Signalling Officer.
            9   Intelligence Officer.
           10   Medical Officer.
           11   War Diary

Volume # 35

WAR DIARY
or
INTELLIGENCE SUMMARY.

1/4 Batt. GORDON HIGHRS   Army Form C. 2118.

Place	Date	Hour	Summary of Events and Information	Remarks and references to Appendices
ROCQUIGNY	1/10/17		Arrived at hut in ROCQUIGNY at 1.30 a.m. Battalion ad half an hour in which. Received orders to move to BERTINCOURT and marched for then at 10 a.m. Arrived BERTINCOURT at 11.30 a.m. and found the Billets allocated to the Battalion still occupied by R.A.M.C. Ultimately managed through our Senior Capar & 2hr received orders to move to BEUGNY and march the Bn to this place at 3.25 pm. Just before starting the attempts the Bath was met by Brigade officer and informed that no billets were available and what Battalion was to move to LOVERAL by some other route at 7 pm. Ent. my cooker at once and made in other vehicles for the following day. Left BEUGNY on 20 Georges at 7 with and after a good deal of delay in which the senior guide thought by leg 4 Company matched the senior mere LOVERAL, and followed by B Coy from a point in road sort of Heucheu on old British frontiers. Got away an under own Bn order taken at 7 pm. Spanly Batt. for tonight.	
Near Belul Ment	2/10/17		Bn and. Tuesday Smith arrangt Officers Sapling Stall M.O. eventiving hunt day in front hivee HUEUVRES. Left at Brigid Hootsnee at 10.30 pm and relieved 3rd London Regt. Arth in tranches E. 19 a & 8. 19 a & e (in front of NUUEUVRES). Except for occasional shelling owing to Buy Moonlight night Bath working part all might night.	
Bruch	3/10/17		Bn holding tranches anent working ats at 6 Vary N.S. Shelly landstites of entrance to Bn Hyp causing very heavy casualties. Bn carrillies No carnettia. Heavy shelling of everything in retry throughout the day. Twinnelith our support line and	

WAR DIARY 1/4 Batt GORDON HIGHRS.
or
INTELLIGENCE SUMMARY

(Erase heading not required.)

Army Form C. 2118

Place	Date	Hour	Summary of Events and Information	Remarks and references to Appendices
Heneka	3/12/17		in the vicinity of Bn. H.Qrs. Lt/Col. Shilling wounded by bullet about 7pm. Lt/Col R.L. Meiklejohn wounded in leg by bullet about 7pm	
	4/12/17		Quiet — had post. tomorrow. Shelling during the day. Several Other ranks Brigade spare men not sent up the working wires. half finished. Working party and Companies got about carrying so enormously supplies and Companies out over at trench fires to HOUND STREET & BUTTE JUNCTION. Rain fell and cruft often aeroplane scouts came up of night at trouble in front line. Battn. Junction — One platoon at 1.30 am A + B each leaving 1 platoon in front line + D Coy ⟶ one platoon plus 1 Lewis Gun in support. Coy HQ at 3.5.5 the platoon of B Coy moved thro' off Sentine Fm. Battn HQrs at Mabon at Coy. Hacking through Flanders ⟶ D Coy support line. At 4.45 am the platoon along with Battn Hqrs mental Mt. during the attack was received all ranks came forward entered and thro'out came at during the barrage and minority came at being front line Carry. 2nd Battn Gordons Harkend mercied back Indyendent to little in FRENICOURT — Tuesday Battn + 152 Inf. Bde. Gordons and Harkens marched arriving Feet Point at 8 P.M. Tuesday hand frost. Unknowing 4 C's and 4 Others wounded, officer 9 killed 19 wounded O.R.	
do	5/12/17			

WAR DIARY or INTELLIGENCE SUMMARY

Army Form C. 2118.

1/4 Batt GORDON HIGHRS

Place	Date	Hour	Summary of Events and Information	Remarks and references to Appendices
FREMICOURT	6/10/17		Men had foot, foot being inspected also Rifles any being found by Armourer Sgt. Echelon B apparently laying out Transport lines along with transport of 7th Div arrived.	
	7/10/17	5pm	Had foot. Several aerial bombs dropped in vicinity of Billet about 5pm the casualties in Battn. but several on neighbouring units. Battalion training in forenoon.	
	8/10/17	10am 4pm	Med. Bath. training during forenoon on ground near Ecoust-St-Mein. Lieut Col G.S. Brakenbury G.S.O. Eastern Comd. paid Battn. a visit. Men training during forenoon. Church service had to be cancelled owing to rain. Bullets transport arrived ont to Ecoust not of splendon from aerial bombs.	
	9/10/17		Med. Bath at BEUGNY. training continued.	
	10/10/17	9am	Med. 3 Officers & 110 Mr on fatigue at Divisional Wash-em supplies working in tank for fifteen other Officers. Eleven carried on during day.	

WAR DIARY
or
INTELLIGENCE SUMMARY.

Army Form C. 2118.

1/4 Batt: Gordon Highrs

Place	Date	Hour	Summary of Events and Information	Remarks and references to Appendices
FREMICOURT	12/7/17		Slight frost. Very heavy shelling on left of our front about 6.15 am today. 7th & 5th am same again on German and throughout evenings. Classes carried on during day. Officers outside carrying on RABBIT ALLEY up to stores during the night. Billet during day.	
	13/7/17		Mild. Heavy shelling as left early morning during most of day. Classes carried on during day. 4 officers + 200 o/rs working on RABBIT ALLEY during evening. Reinforcement of 17 o/rs arrived this morning.	
	14/7/17		Very mild. Coys training and working on things in trenches. Two Lewis Guns mounted at Gnd. Lewis Gunners. Two hostile bombing aircraft coming over. No news of hostile party called for tonight. Co. 2nd Boy officers inspecting party called for tonight. Remaining men during afternoon.	
	15/7/17		Slight frost. Hostile aircraft over vicinity of Billet about 1 am. Bombs dropped in neighbourhood of village. D Coy inspected by B.G.C. B & C Coys at Range.	
	16/7/17		Mild. Church service in 'CINEMA HOUSE' at 10.45. Billet inspection by C.O. at noon. Battn. dinner 5 Gordons in afternoon. Pres. Major and A/78 Coys.	

WAR DIARY
or
INTELLIGENCE SUMMARY.
(Erase heading not required.)

Army Form C. 2118.

1/4 Batt Gordon Highlanders

Place	Date	Hour	Summary of Events and Information	Remarks and references to Appendices
	11/10/16		Coys in Quarter Road I 19 + 11 A and C + D Coy in Quarter Road in I 7 + A. Men being ordered to shelter anyone in shelter anyone. A Coy in Caves. Quiet men confid of one Bombet [illegible] of Coy - men ordered had an extra blanket sent up to transport as they were not in coys. Report of the number of D men - are were missed to Egypt. Bill for tactical purposes. A M dept Brigton considering this which does wish D Coy carit marked neither 252nd Tunnelling Co. Listed roof - our gun over night.	
F. 9. 2.	17/10/16		Very quiet over night. All carrying parties working working one 75 [illegible] and 15 [illegible] working carrying rations + barbed wire. NCOs reconnoitering [illegible] position - front line.	
	18/10/16		Very hard frost and ten thick. About women to rifle and came number by night working as carrying. Enemy artillery active during evening. 1/4th relief tonight. Working on fatigue tonight.	

Army Form C. 2118.

WAR DIARY
or
INTELLIGENCE SUMMARY.

1st Buff's Own High'rs

(Erase heading not required.)

Instructions regarding War Diaries and Intelligence Summaries are contained in F. S. Regs., Part II. and the Staff Manual respectively. Title pages will be prepared in manuscript.

Place	Date	Hour	Summary of Events and Information	Remarks and references to Appendices
Z.17b	19/10/17		[illegible handwritten entry]	
	20/10/17		[illegible handwritten entry]	
	21/10/17		[illegible handwritten entry]	
	22/10/17		[illegible handwritten entry]	
FREMICOURT	23/10/17		[illegible handwritten entry]	

1/4 Batt Gordon Highrs

Army Form C. 2118.

WAR DIARY
or
INTELLIGENCE SUMMARY.
(Erase heading not required.)

Place	Date	Hour	Summary of Events and Information	Remarks and references to Appendices
FREMICOURT	23/10/17	6pm	of bombing by troops encamped in village & neighbouring from 6 to 7pm. Fine weather in Battalion. Slightly wounded but circumstances considered when hit and several hit. Reinforcement of 9 other ranks on D.14 Major.	
	24/10/17	6am	Went out earlier that day. "D" Coy at ranges near the village. A B.C Coy marched to field south of Haringhirst lane and engaged in training during further specialist lessen advanced again. Rev Battalion B formed Command to rear. Enemy storm. Holiday Special Service to men.	
	25/10/17	6pm	Snowing during day. Hard frost during night.	
	26/10/17	—	Frosty and snowing during morning. Superior G.S Hebron Bac cancelled owing to weather. Men engaged in digging Shelter Trenches.	
	27/10/17		Frosty. Battn. at Baths in forenoon. Rifles inspected by Arm. Sgt. C.O. try which according one to be taken over a stately weather.	
	28/10/17	9pm	Frosty morning. 2nd Lt. Hutton took part in Musketry Competition with Hutton team and Battalion of the Brigade won through (Captain) was given for the next Lutin Scam. G R Scott	

WAR DIARY
or
INTELLIGENCE SUMMARY.
(Erase heading not required.)

Army Form C. 2118.

1/4 Batt. Gordon High[landers]

Place	Date	Hour	Summary of Events and Information	Remarks and references to Appendices
FREMICOURT	29/12/17 8pm		Rest of Battalion training in forenoon. 5 officers & 250 o/r as first para of reinforcement of 20 o/r arrived.	
	30/12/17 pm		Frosty. Training during forenoon. 3 officers reinforcement arrived.	
	30/12/17 10pm		Made this movement. Dinners at 11.30 am and commenced moving off to trenches at 12.45pm. Relieved 6th Seaforths in trenches North of BOURSIES. Relief complete by 5pm. Very quiet. Our own artillery active overnight. South of divisional front enemy artillery not very active.	
	31/12/17 8pm		Slight snow today. Dull. Very quiet.	

J. Rowbotham Lt Col
Comdg 1/4th Gordon H'rs

31/12/17

Operation Order No. X5 by Lt.Col.J.Rowbotham,D.S.O.,M.C.,
Commanding 1/4th Battalion The Gordon Highlanders.
In the Field....4th December,1917.

1. The present front British Line is to be withdrawn to-night.

X. The original British Front Line will be re-established by the 152nd Infantry Brigade. Trenches now held by 1/4th Gordon Highlanders will be vacated. The Battalion will pass through the 152nd Infantry Brigade and proceed to billets at FREMICOURT.

2. ROUTE. HOUNDSDITCH - BISHOPSGATE, CAMBRAIN - BAPAUME Road. On reaching cross roads at J.9 b.7.2 (late debussing point) troops will move by any track south of main road, but avoid road if possible.

3. O.C. 'D' Coy. will detail 1 platoon to load limbers at HOUND Dump. On completion of loading this party will proceed to billets. O.C. 'D' Coy. will post 1 platoon in trench in vicinity of Battalion H.Qrs. This platoon will lie behind the parados in order to keep trench clear. This will be completed by 1 a.m., 5th inst. Officer in Charge will take command of Machine Gun at E.19 c.35.40 and be responsible that exit trench to HOUNDSDITCH is clear.
At 2 a.m. balance of 'D' Coy. will move off, O.C. reporting to Battalion Headquarters.

4. At 2 a.m. all 'C' Coy. will move off. O.C.Coy. reporting at Battalion Headquarters.

5. WITHDRAWAL OF FRONT LINE. At 1.20 a.m. three platoons of 'B' Company will move off, O.C. Coy. reporting to Battalion H.Qrs.

6. At 1.30 a.m. three platoons of 'A' Company will move off, following 'B' Company. O.C. Coy. will report to Battalion H.Qrs.

7. At 1.30 a.m. remaining platoon of 'B' Company under 1 Officer will vacate 'B' Coy's sap, and take up position at head of C.T. leading into front line at E.19 b.1.1.
The remaining platoon of 'A' Company will continue to hold 'A' Company's Sap.

8. Great care must be taken to minimize noise. Ordinary trench routine should be carried out to the last moment, i.e. sniping and firing flares.

9. At 3.55 a.m. last platoon of 'A' Coy. will move out of front line and proceed to billets. One N.C.O. will report move at Battalion H.Qrs.
Remaining platoon of 'B' Coy. will follow, one N.C.O. reporting as above. This platoon should have a bombing squad in rear ready for action.

10. REARGUARD. The remaining platoon of 'D' Company with Machine Gun and Battalion Headquarters will move off at 4.45 a.m.

11. Os.C. Coys. are responsible for taking with them any men from other Coys. or units who may be in their sector.

12. Company and Platoon Commanders are held responsible that all men are completely equipped, especially as regards Lewis Gun Carriers and Pans.
In addition to this all ranks will carry out some salved article, S.A.A. or Bombs etc. which will be dumped at J.6 a.4.2 (where sunken road crosses old British Front Line Trench)

Sheet 3.

12 (contd.)
Sgt. Carnegie will indicate the spot and 4 guides are posted at intervals along route to this point.

13 Transport for Lewis Gun Pans, Bomb Buckets etc. will be at west end of BOURSIES (J.5 c.8.9)
Sgt. Calder will be responsible for loading.
Stretchers will be loaded on these limbers.

14 Billeting has been arranged.

15 Reference Map MOEUVRES 1/20.000 and 57 c.

16 Acknowledge.

(sgd) J.R.Thomson, Lieut. & Adjutant,

1/4th Battalion The Gordon Highlanders.

Hn. J. M. Gordon Gld.
H in the Garden Gld.   Vol 35

War Diary   Volume No. 36

January 1918.

VOLUME 36

4th Batt Gordon Highrs

WAR DIARY or INTELLIGENCE SUMMARY
Army Form C. 2118.

(Erase heading not required.)

Place	Date	Hour	Summary of Events and Information	Remarks and references to Appendices
Trenches	1/1/16		Front Trench. Very quiet.	
	2/1/16		do. do. Artillery activity	
	3/1/16		Slight midday Zeredemka aerial activity. SE & coast rest line about 11 am. One turned and came down inside contd in enemy lines near MOEUVRES A+B Coy relayed C+D Coy as front line during afternoon. Our artyh is vb active today	
	4/1/16		Fresh. Very quiet.	
	5/1/16		do. Slight aerial activity. Aug 6th arrived	
	6/1/16		do. do. Very quiet. Raining at night	
	7/1/16		Slight miller. Very wet and windy.	
	8/1/16		Very wet overnight. Shrapnel very wet and windy. Relieved by 10th Gordons in afternoon. Complete by 4.15 pm. Marched back to Station by Battns. 2nd DLI LINDUP C+ M.O. train 2REMICOURT arriving Station 6.10, off to work lift Bland. Reached billets by 1.30 am. First chefs of Officers, Station + cooking party arriving by 10 am.	
2REMICOURT	8/1/16		Cloudy. Clearing up in forenoon. Draft of 9 NCO arrived	

WAR DIARY or INTELLIGENCE SUMMARY.

4th Bn Queens Regt

Army Form C. 2118.

Place	Date	Hour	Summary of Events and Information	Remarks and references to Appendices
FREVICOURT	8/1/18		General training. Brigade expected to F.G.C.O. in Regimental Officers Boys etc. left at 2.30 pm up on scout train near JUIGNIES and returned about 2.30am next morning - Train was too heavy and train did not reach Still frosty. Both during the day. Depth of snow 9ins covered.	
"	9/1/18			
"	10/1/18		Milder. Officers 3rd M Lewis Gun Course at BEAUMETZ from 9am till 1pm. Raining during afternoon & evening.	
"	11/1/18		Snow + ice almost disappeared. Training up in forenoon. Officers 10.30/4.30 working on cable trench near BEAUMETZ from & to the Hills 3.30pm onwards to sundown in drain party only reached camp 10.30pm	
"	12/1/18		Mild rain. Church Service in forenoon. Battalion at Bath.	
"	13/1/18		Mist turning during morning forenoon. Training carried on Mist ending forenoon. All being rubbed with oil.	
"	14/1/18	9am	Raining during morning forenoon. Training to move up to trenches Received 6 Leafforth 6 Lunches and CTs in afternoon. Very rainy during that no CTs and ship had off to the true overland. Great	

4th Batt Gordon Highrs

Army Form C. 2118.

WAR DIARY
or
INTELLIGENCE SUMMARY
(Erase heading not required.)

Place	Date	Hour	Summary of Events and Information	Remarks and references to Appendices
TRENCHES	16/1/18		Very quiet. Dry and Trenches improving. Enemy aircraft more active over trenches. Practically no shelling had on Lancashire Regt. reconnoitring line during day.	
	17/1/18		Very quiet and trenches again very bad. Quiet no artillery activity. C.O. left this morning to proceed to Staff Council at R.T.C. Battalion under command of MAJOR GORDON.	
	18/1/18		Still wet. Cleared out during forenoon very close trenches, more hostile artillery activity today. Relieved by Leicester Regt. in trenches from relief - complete by 6 p.m. Battalion marched back to LUDOT CAMP FARMICOURT. Casualties for trip 2 wounded.	
FREMICOURT	19/1/18		Cleaning up in forenoon. All men who were in trenches, except Lewis Gun and Intelligence officers entrained at FREMICOURT STATION at 3 p.m. and proceeded to ACHIET LE GRAND and marched from here to their Billets. Battalion B and C Companies entraining arriving then by 5.30 p.m. at COURCELLES and marched at 11 a.m. and marched those who were not in trenches paraded at 1.30 p.m. all the way to COURCELLES arriving their about 4.30 p.m.	
COURCELLES	20/1/18		Left at 8.45 a.m. and marched with Brigade to BAILLEULVAL arriving then at 1.30 p.m. Men marched very well, only one man falling out. Dinners served on arrival. Men resting for balance of day. Billets only fair and very crowded.	

4 Batt Gordon Highrs

Army Form C. 2118.

WAR DIARY
or
INTELLIGENCE SUMMARY
(Erase heading not required.)

Army Form C. 2118.

Place	Date	Hour	Summary of Events and Information	Remarks and references to Appendices
BAILLEULVAL	21/1/18 Sat		Battalion at Baths and cleaning up. Draft of 4 Officers and 37 ORs arrived today. Very mild weather.	
	22/1/18 Sun		Training commenced. Conformed from 9.15 am till 1.15 pm. Officers & NCOs class in afternoon. Recreational training in afternoon.	
	23/1/18 Mon		Training continued during forenoon. Short in afternoon. C.O. returned today.	
	24/1/18 Tue		Training continued. Training contained. Short in afternoon.	
	25/1/18 Wed		Still very mild.	do
	26/1/18 Sat		Mild	do
	27/1/18 Sun		Battalion at Baths. Owing to a case of Diphtheria. No 11 Platoon isolated. Church Service in forenoon. Short in afternoon.	
	28/1/18		Training continued.	
	29/1/18		do	do
	30/1/18		do	do Hand Foot
	31/1/18		Hand Foot. Training continued.	

31/1/18
R. D. Shaw Lt Col
Comdg 1/4 Batt Gordon Highrs

Vol 34

1st Battalion McGordon Highl.

War Diary

Volume No. 35

December 1917

War Diary

Mr Bazentin — the Seven Highlanders.

February, 1918

Volume No 37

VI 36

SECRET

VOLUME 37.   4 Bn. Gordon Highlanders   Army Form G. 2118.

WAR DIARY
or
INTELLIGENCE SUMMARY.
(Erase heading not required.)

Place	Date	Hour	Summary of Events and Information	Remarks and references to Appendices
BAILLEULVAL	1/9/18		Militia. Training continued.	
	2/9/18		Battalion marched off (less No.11 Platoon) at 9am and proceeded to Hink near LOGEAST WOOD arriving thereat 1.30pm.	
LOGEAST WOOD	3/9/18	9pm	Church Service in forenoon. Clearing up during rest of day, and improving camp.	
	4/9/18		Training and improving camp	
	5/9/18		Battalion at Bath at ABLAIN ZEVELLE. Improvement of camp carried out.	
	6/9/18		Training, improving camp continued. Slight improvement to Brigade. I took the Brigade this morning and proceeded to join One Division.	
	7/9/18	9pm	Tactical attack on village of ABLAINZEVELLE by Battalion. Bath at Baths during day. Digging shelter trenches continued.	
	8/9/18	9pm	Raining most of the day. Training carried on. Going out of Brigade. Training, digging trenches work continued and improving camp. Lieutenant Fraser just arrived Birmingham. Completion of training [illegible] [illegible] [illegible] (No 3 Platoon) became Pte 2. Light Morris [illegible]	

4 Batt Walter Hughes Army Form C. 2118.

WAR DIARY
or
INTELLIGENCE SUMMARY.
(Erase heading not required.)

Place	Date	Hour	Summary of Events and Information	Remarks and references to Appendices
LOCEAST WOOD	9/7/18		Training continued. 5th Platoon Expedition on the Brigade for much discipline. Rigging turn tape today. 2nd & 3rd R.T. Recruits march brigade. 2nd & 3rd R.T. Hughes and 3rd & 4th military (3rd & 4th Rigging Tape 7.05 p.m. Major Record & Gorton Hughes (5.015 Hasson) and Major & Seton Hughes	
	10/7/18		Since last entry had the pick off owing to weather. Improvements in camp carried on unit.	
	11/7/18		Training continued. Staff of "Offices" (off. Rd High) and 11 O.R. carried today. Battalion at P.O.P.H. which took down each in person.	
	12/7/18		Dry mild. Battalion engaged cleaning at camp & equipment. Returning drying dry ppl Both Demonstration with Gas Projectors at 5.30 pm attended.	
	13/7/18		7am met. Marched off from Camp at 9.40 am and proceeded to LINDIT CAMP TREMICOURT arriving there at 1pm.	

A5834 Wt.W4473 M687. 750,000 8/16 D.D. & L. Ltd. Forms/C.2118/13.

4 Batt Gordon High[landers]

Army Form C. 2118.

WAR DIARY
or
INTELLIGENCE SUMMARY

(Erase heading not required.)

Place	Date	Hour	Summary of Events and Information	Remarks and references to Appendices
LINDUP CAMP FREMICOURT	14/7/18	10 am	Still [performing?] camp. Working party of 5 officers + 100 other ranks out at night burying cable. Battalion's at rest during day.	
	15/7/18	9 pm	6 Officers + 250 OR burying cable during day. Remainder carrying on with camp improvements. AMS Coy inspected for scabies. 13 cases. Improvement.	
	16/7/18	8 am	Same size of party again out with C/O Coys transport and camp trying cable. 19 Cases to hospital. Men inspected for scabies. 19 cases out burying cable. Remainder at Kort Root.	
	17/7/18	8 pm	Baths and working in camp.	
	18/7/18	frosty	6 Officers + 250 OR again out burying cable.	
	19/7/18	8 am frosty	Battalion working on camp with exception of 50 OR working at dugouts near YELU.	
	20/7/18	9 am	Same party of 50 out at YELU again today. Relieved 6th Battalion Seaforth Hldrs in Sector North of CARTSROI – BAPAUME ROAD. No casualties.	

WAR DIARY
or
INTELLIGENCE SUMMARY
(Erase heading not required.)

Army Form C. 2118.

4th GORDON H⁻rs

Place	Date	Hour	Summary of Events and Information	Remarks and references to Appendices
TRENCHES	21/2/18	—	BOORSIES shelled. RIGHT FRONT Coy slightly shelled. CASUALTIES 4.O. Ranks wounded. Working on posts in front line e.T's + wiring support lines	
"	22/2/18	—	Slight shelling on Battalion Area. Casualty 1.O. Rank. Patrols out. Work as above.	
"	23/2/18	—	Very quiet day. No casualties.	
"	24/2/18	—	Slight Shelling. No casualties	
"	25/2/18	—	Slight Shelling. No Casualties	
"	26/2/18	—	Very Quiet day. Heavy Patrol went out under 2nd Lieut DUNCAN. Two O. Ranks got through enemy wire at HOUNDSDITCH. M.G. fire was opened. Casualties 2nd Lieut DUNCAN & 1 Other Rank wounded.	

J Rowbottom Pte
Comdg 4th Gordon H⁻rs

51st Division
154th Infantry Brigade.

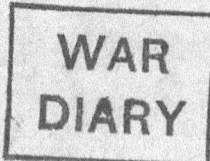

1/4th BATTALION

GORDON HIGHLANDERS

MARCH 1918

Attached :- Report on Operations 21st-26th March

WAR DIARY
or
INTELLIGENCE SUMMARY.

Army Form C. 2118.

Volume 38

Instructions regarding War Diaries and Intelligence Summaries are contained in F. S. Regs., Part II. and the Staff Manual respectively. Title pages will be prepared in manuscript.

(Erase heading not required.)

Place	Date	Hour	Summary of Events and Information	Remarks and references to Appendices
Trenches	1/3/18	AM	Battalion moved to new (BEAUCOURT) Sector S of CAMBRAI = RAPAUME ROAD. Batt H.Q in Sunken road SW of DOIGNIES at BRUNO MILL. D Coy attached 4th Seaforth. "C" Coy in INTERMEDIATE LINE. B Coy in SUPPORT. A Coy in Reserve at LE BUCQUIERE	
"	2/3/18	AM	All companies employed in Trench improvements. Weather very fine.	
"	3/3/18	AM	Working parties found daily and nightly for work on front line largely under R.E. Rate storm.	
"	4/3/18	AM	Weather continued fine. No shelling and no aerial activity noticed.	
FRONT LINE	5/3/18	AM	Battalion proceeded to front line. A Coy on right. B Coy in centre. C Coy on left. D Coy in Support. Day light relief in spite of very bright day. Batt relieved 4th Seaforths. Batt H.Q in Sunken road S of DEMICOURT.	
"	6/3/18	AM	Work carried on in front front line. Weather fine. Reinforcements 29 O.R.s	
"	7/3/18	AM	Work by all companies day and night on wire in front of	

A5834 Wt. W4973 M687 750,000 8/16 D. D. & L. Ltd. Forms/C.2118/13.

WAR DIARY
or
INTELLIGENCE SUMMARY.
(Erase heading not required.)

Army Form C. 2118.

Place	Date	Hour	Summary of Events and Information	Remarks and references to Appendices
FRONT LINE	7/3/18		Front line.	
	8/3/18		Fine weather. No enemy shelling of front line. Some intermittent shelling of DEMICOURT and SUNKEN ROAD by 5.9's.	
	9/3/18		Fine weather. During this turn in trenches a considerable amount of work was done on wire both in front of front line and in front of Support Line. A new belt of double belt was put up to N & and N.W. of DEMI COURT. Battalion relieved by 1st A & S.H. and 4th Seaforth Highlanders at about 6.30 p.m. Battalion proceeded to AMBULANCE CAMP – LEBUCQUIERE	
LEBUCQUIERE	10/3/18		Day spent resting and cleaning.	
	11/3/18		Stand to 4 A.M. Work stated improving Camp. Huts, new Cookhouse for A & B Coys, mens huts etc. Reinforcements – 5 O.R. arrival.	
	12/3/18		H.V. gun fires about 30 shells on S. side of village LE BUCQUIERE. Weather fine. Work in Camp continues.	
	13/3/18		Training carried out in morning. Gas Inspection by C.O.	
	14/3/18		Training continued	
	15/3/18		Battalion moves to line – right sub-section of DEMICOURT	

Army Form C. 2118.

WAR DIARY
or
INTELLIGENCE SUMMARY.
(Erase heading not required.)

Instructions regarding War Diaries and Intelligence Summaries are contained in F.S. Regs., Part II. and the Staff Manual respectively. Title pages will be prepared in manuscript.

Place	Date	Hour	Summary of Events and Information	Remarks and references to Appendices
TREIVCRES FRONT LINE	16/3/18		Sector. Battalion left LE BUCQUIERE 1.45 p.m. Quiet relief. C & D Coys Front Line. D Coy right, C Coy left. B Intermediate line. A Coy REAUMETZ - MORCHIES LINE. Quiet and fine.	
	17/3/18		Quiet. E.A. observed to fire in direction of BOURLON WOOD. Bombardment of enemy Front line with gas projectors at night.	
	18/3/18		Some enemy airieens activity against DOIGNIES all day with sgr. Also BOURSES and main CAMBRAI ROAD.	
	19/3/18		Quiet and some rain.	
	20/3/18		Quiet.	
	21/3/18	5 am -6.30	Intermittent shelling in Battalion Front. Some gas shell. Heavy bombardment started on left at 4.30 am. No attack developed on Battalion Front. Front line trenches commencing 1.30 am and Battalion took up position in HERMIES SWITCH. B Coy in INTERMEDIATE LINE being on right C & D Coy in SPITLOCK TRENCH. A Coy from left touching onto 4th SEAFORTHS. Attack developed on left of DOIGNIES. HERMIES ROAD. Defences flank at BRIAN MER.	
	22/3/18	10 am 10.45 am	Troops on left gave way but on right saw advance on left. He was held also along Battalion Front.	

A5834 Wt.W4973 M687 750,000 8/16 D.D. & L.Ltd. Forms/C.2118/13.

Army Form C. 2118.

WAR DIARY
or
INTELLIGENCE SUMMARY.
(Erase heading not required.)

Instructions regarding War Diaries and Intelligence Summaries are contained in F.S. Regs., Part II. and the Staff Manual respectively. Title pages will be prepared in manuscript.

Place	Date	Hour	Summary of Events and Information	Remarks and references to Appendices
22/3/18		9.0 a	Lt Col J Row ROTHAM. D.S.O. M.C. wounded.	
		11.15 am	Violent attack in A Coy from about Jrune Rd. Remainder of day quiet. Major GORDON M.C. assumed command of Batt.	
	23/3/18	1 am	Battalion proceeded to huts at LEBUCQUIERE	
		8 a	Slept out & huts. SUNKEN ROAD manned	
		10 a	Troops in late returns, Batt were unfed/less to relieve to GREEN LINE.	
		5 pm	Orders received to proceed to BANCOURT line taken up NW of BANCOURT. Line taken up SE of BEAULENCOURT A & SH on Right. 47 Seaforths on left. Battalion Slowly retired in front of enemy attack to WARLENCOURT.	
	24/3/18	am	Line taken up E of WARLENCOURT will inform to have at all costs the 1 hr when these Divisions were to relieve Battalion. Batt. held on the 1.30h. to former enemy and Rearguard action fought to day to PYS AU MONT. A & SH on left. 4/5 Seaforths in right. Strong enemy attack developed from direction of LOUPART WOOD and Patrols withdrew...	

Army Form C. 2118.

WAR DIARY
or
INTELLIGENCE SUMMARY.
(Erase heading not required.)

Instructions regarding War Diaries and Intelligence Summaries are contained in F. S. Regs., Part II. and the Staff Manual respectively. Title pages will be prepared in manuscript.

Place	Date	Hour	Summary of Events and Information	Remarks and references to Appendices
COLINCAMPS	25/3/18		Major A STEIN, M.C. took command of Batt.	
	26/3/18		Battalion withdrew to COLINCAMPS and took up his S.F.O.	
			SAILLY-AU-BOIS	
		9 a.m.	Battalion withdrew to SOUASTRE and recovered reserve line to Brigade	
		6 p.m.	Batt. relieved by Australians and marched to PAS	
			Casualties during Battle	
			Officers wounded 9 ⎫ 18	
			missing 9 ⎭	
			O.R. Killed 10 ⎫	
			wounded 97 ⎬ 400	
			missing 293 ⎭	
PAS	27/3/18		Batt. entrained for BARLY	
BARLY	28/3/18		Day spent resting and cleaning	
"	29/3/18		Left BARLY 12 noon & marched to FREVENT entrained about	
		4 p.m.	reached LILLERS about 9.30 p.m. marched to L'ECLEME	
L'ECLEME	30/3/18		Day spent resting and cleaning	
	31/3/18		Church Service 10.30 a.m.	

A6945 Wt. W14422/M1160 350,000 12/16 D. D. & L. Forms/C/2118/14

SECRET
*****

~~154th Infantry~~
4th Battalion GORDON H'DRS
OPERATION ORDER No 2

REFERENCE MAP.
MOEUVRES. Scale 1/20.000.   8th March 1918.

1) 7th A & S. Highlanders will relieve 4th GORDON H'DRS in DEMICOURT SECTOR on 9th March. On relief 4th GORDON H'DRS will proceed to LEBUCQUIERE & become RESERVE Battalion.

~~3)~~ 2) Relief will be carried out in daylight visibility permitting. If visibility is good code word "LUX" will be sent ~~otherwise~~ & relief will commence at 6. p.m.

~~2)~~ 3) "A" Coy ~~7th A & S.H will be relieved~~
4th GORDONS will be relieved by "B" Coy 7th A & S.H. RIGHT FRONT Coy
"B" "   "   "   "   "   "   "C" Coy " " CENTRE Coy
"C" "   "   "   "   "   "   "D" Coy " " LEFT FRONT Coy
"D" "   "   "   "   "   "   "A" Coy RESERVE Coy
COMPANIES will arrive in following order. H.Q. RIGHT FRONT, LEFT FRONT CENTRE Coy & RESERVE Coy.

4) Guides.
No guides will be provided.

5) Air Photographs. Maps. trench stores and work in hand & proposed will be handed over on relief. Platoons at work on Dug-outs will be relieved by their opposite numbers. No cessation of work will take place.

6) TRANSPORT
Transport ~~will be~~ for L. Guns etc will be at Junction of Demicourt

MAIN STREET & ROACH AVENUE J12d 6.3.
L.Guns Limbers & Water carts will proceed to LEBUCQUIERE.

7. Echelon "B" will rejoin Battalion
   List of new Echelon "B" will be forwarded to Bn. H.Q. by 10. a.m. on 10th inst.

8. Completion of relief will be wired by usual CODE.

9. ACKNOWLEDGE

File
C.H.Q.
Compnys
Trench o O
  Assistant A12
Relieving Battn / 2 copies

1/4 Battn GORDON HIGHLANDERS.

REPORT ON OPERATIONS FROM 21st MARCH to 26th MARCH 1918.

Reference Maps :- France 1 / 20000 57.c N.W.

France 1 / 20000 57.c. S.W.

Hermies 1 / 10000 57.c. N.E.3.

Lens. 11.

21st March 1918.

The Battalion was holding the Right Sub. Sector (Demicourt) of the Divisional Front.
The Dispositions of the battalion were as follows :-
"D" Coy - Right Front Coy - holding Front on support lines.
"C" Coy - Left Front Coy - holding Front & Support Lines.
"B" Coy - Near Battn Hqrs - in DEMICOURT - HERMIES ROAD, with 1 Platoon in intermediate Line.
"A" Coy - in BEAUMETZ - MORCHIES LINE.

From 5.0. to 6.30.a.m. intermittent shelling on battalion front - proportion of gas shells being used. Respirators worn for two hours - no casualties sustained - no hostile Infantry attacks.

22nd March 1918.

In accordance with instructions received, British Front Line held by battalion was vacated, commencing at 1.30.a.m., and battalion proceeded to HERMIES SWITCH as ordered.
There were no troops in this trench at 3.0.a.m., but all trenches South were packed.
Accordingly the companies available, B, C, & D, were put into the following despositions - "B" Coy in the Intermediate Line touching on our Right "C" & "D" in SPIT LOCK trench which was only 18 inches deep, in front of the HERMIES SWITCH.
H.Q. manned the Left portion & touched with 4th Seaforths on HERMIES - DOIGNIES ROAD.
Tools, Ammunition, Rations, Rum, & Water were issued, and men fairly dug in by 5.0.a.m., when a slow bombardment began.
The bombardment increased and it soon became evident that an attack would be delivered along the Battalion Frontage.
"A" Coy, who had previously occupied our Flank Defence Position at BRUNO MILL, received orders from Brigade to rejoin the Battalion.
This Company failed to get into touch with the Battalion, so it took up a position in the HERMIES SWITCH from N end of village to the HERMIES DOIGNIES ROAD.
This trench was also garrisoned thinly by a Company of 7th Lincolns. "A" Coy was in position at 5.30.a.m. About 9.15. a.m. touch has been lost with Division on Right in the Intermediate Line. This was however partly compensated by trenches strongly manned in the Rear.
Casualties were moderate & men in good spirits, though shelling was extremely hard.
About 10.0.a.m. the attack was in progress, as musketry fire was taking place all along the line, and at this time the Right gave way, but was in hand, owing to men in the Rear trenches
Bombing in the Intermediate Line was heavy.
Remainder of Hqrs & stragglers of various regiments were made into a Flank Defence along the DOIGNIES - HERMIES ROAD.
At about 10.45.a.m. the troops 300 yds left of the DOIGNIES - HERMIES ROAD commenced to withdraw.
The enemy was then seen to be advancing on our left, though checked all along our Front.

(over)

The men in this part were badly enfiladed and knowing their position fought to the last.

At this junction Lieut. Colonel J. Rowbotham was wounded.

About 11.15 the positions held by "A" Coy. in the HERMIES SWITCH were heavily attacked, but without success. – Four efforts were made to break our lines, but on each occasion the enemy was driven off with heavy loss.

The remainder of the day was quiet and the Battalion was re-organised.

23rd March, 1918.

At 1 a.m. relief orders were received and the Battalion proceeded to Huts at I.35.b.

Arrived there at 5.30 a.m.

At 8 a.m. Hutments heavily shelled.

The Huts were cleared and the Battalion manned the Sunken Roads.

About 10 a.m. troops were observed, withdrawing on our Right and Left, and the Battalion then took up positions in the GREEN LINE at approximately I.35.a.9.4. The Battalion remained in this line till 5 p.m. when orders were received for the Battalion to proceed to BANCOURT.

The Battalion arrived at BANCOURT at 7.30. p.m. and took up positions at approximately N.5.b.

Previously to this Echelon B and a draft from Divisional Wing had been ordered to report to G.O.C. 153rd Infantry Bde. at N.35.a.8.3. They were held in tactical reserve during the night and rejoined the Battalion at N.5.c.9.4 at 11 a.m. on morning of 24th, taking up line N.5.c.6.2. to N.11.a.9.4.

? BEAULENCOURT

24th March, 1918.

About 1 p.m. the Battalion was ordered to take up line S.E. of BULLECOURT at N.17.c., Echelon "B" at N.17.d., 7th A. & S. Highrs. on left.

About 3 p.m. the Battalion received orders to withdraw to valley, E. of BULLECOURT, and took up position approximately N.16.a.1.6 – 7th A.& S. Highrs. on left. No touch on right.

Orders were received to assist 6th Gordon Hrs. if required, and if they withdrew to cover their withdrawal.

For this purpose positions were taken up in CABLE TRENCH, approximately N.10.d. and N.11.c. 7th A. & S. Highrs. on Right 4th Seaforth Hrs. on Left. This position was maintained till 6th Gordon Hrs. had withdrawn, and an attack had developed on our Left, strong forces pushing through BULLECOURT under cover of heavy Machine Gun Fire.

In accordance with orders and communication being maintained with our Flank, the Battalion withdrew to a position approximately N.9.b. and N.10.a., when Battalion was again re-organised and marched back to 300 yards West of X roads at N.11.a. (WARLEN: COURT). The Battalion arrived at WARLENCOURT at 11 p.m.

25th March, 1918.

At Commanding Officer's Conference orders were received from G.O.C. to take up position in depth, on high ground at M.11.b. 7th A. & S. Highrs. on Left, 4th Seaforth Hrs. on Right.

Orders were received to hold on to this position as long as possible. This position was maintained till after 1.30 p.m., when both flanks were turned, and the Battalion withdrew to position on high ground at M.8.b. and from there again to position at M.2.a.

About 4 p.m. a strong enemy attack developed on a frontage from LOUPART WOOD, Southwards, on a wide front, under cover of heavy Machine Gun Fire.

From this point, owing to both flanks being turned, the Battalion was forced to withdraw, and orders were received to march back to COLIN CAMPS, which was reached about 9.30 p.m. and the Battalion then proceeded to SAILLY-AU-BOIS, arriving there about 10.30 p.m.

March, 1918.

Cookers arrived about 4 a.m. and a hot meal was provided.

At dawn an outpost line was taken up S.E. of SAILLY-AU-BOIS. – 7th A.& S.

7th A. & S. Highrs. on Right, 4th Seaforths on Left.

About 9 a.m. in accordance with orders, the Battalion withdrew to SOUASTRE and occupied Reserve Line for the Brigade.

At 6 p.m. the Battalion was relieved by an Australian Battalion, and the Battalion marched back to PAS.

Total Casualties sustained were :-

OFFICERS - Killed...........1
           Wounded..........9
           Missing..........9   TOTAL...19

           Killed 10
O/RANKS. - Wounded........97
           Missing.......293   TOTAL..400

[signature] Major,
Commanding 1/4th Bn. The Gordon Highlanders.

1st April, 1918.

In accordance with orders and communication being maintained with our Flank, the Battalion withdrew to a position approximately N.9.b. and N.10.a., when Battalion was again re-organised and marched back to 300 yards West of X roads at N.11.a. (WARLENCOURT). The Battalion arrived at WARLENCOURT at 11 p.m.

25th March, 1918.
At Commanding Officer's Conference orders were received from G.O.C. to take up position in depth, on high ground at M.11.b. 7th A. & S. Highrs. on Left, 4th Seaforth Hrs. on Right.

Orders were received to hold on to this position as long as possible. This position was maintained till after 1.30 p.m. when both flanks were turned, and the Battalion withdrew to position on high ground at M.8.b. and from there again to position at M.2.a.
About 4 p.m. a strong enemy attack developed on a frontage from LOUPART WOOD, Southwards, on a wide front, under cover of heavy Machine Gun Fire.
From this point, owing to both flanks being turned, the Battalion was forced to withdraw, and orders were received to march back to COLIN CAMPS, which was reached about 9.30 p.m. and the Battalion then proceeded to SAILLY-AU-BOIS, arriving there about 10.30 p.m.

26th March, 1918.
Cookers arrived about 4 a.m. and a hot meal was provided.
At dawn an outpost line was taken up S.E. of SAILLY-AU-BOIS, - 7th A. & S. Highrs. on Right, 4th Seaforths on Left.
About 9 a.m. in accordance with orders, the Battalion withdrew to SOUASTRE and occupied Reserve Line for the Brigade.
At 6 p.m. the Battalion was relieved by an Australian Battalion, and the Battalion marched back to PAS.

Total Casualties sustained were :-

OFFICERS - Killed............1.
          Wounded...........9.
          Missing...........9.   TOTAL...19

          Killed............10.
O/RANKS. - Wounded..........97.
          Missing...........293.   TOTAL..400

Alan STEIN Major,
Commanding 1/4th Bn. The Gordon Highlanders.

1st April, 1918.

S E C R E T.   Copy No.

OPERATION ORDER No. 13
BY
Lt. Col. J. Rowbotham, D.S.O., M.C.,
Commanding 1/4th Battalion The Gordon Highlanders.
In the Field....14th March, 1918.

PART 11 - ADMINISTRATIVE.

1. **BLANKETS, VALISES etc.**

    Blankets with the exception of those of 'A' Coy. will be rolled by Sections by 10 a.m. and will be stored in Pack Store at Echelon 'B' opposite present Battalion Orderly Room.
    Officers Valises and surplus kit, with the exception of those of 'A' Coy., will be dumped at same time and same place as above.
    'A' Coy. will dump valises and Blankets in front of Orderly Room by 12 noon.
    Mess Boxes will be dumped in front of Orderly Room by 1 p.m.
    Os. C. Coys. will detail 1 man per Coy. to be at Orderly Room by 12 noon to store blankets, valises etc.

2. **DRESS** ....Full Marching Order. Leather Jerkins will be worn. Waterproof Sheets will be carried under flap of Pack. Flashes will be worn.

                        (sgd) B.C.Brodie, Capt. & A/Adj.,

                        1/4th Battalion The Gordon Highlanders.

        Copy No. 1 - File.
                 2 - O. C. 'A' Coy.
                 3 -   'B' "
                 4 -   'C' "
                 5 -   'D' "
                 6 -   Headquarters.
                 7 - Second in Command.
                 8 - Quartermaster.& Transport Officer.

SECRET.

Copy No. 1

10/3/18.

DEFENCE SCHEME

BATTALION IN REST.

1. Battalion in REST is at one hour's notice.
2. In the event of action it will proceed to BEAUMETZ - MORCHIES LINE and take up position covering whole Brigade Frontage.
3. DISPOSITIONS.
   'A' Company on RIGHT, 'B' Company in CENTRE, 'C' Company on LEFT and 'D' Company in RESERVE.
   Battalion H.Q. will be in sunken road at J.21.d.5.2.
   RIGHT COMPANY will have 2 Platoons in the line from the right Div. Boundary at J.28.a.80.15 to J.28.a.30.85., and 2 Platoons in the sunken road running southwards from Cross Roads at J.28.a.40.05.
   CENTRE COMPANY will be in the line holding from J.26.a.30.85 to J.21.b.6.0.
   LEFT COMPANY will be in the line holding from J.21.b.6.0 to J.21.a.9.2.
   RESERVE COMPANY will be in sunken road from J.27.b.70.95. to J.21.d.4.3.
4. MACHINE GUNS.
   2 Machine Guns will be at each of the following positions -
   J.28.a.70.25   J.21.b.0.2.
5. LEWIS GUNS.
   Good positions for Lewis Guns are as follows -
   J.28.a.32.60.   J.21.d.78.82.
   J.28.a.31.76.   J.21.b. 7. 0.
   J.28.a.26.92.   J.21.b.31.15.
6. On arrival Coys. will report to Battalion H.Q. by Runner.
7. O.C. Echelon 'B' will arrange to have cookers sent up with meals. He will at once send for horses to take Cookers and Water Carts to their Companies.

All Defence Schemes issued for the DEMICOURT SECTOR are cancelled and will be destroyed. Maps will be retained. Schemes for new dispositions will be issued shortly.

(sgd) B.C.Brodie, Capt. & A/Adj.,
1/4th Battalion The Gordon Highlanders.

Copies to all recipients of DEFENCE SCHEME.

SECRET.
░░░░░░░░░░░░░

Copy No. 1

DEFENCE SCHEME

10/3/18.

BATTALION IN REST.

1. Battalion in REST is at one hour's notice.
2. In the event of action it will proceed to BEAUMETZ - MORCHIES LINE and take up Position covering whole Brigade Frontage.
3. DISPOSITIONS.
   'A' Company on RIGHT, 'B' Company in CENTRE, 'C' Company on LEFT and 'D' Company in RESERVE.
   Battalion H.Q. will be in sunken road at J.21.d.5.3.
   RIGHT COMPANY will have 2 Platoons in the line from the right Div. Boundary at J.28.a.80.15 to J.28.a.30.85., and 2 Platoons in the sunken road running Southwards from Cross Roads at J.28.a.40.05.
   CENTRE COMPANY will be in the line holding from J.28.a.30.85 to J.21.b.6.0.
   LEFT COMPANY will be in the line holding from J.21.b.6.0 to J.21.a.9.8.
   RESERVE COMPANY will be in sunken road from J.27.b.70.95. to J.21.d.4.3.
4. MACHINE GUNS.
   2 Machine Guns will be at each of the following Positions -
   J.28.a.70.25   J.21.b.0.8.
5. LEWIS GUNS.
   Good Positions for Lewis Guns are as follows -

   J.28.a.38.60.   J.21.d.78.88.
   J.28.a.31.76.   J.21.b. 7. 0.
   J.28.a.28.92.   J.21.b.31.15.
6. On arrival Coys. will report to Battalion H.Q. by Runner.
7. O.C. Echelon 'B' will arrange to have cookers sent up with meals. He will at once send for horses to take Cookers and Water Carts to their Companies.

(sgd) E.C.Brodie, Capt. & A/Adj.,
1/4th Battalion The Gordon Highlanders.

```
Copy No. 1 - File. ✓
        2 - O.C. 'A' Company.
        3 -  "   'B'    "
        4 -  "   'C'    "
        5 -  "   'D'    "
        6 -  "   Headquarters.
        7 -  "   Echelon 'B'.
        8 - Transport Officer.
        9 - Quartermaster.
```

SECRET.   Copy No.

1/4th BATTALION THE GORDON HIGHLANDERS.

DEFENCE SCHEME.
DEMICOURT SECTOR.

REFERENCE MAP - MOEUVRES, 1/20.000 issued.

1. GENERAL PRINCIPLES.
    In the event of FRONT LINE being penetrated at any point, troops will not fall back from one line to another but hold on till line is re-established by COUNTER ATTACK.

2. DISPOSITIONS.
    (a) Three Companies in the line, each Company on a two Platoons FRONTAGE with two Platoons each in SUPPORT LINE.
    (b) FRONT LINE is held by 16 Posts.
    (c) RESERVE COMPANY is situated in ROAD J.7.c. & d. and J.13.b.
    (d) COMPANY of SUPPORT BATTALION has two Platoons at J.18.a.8.9 and two Platoons at J.18.d.Central.

3. ACTION.
    (a) If attacked, POSTS in FRONT LINE will stand fast.
    (b) Platoons in SUPPORT LINE will man fire steps and be prepared to either fight in SUPPORT LINE or COUNTER ATTACK.
    (c) COMPANY in RESERVE LINE will hold from K.13.b.9.3 to road junction (inclusive) at K.7.c.90.55 with three Platoons. Remaining Platoon will hold from K.7.c.90.55 to ALDGATE (inclusive) J.12.d.7.6.
    (d) COMPANY OF BATTALION IN SUPPORT will man positions as follows:-
       One Platoon of Support Battalion accommodated at J.18.a.9.0 and employed spoiling new dug-out at K.7.c.55.95 will garrison the Support Line at their work.
       One Platoon of Support Battalion accommodated at J.18.a.9.9 and employed spoiling new dugout at J.12.b.4.0 will garrison the Support Line at their work.
       One Platoon of Support Battalion at J.18.a.9.9. will be allotted fire positions for 2 Sections (to include Lewis Gun Section) in small work at J.12.b.1.1. and for 2 Sections in ROACH AVENUE West of Cemetery at J.12.b.1.4.
    (e) BATTALION H.Q., COMPANY H.Q., and two Platoons of SUPPORT BATTALION at J.18.d.3.8 will "stand to" in their dugouts.

4. COUNTER ATTACK.
    All Commanders will counter attack on their own initiative WHEN SITUATION IS RIPE for a successful counter attack. A garrison must always be left in the trench from which counter attack is launched.

                    (sgd) B.C.Brodie, Captain & A/Adjutant,
                        1/4th Battalion The Gordon Highlanders.

    Copy No. 1 - File.
             2 - O.C. 'A' Company.
             3 - "   'B'   "
             4 - "   'C'   "
             5 - "   'D'   "
             6 - "   Headquarters.
             7 - "   Coy. in INTERMEDIATE LINE.   ) SUPPORT
             8 - "   Coy. in RESERVE to Battn.in Line) BATTALION.

S E C R E T.
****

Copy No. 1

1/4th BATTALION THE GORDON HIGHLANDERS.

PROVISIONAL DEFENCE SCHEME.

REFERENCE - SKETCH 'P'

1. **SUPPORT BATTALION.**
   The Support Battalion with Battalion Headquarters at BRUNO MILL, J.16.c., will be disposed as follows :-
   One Company under tactical control of O.C.Front Battalion.
   Company Headquarters and 2 Platoons at J.12.d.4.7.
   2 Platoons at J.12.a.9.9.
   One Company, less 1 Platoon, in Intermediate Line, with Company Headquarters in QUARRY at J.24.a.6.4.
   One Platoon employed as spoilers on dugout at J.12.b.4.9. being temporarily accommodated in dugout in 152nd Brigade Area at J.6.d.3.1.
   One Company in SUNKEN ROAD at J.21.d.5.3.
   One Company in LEBUCQUIERE until such time as accommodation is made in J.21.c. and J.20.b.

2. **ACTION.**
   (a) One Platoon of Support Battalion accommodated at J.12.a.9.9. and employed spoiling new dugout at K.7.c.55.95 will garrison the Support Line at their work.
   One Platoon of Support Battalion accommodated at J.6.d.3.1, and employed spoiling new dugout at J.12.b.4.9. will garrison the Support Line at their work.
   One Platoon of Support Battalion at J.12.a.9.9. will be allotted fire positions for 2 Sections (to include Lewis Gun Section) in small work at J.12.b.1.1. and for 2 Sections in ROACH AVENUE West of Cemetery at J.12.b.1.4.
   (b) In the event of hostile attack, all troops will man their fire positions and hold them, it being clearly understood that the Support and Reserve Lines are not to be denuded of their Garrisons in order to reinforce the Front or Support Lines respectively.
   (c) In the event of a hostile raid, or temporary penetration, by the enemy of our Front Line at any point demanding immediate counter-attack, Platoons holding the Support Line will be used. A garrison in all cases will be maintained in the Support Line on each Company Front.
   (d) In the event of the enemy penetrating the front of the Brigade on the Right, O.C. Front Battalion will form a defensive flank on the line of BETTY AVENUE.
   (e) The garrison of the INTERMEDIATE LINE will maintain its position and fight there.
   (f) The Company of the Support Battalion located in Sunken Road at J.21.d., will, if there are indications of hostile attack, occupy the best possible positions to hold the whole of the BEAUMETZ - MORCHIES Line within the Brigade Area.

3. **S.O.S.**
   S.O.S. Signal is a Rifle Grenade bursting into 2 GREEN and 2 WHITE lights.
   The S.O.S. for the Division and Corps on the Right is 2 RED and 2 WHITE Lights.

(sgd) B.C.Brodie, Capt. & A/Adj.,
1/4th Battalion The Gordon Highlanders.

Copy No. 1 - FILE ✓
        2 - O.C. 'A' Coy.
        3 -   'B'
        4 -   'C'

No. 5 - O.C. 'D' Coy.
    6   Signalling Officer
    7 - Transport Officer.

SECRET.   Copy No.

1/4th BATTALION THE GORDON HIGHLANDERS.

DEFENCE SCHEME.

RIGHT SUB SECTOR DEMICOURT SECTOR.

REFERENCE MAP – (MOEUVRES, 1/20.000.
               (SKETCH 'R'.

1. **GENERAL PRINCIPLES.**
    In the event of FRONT LINE being penetrated at any point, troops will not fall back from one line to another but hold on till line is re-established by COUNTER ATTACK.

2. **DISPOSITIONS.**
    These are shown on Map. R
    One Company at SUNKEN ROAD at J.21.d.
    One Platoon in INTERMEDIATE LINE.

3. **ACTION.**
    (a) If attacked, Posts in FRONT LINE will stand fast.
    (b) Platoons in SUPPORT LINE will man fire steps and be prepared to either fight in SUPPORT LINE or COUNTER ATTACK.
    (c) Platoons in SCOTCH STREET will man RESERVE LINE from K.13.b.5.9 to K.7.c.90.55. One Platoon of LEFT FRONT COY. will be prepared to proceed to BETTY AVENUE to form a Defensive Flank or to reinforce any part of FRONT or SUPPORT LINE.
    (d) Platoons at Battalion H.Qrs. will be prepared to move to any part of the line.
    (e) Battalion H.Q. will be prepared to fight in positions in old Gun Pits at K.13.c.
    (f) Platoon in INTERMEDIATE LINE will fight there.
    (g) Company in BEAUMETZ – MORCHIES LINE will be prepared to move to any portion of Battalion Frontage.

4. **COUNTER ATTACK.**
    All Commanders will counter attack on their own initiative WHEN SITUATION IS RIPE for a successful counter attack. A garrison must always be left in the trench from which counter attack is launched.

                                (sgd) B.C. Brodie, Capt. & A/Adj.,

                        1/4th Battalion The Gordon Highlanders.

    Copy No. 1 – File.
             2 – O.C. 'A' Company.
             3 –   'B'   "
             4 –   'C'   "
             5 –   'D'   "
             6 –   Headquarters.
             7 –   BATTALION ON RIGHT
             8 –   BATTALION ON LEFT.

Addendum to PROVISIONAL DEFENCE SCHEME.

At the end of Para. 2 (f), add the following :-

"The Company of the Support Battalion located in LEBUCQUIERE, will, on receipt of orders to move from Brigade H.Qrs., march by the most direct route to Sunken Road at J.20.b.8.2 and be prepared from there, either to take over defence of BEAUMETZ - MORCHIES Line from about J.21.d.8.7.Northwards, or to re-inforce any portion of this line within the Brigade Area. This Company will be at one hour's notice.

All officers of above two Coys. will thoroughly reconnoitre the line."

(sgd) B.C.Brodie, Capt. & A/Adj.,
1/4th Battalion The Gordon Highlanders.

1st March,1918.

1 PLATOON

3 PLATOONS
SUPPORT
COY HQ

1 PLATOON
WASH

TROJN TRENCH

COY HQ

BATT HQ

COY HQ

SECRET.

COPY No. 5

1/4th BATTALION THE GORDON HIGHLANDERS.

DEFENCE SCHEME.

Reference Map - SKETCH 'Q' Attached.

This cancels all previous Defence Schemes, which will hereby be destroyed.

1. GENERAL PRINCIPLES
   In the event of the FRONT LINE being penetrated at any point, troops will not fall back from any part of our line to another, but hold on till line is re-established by Counter Attack.

2. DISPOSITIONS.
   See Sketch 'Q' attached.

3. ACTION.
   If attacked, POSTS in FRONT LINE will stand fast.
   Platoons in SUPPORT LINE will man the fire steps and be ready to either fight in SUPPORT LINE or COUNTER ATTACK.
   Platoons of SUPPORT COMPANY and FIELD COY. R.E. situated in ROAD J.5.c.95.20 to J.4.a.s.s will man the ROAD and be prepared to either fight in position or COUNTER ATTACK.
   FIELD COY. R.E. is allotted from J.5.c.1.2. to LEFT BOUNDARY.
   Platoons of SUPPORT COMPANY will man SUNKEN ROAD on both sides of FISH AVENUE.
   In every case where Counter Attack is ordered from any line, a sufficient garrison will be left in the line to hold it.
   Reconnaissance of SUNKEN ROAD will be carefully made. Positions selected for L.G. etc. and routes to SUPPORT LINE known.
   All Platoons in LOUVERVAL LINE will stand fast and fight in this line. They will however be prepared to guide in a relief and themselves move to any portion of ROAD J.5.c.95.20 - J.4.b.05.20.

b.20.05

Captain & A/Adjutant,
1/4th Battalion The Gordon Highlanders.

```
Copy No. 1 - FILE
        2 - O.C. 'A' Coy.
        3 -  "   'B'  "
        4 -  "   'C'  "
        5 -  "   'D'  "
        6 -  "   Headquarters.
        7 -  "   Relieving Battalion
        8 -  "   Battalion on LEFT.
        9 -  "   404th Field Coy. R.E.
```

SECRET.   Copy No.

1/4th BATTALION THE GORDON HIGHLANDERS.
DEFENCE SCHEME.
RIGHT SUB SECTOR DEMICOURT SECTOR.

REFERENCE MAP – (MOEUVRES, 1/20.000.
              (SKETCH 'R'

1. **GENERAL PRINCIPLES.**
    In the event of FRONT LINE being penetrated at any point, troops will not fall back from one line to another but hold on till line is re-established by COUNTER ATTACK.

2. **DISPOSITIONS.**
    These are shown on Map.
    One Company at SUNKEN ROAD at J.21.d.

3. **ACTION.**
    (a) If attacked, Posts in FRONT LINE will stand fast.
    (b) Platoons in SUPPORT LINE will man fire steps and be prepared to either fight in SUPPORT LINE or COUNTER ATTACK.
    (c) Platoons in SCOTCH STREET will man RESERVE LINE from K.13.D.5.8 to K.7.c.80.55. One Platoon of LEFT FRONT COY. will be prepared to proceed to BETTY AVENUE to form a Defensive Flank or to reinforce any part of FRONT or SUPPORT LINE.
    (d) Platoons at Battalion H.Qrs. will be prepared to move to any part of the line.
    (e) Battalion H.Q. will be prepared to fight in positions in old Gun Pits at J.13.c.
    (f) Platoon in INTERMEDIATE LINE will fight there.
    (g) Company in BEAUMETZ – MORCHIES LINE will be prepared to move to any portion of Battalion Frontage.

4. **COUNTER ATTACK.**
    All Commanders will counter attack on their own initiative WHEN SITUATION IS RIPE for a successful counter attack.
    A garrison must always be left in the trench from which counter attack is launched.

                    (sgd) E.C. Brodie, Capt. & A/Adj.,
            1/4th Battalion The Gordon Highlanders.

    Copy No. 1 – File.
             2 – O. C. 'A' Company.
             3 –   'B'   "
             4 –   'C'   "
             5 –   'D'   "
             6 –   Headquarters.
             7 –   BATTALION ON RIGHT
             8 –   BATTALION ON LEFT.

INSTRUCTIONS ON PROCEEDING TO TRENCHES.

1. All ranks will stand to arms at 4 a.m. and stand down when enemy trenches can be seen clearly. Company in BEAUMETZ - MORCHIES LINE is included.
2. S.O.S. is 3 GREEN and 3 WHITE.
   S.O.S. on CORPS on RIGHT is 3 RED and 3 WHITE.
3. Any heavy Bombardment must be immediately reported to Battalion H.Q. Also use of Smoke Bombs.
4. Respirators will be worn during any heavy bombardment and all ranks except the sentry will wear box respirators for 1/2 hour during stand to in the evening. Inspection of respirators will take place then and should any be found faulty a reserve is available at Battalion H.Q.
   Respirators will also be worn by off going sentry for few minutes after he has been relieved. He will fire two rounds at the same time at a target with respirator on.
5. Attention is again drawn to the necessity of quick transmission of Patrol Reports.
6. S.A.A. and Bombs require organization into Boxes or Shelters in FRONT and SUPPORT line. INTERMEDIATE and BEAUMETZ-MORCHIES Line also require adjustment.
7. COOKHOUSES....One will have to be made in SUPPORT LINE or SUNKEN ROAD to cook for the 6 Platoons in the FRONT and SUPPORT LINES. Cookhouse for two Platoons at Battalion H.Q. will be improved and water tank made.
   Report on situation of Cookhouse for platoon in Intermediate Line to be rendered to Orderly Room by 2 p.m. on 16th inst.
8. All Coys. will arrange to have salvage taken to their Cookhouses where it will be loaded on RATION LIMBERS nightly. Q.M. will send duplicate of list of salvage to Battalion H.Q. daily.
9. H.Q. Scouts will collect tin, make notice boards of good size, and put up in Sector.
10. Work in trenches will be continued in usual manner.
    All ranks will work 1 hour at morning stand to and 1/2 hour at evening stand to. This will be on fire position berms etc. All ranks in FRONT LINE will also work from 10 a.m. to 12 noon and 2.30 p.m. to 4.30 p.m.
    Work must be carefully detailed.
    L/Cpl. Stewart and Pte. Mann of 'B' Coy. will be employed on work on deep dugouts in FRONT LINE. The garrison situated there will assist.
    O.C. 'B' Coy. will detail Pte. Mann to report to Battalion H.Q. before proceeding to trenches.
    Platoons not in Front Line will have tasks detailed to them.
11. All Coys. will take over work in hand handed over and send statement of parties etc. to Battalion H.Q. by 10 p.m. on 15th.
12. Attention is drawn to TRENCH ORDERS. Considerable slackness has crept in especially as regards cleanliness of men, reporting of posts, saluting, wearing of equipment, and gas respirators. It is pointed out that all Officers and N.C.Os. are neglecting to do their duty if they do not check men, whether they are in their own platoon or not. The same applies to men of other units in the Sector.

(sgd) B.C.Brodie, Capt. & A/Adj.,
1/4th Battalion The Gordon Highlanders.

14/5/18.

SECRET.
****

O.C.
    4th Seaforth Highrs.
    4th Gordon Highrs.
    7th A. & S. Highrs.
    154th T. M. Battery.
H.Q.
    152nd Infantry Brigade.
    51st (H) Division "G".

Reference Sheet BETHUNE 1/40,000, Edition 6.
Special Sheet SAILLY - LABOURSE 1/5,000 (Issued to O.C. Bns.).

        SCHEME FOR OCCUPATION OF DEFENDED LOCALITY
       OF SAILLY - LABOURSE BY 154th INFANTRY BRIGADE.

1.   In the event of 51st (H) Division being required to reinforce Ist Corps front, 154th Infantry Brigade will occupy the SAILLY - LABOURSE locality from about L.9.b.7.7. to F.21.d.7.8.
    4th Gordon Highrs. will be on the right.
    7th Arg. & Suth'd. Highrs. on the left.
    Boundaries between Battalions in the front line will be - M.G. emplacement at L.4.a.40.95. inclusive to 4th Gordon Highrs.
    4th Seaforth Highrs. will be in close reserve in open ground F.27.a. and c. on the North side of the BEUVRY - SAILLY-LABOURSE Road.
    Battalion Headquarters will be as follows :-
    4th Gordon Highrs. House about F.3.b.5.0.
    4th Seaforth Highrs. and 7th A. & S. Highrs.
            CHATEAU DE PRES, F.27.d.1.6.
    154th T. M. Battery, if equipped with guns, will place 2 Mortars in action on right Battalion front and 2 on left Battalion front, remainder of the guns and teams will remain in reserve with 4th Seaforth Highrs.
    If not equipped with guns, the Battery will remain with 4th Seaforth Highrs.
    Advanced Brigade Headquarters will be at CHATEAU DE PRES.

2.   The defended locality on the right of 154th Brigade will be held by 152nd Infantry Brigade, that on the left will be held by 55th Division.

3.   The locality of ANNEQUIN due East of 154th Brigade is held by 11th Division.
    Units of 154th Brigade may be ordered to reinforce this locality. Best means of approach must therefore be decided on by O.C. Battalions.

4.   If ordered to occupy SAILLY - LABOURSE locality at short notice, the following lorries will report at billets of Units :-
        Brigade Headquarters, GONNEHEM   1 lorry.
        4th Seaforth Highrs., BUSNETTES   9 lorries.
        4th Gordon Highrs., L'ECLEME   10 "
        7th A. & S. Highrs., CANTRAINNE 10 "
    These lorries will make two journeys. O.C. Units will, however, arrange that as many fighting men as possible go with the first lorry.
    T. M. Battery will move in the second trip of the 1 lorry from GONNEHEM.
    If the situation admits, the 4th Gordon Highrs. and 4th Seaforth Highrs. will debus on the BEUVRY - SAILLY-LABOURSE Road in or as near as possible to the village of SAILLY.

                                                7th Arg. /

** 2 **

7th Arg. & Suth'd. Highrs. will debus on the BEUVRY - ANNEZIN Road as near the left flank of the locality as possible.

5. Before moving off, S.A.A. on the man will be made up to 220 rounds. All Lewis Guns which can be manned will be taken in the lorries, also the necessary drums.
There are ~~250~~ 150 boxes S.A.A. at CHATEAU DE PRES.

6. Battalions will issue all available tools from their Mobile Reserve and take them up in the lorries.
Tools are also available at the R.E. Dump at SAILLY - LABOURSE near the Church.

7. O.C. Units will ensure that all men embus with full water bottles.

8. All surplus stores, packs, blankets, etc. will be left in present billets under a small guard.
Either greatcoats or jerkins to be carried on the man.

9. Maps of SAILLY - LABOURSE locality (1/5,000) have been issued to all concerned to-day.

10. ACKNOWLEDGE.

Captain,
Brigade Major,
154th Infantry Brigade.

2nd April, 1918.

OC   HQ
      1. A Coy
      2. C Coy
      3. Sp Coy
      4. HQ Coy
      Please in turn
           A.B.
           4.16

Operation Order

S E C R E T.
****

O.C.
    4th Seaforth Highrs.
    4th Gordon Highrs.
    7th A. & S. Highrs.
    154th T. M. Battery.
    401st Field Coy. R.E.
    2/1st (H) Field Ambulance.
    No. 2 Coy. A.S.C.

Reference Sheet 36.B. 1/40,000.

WARNING ORDER.

1.   154th Infantry Brigade Group and 8th Royal Scots will move in the near future to construct defences in HERSIN - COUPIGNY - BRACQUEMONT and SAINS-EN-GOHELLE.

2.   One Battalion will be available for training every day and two Battalions will be employed at work on defences.

3.   Brigade Group will be accommodated as follows on completion of move :-

Brigade Headquarters	CHATEAU, COUPIGNY.
4th Seaforth Highrs.	Huts, COUPIGNY, Q.17.a.3.9.
4th Gordon Highrs.	" " Q.12.d.0.2.
7th A. & S. Highrs.	SAINS-EN-GOHELLE - FOSSE 10 - R.8.b.
154th T.M. Battery.	COUPIGNY.
401st Field Co.R.E.	" Q.5.b.1.8.
2/1st (H) Fld. Amb.	" Q.11.a.9.5.
No. 2 Coy. A.S.C.	SAINS-EN-GOHELLE, R.2.c.3.5.

                            Captain,
                       Brigade Major,
            154th Infantry Brigade.

4th April, 1918.

Copy to Staff Captain.

51st Division
154th Infantry Brigade.

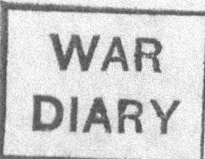

1/4th BATTALION

THE GORDON HIGHLANDERS

APRIL 1 9 1 8

Attached :- Report on Operations
9th - 12th April.

Vol 38

SECRET

11th Battalion The Gordon Highlanders
1st/S-1

War Diary.

Volume No. 29

April, 1918.

Army Form C. 2118.

WAR DIARY
or
INTELLIGENCE SUMMARY.
(Erase heading not required.)

Place	Date	Hour	Summary of Events and Information	Remarks and references to Appendices
LECLERS	1/4/18		Reorganise Reinforcements 20 O/R	
	2/4/18		Reorganise and receive Reinforcements 9 O/R	
	3/4/18		2/Lt Major Buckner's arrived Command, Major Brown attached training	
			orders received	
	4/4/18		2/Lt LECLERS 10.7am marched to AUCHEL, billeted	
AUCHEL	5/4/18		Running bath, cleaning up	
	6/4/18		with another Regt Reinforcements 5 O/R	
	7/4/18		Church Service, Reinforcements 102 O/R	
	8/4/18		Left AUCHEL at 9pm marched to BUSNETTES, billeted	
	9/4/18		Struck by rounds 11.30 am rapid German attack on Portuguese front battalion	
			Moved 1.30pm to Brigade Reserve at LES CAUDRONS	
	10/4/18		1am rec'd reinforcements, moved forward to TOMBE WILLOW FARM	
	11/4/18		Transport moved to LA MIQUELLERIE, Reinforcements 78 O/R Major Steenkirk in B	
	12/4/18		Regt at ST-VENANT-B, moved forward towards front	
	13/4/18		Transport moved back to HAM-EN-ARTOIS, moved to South side of canal to trenches	
	14/4/18		Moved back to BUSNES and billets	

Army Form C. 2118.

WAR DIARY
or
INTELLIGENCE SUMMARY.
(Erase heading not required.)

Instructions regarding War Diaries and Intelligence Summaries are contained in F. S. Regs., Part II. and the Staff Manual respectively. Title pages will be prepared in manuscript.

Place	Date	Hour	Summary of Events and Information	Remarks and references to Appendices
ROBECQ	12/4/18		Moved forward to ROBECQ. C Coy right flank, D Left. B support. A in reserve H.Q.	
	13/4/18		Front line posts shelled at intervals	
	14/4/18		Posts shelled at intervals. Lt KNOX and 2/Lt FRICKER joined and 187 O.R.	
	15/4/18		Out of line. [illegible]	
	16/4/18		C Coy to left and D right flanks. Lt J F Walker joined	
	17/4/18		Fairly heavy German shelling	
	18/4/18		Wiring in front of village. Capt Bate and 2/Lt Scott-Cleiss and Revd. joined	
	19/4/18		Moved to billets in LA MIQUELLERIE. Details at transport lines joined	
	20/4/18		Resting & cleaning. Working order received. 69 O.R. Reinforcements	
LA MIQUELLERIE	21/4/18			
ST HILAIRE	22/4/18		Moved to ST. HILAIRE and billeted. Reinforcements 3 O.R.	
	23/4/18		Training commenced. A Bn Coys on Range. Medical Inspection	
	24/4/18		Training. D Coy on Range. Draft inspection by Commanding Officer	
	25/4/18		Training. Inspection of Box Respirators	
	26/4/18		Trained hard. Lecture to pris & Instructors from Brigade	
	27/4/18		Church Parade. Protection Conference by Commanding Officer on [illegible]	
	28/4/18		Training. 28 O.R. Reinforcements. M.G. on recent operations. A.C. Coys on Ranges	

Army Form C. 2118.

WAR DIARY
or
INTELLIGENCE SUMMARY.
(Erase heading not required.)

Instructions regarding War Diaries and Intelligence Summaries are contained in F. S. Regs., Part II. and the Staff Manual respectively. Title pages will be prepared in manuscript.

Place	Date	Hour	Summary of Events and Information	Remarks and references to Appendices
ST HILAIRE	Sept/18		Training carried out in training area.	

D.H. Bickmore, Lt Col
O/C 1/4 Bn The Gordon H'rs

4th Gordon H.

HISTORY OF OPERATIONS
9th to 12th April, 1918.

Ref. Map.. Sheet 36 A. S.E

April, 9th, Tuesday.
On this date the Battalion was in billets at BUSNETTE. At 11 a.m. orders arrived that the Battalion was at half an hour's notice to move. Shortly afterwards orders arrived to move to ESSARS. At 1.30 p.m. Battalion moved, marching via LANNOY & OBLINGHEM - to VENDIN - BETHUNE; here orders were received to move to LES CAUDRONS.

Battalion reached LES CAUDRONS during the late afternoon and was put in Brigade Reserve taking up positions in artillery formation in W.12.a.

When darkness fell Battalion was billetted in farms W.6.c.

April, 10th, Wednesday.
At about 8 a.m. 'A' Company was ordered to dig in X.1.c, remainder of Battalion remaindd in billets.

April, 11th Thursday.
During the early morning Battalion was moved up to position in Support Line.
Situation.
Enemy held foot bridge and farm in X.3.a. from which position an attack delivered during the previous afternoon had failed to eject him.
Enemy was also reported to be marching down RUE DE LANNOY - ZELOBES Road in force and to be advancing West in the vicinity of R.14.
Dispositions and action
Elements of 6th Seaforth Highrs and 5th Seaforth Highrs. were holding road at ZELOBES-LELOBES and line facing E. from VIEILLE CHAPPELLE along CANAL BANK, 7th Argyll & Sutherland Highrs. were on the Right flank of the latter line.
4th Battalion Gordon Highrs. took up positions as follows:-
'C' and 'A' companies along road from R.32.c.85.20. to R.31.a.2.7.
3 Platoons were in line and 1 platoon in Support.
'C' Coy. were in Right, 'A' Company in Left having on Right flank 7th Argyll & Sutherland Highrs and on their Left Pioneers 2nd S.W.B.
'B' Company was astride the road X.1.b. facing E.
'D' Company was under orders of 6th Seaforth Highrs. and were disposed as follows:- 2 Platoons in support of 6th Gordon Highrs. in front of FARM X.3.a. and 2 Platoons in vicinity of R.32.Central.
At about 3 a.m. the 2 Platoons of 'D' company in support of 6th Gordon Highrs. passed through the Front Line and advanced towards the FARM Foot bridge X.3.a.2.9.
Lieut.F.N.Robertson was in command of Left platoon and Lieut. H.Murray, Right platoon. On advancing these two platoons came under considerable M.G. fire and suffered some casualties. The platoons retired but the two Officers went back and rallied and re-organised the platoons and took up new positions. I wish to make special mention of Lieut. Robertson and Lieut.Murray for the above action. Lieut.Robertson was wounded and as no further information has been obtained it is feared he is missing.

At about 5 a.m. it became apparent that an attack was about to develope. Some M.G. fire opened which increased until it became exceedingly heavy. It was accompanied by some shell fire.

At about this time the enemy made vigourous attempts to thrust forward in a W.S.W. direction and at the same time to turn the flank of 'C' Coy. by a vigourous attack between 'C' Coy. and 7th Argyll & Sutherland Highrs.

The immediate result of this operation was to force the elements of 152nd Inf. Bde. to retire West and to form a defensive flank facing East in R.25.c. and to compel the Right flank of 'C' Coy. to retire about 100 yards.

The two platoons of 'D' Coy. from R.32.Central and the remnants of the depleted platoons who were in support of 6th Gordon Highrs. participated in this operation and reported to O.C. 'A' Coy., eventually taking up position on left of 'A' Coy. about R.31.a.4.8.

While this operation was in progress attacks were being made with increasing violence and as there appeared some liklihood of the Right flank having to withdraw 'B' Coy. was moved to protect 'C' Coy's. flank and prevent/

prevent any possibility of a breakthrough between 'C' Coy. and 7th Argyll & Sutherland Highrs.

Meanwhile M.G.fire had increased and was now extremely heavy. At 9.30 a.m. O.C. 'C' Company, Captain J.Strachan M.C., was wounded in the finger but although the finger was almost shot away he remained on duty. At 11 a.m. he was again wounded and before he could be removed by stretcher bearers he died of his wounds.

I wish to draw special attention to this Officer's conduct who all through the operations was remarkable for his ability as organiser no less than for the noble example he set to all by his disregard for his own personal suffering when wounded and by his devotion to duty at a time when cheerfulness and perseverance were qualities of the first importance.

Soon after noon information was received that the troops on the Left flank were retiring and that 'C' Company was having difficulty in maintaining its position as the Right flank was slowly retiring.

At about 1 p.m. 200 reinforcements of Seaforths were placed under my orders and were ordered to take up position in support of 'C' Coy.

At 1 p.m. information was received that the Right flank was retiring. 'A' Coy. was still resisting and made a strong defence right up to the minute when it was found necessary to order withdrawal. 'B' Coy. formed a defensive flank and covered the operation.

An orderly retirement was effected and a new line was taken up from X.1.b.10.35. to Q.36.d.95.20.

The Battalion was reorganised as two companies. This was rendered necessary on account of casualties. 'B' Coy. was on the Right and 'A' Coy. on the Left. On the RIGHT flank of Battalion were 7th Argyll & Sutherland Highrs and on the LEFT flank a force of reinforcements to Seaforths in the vicinity of VERTBOIS FERME Q.35.d.

During the late afternoon small parties of enemy were seen working their way forward assisted by Motor M.G.S. from direction of LA C^{IX} MARMUSE R.20. No attack developed and the line was maintained intact until relieved by the S.Fusiliers.

April, 12th, Friday.

On relief the Battalion moved back to W.11.a. and having marched along South side of CANAL took up position in reserve in W.5.c. and W.4.b.
About 2 p.m. as the enemy was observed advancing one company (B) was advanced and formed a defensive flank in Q.34. b. and d facing East.
Three Lewis Guns Sections under 2/Lieut.Fraser were put in position in BOIS de PACAUT Q.33.a.6.5., Q.27.d.3.2., Q.28.Central. Elements of 6th Seaforths were on the Right flank and 1st Gordon Highrs. on the Left.

Owing to strong enemy attack developing in which enemy pushed scouts and M.Guns forward very rapidly and in considerable numbers the most Northerly L.Gun.Section was forced to withdraw from BOIS DE PACAUT, the remaining guns although strongly attacked and by allowing enemy to approach to within close range, inflicted heavy casualties. I wish to mention 2/Lieut.Fraser for his ability in organising the defence and his resolution in holding out.

These Lewis Gun Sections and 'B' Coy. maintained their positions till nightfall when the Battalion was withdrawn to billets.

I wish to draw attention to the conduct of
    CAPTAIN J. STRACHAN, M.C.(Killed)
    LIEUT. H.MURRAY.
    LIEUT. F.N.ROBERTSON (Missing)
    2/LT. H.M.FRASER.

Major,
Commanding 1/4th Battalion The Gordon Highlanders.

17th April, 1918.

WL 39

War Diary

1st Battalion Ka Gordon Highlanders

May 1919.

SECRET

WAR DIARY
INTELLIGENCE SUMMARY
(Erase heading not required.)

Army Form C. 2118.

Place	Date	Hour	Summary of Events and Information	Remarks and references to Appendices
ST HILAIRE	1/5/18		Training carried on in vicinity of village.	
"	2/5/18		Training. Bde Musketry competition with 1/7 Storop. Bn competing. No 5 & No 8 Platoon of A & B Coy competed.	
"			2/Lt Flower returned from hosp. 2/Lt Pollock joined.	
"	3/5/18		Training. 7 & 8 Platoons Bn team shots in afternoon including for Bde match v. 4 G.H.	
"	4/5/18		Mys gadre arrived from Bde H.Q. Training carried on including Tactical Schemes for officers.	
"			6 ofr reinforcements.	
Ecoivres	5/5/18		Bn left ST HILAIRE 8am. Entrained in funny aux near LILLERS. Detrained about 2pm at MAROEUIL & marched to camp at ECOIVRES.	
"	6/5/18		Training in camp. 6 o/r to hosp.	
ROCLINCOURT	7/5/18		Bn marched at 8am to STEWART CAMP ROCLINCOURT & after 2hrs rest move & r/p to Reserve line in HOPPY SECTOR in reserve to 152 Bde. 2/Lt W. Reid to hosp.	
RESERVE TRENCHES				
ROCLINCOURT	8/5/18		Bn in Reserve line. No shelling. 2/Lt R.P. Leslie + 11 o/r reinforcements joined Bn.	
"	9/5/18		Bn relieved by 6th Black Watch & on reach back to STEWART CAMP.	
"	10/5/18		Training in camp. Officers reconnoitred the GREEN LINE. 2/Lt Froom to Div Wing Party.	
RES TRENCHES	11/5/18		Bn proceeded to reserve trenches to relieve 6 Black Watch. MBD Cup BROWNING C/ngr R. A/L BRIERLEY HILL to hosp.	

Sd/t to Hosp.

Army Form C. 2118.

WAR DIARY
or
INTELLIGENCE SUMMARY.
(Erase heading not required.)

Instructions regarding War Diaries and Intelligence Summaries are contained in F. S. Regs., Part II. and the Staff Manual respectively. Title pages will be prepared in manuscript.

Place	Date	Hour	Summary of Events and Information	Remarks and references to Appendices
RES TRENCHES	12/5/18		3o/r to Amp. Quiet day hostility.	
	13/5/18		Bn HQ moved from B.20 b.14 to B.14 c.9.5. Work on line continued. a quiet day.	
	14/5/18		Quiet day. 8 O.R. to Hosp. 16 ORs rejoined from Hosp.	
	15/5/18		Work continued. Visibility good & slight hostile shelling near Bn HQ.	
	16/5/18		Left front sub-sector reconnoitred. Sgt to Amp. Maj. [Crawstron?] to 6th Gds Bn. Lt Dowse O.C. [?] [?]	
FRONT LINE	17/5/18		The Battn relieved 7th R S Ft in Left sub-sector. Dispositions. Army Right front coy. C coy Left	
			front coy. B coy Support (POST LINE) Reny Reserve BROWN LINE. Bn HQ B.15 c. 2.4. 7.o/r to Hosp.	
	18/5/18		Exceptionally quiet day. Had m[?] for POST LINES continued. 2 [?] and [?] [?] 7 o/r to Hosp.	
	19/5/18		In the [?] the first [?] killed Nov 15 [?] [?] and York Place a Coy. Dowse in [?]	
			wounded in Left. 2/Lt Sebart in [?] sector 2/Lt Metropic bar M.C. wounded in watching [?] [?]	
			about B.11 b.11. 4 got behind them but [?] to [?] [?] would not effect [?]	
	20/5/18		Quiet day. work continued on line. Capt Bridge to Hosp. [?] [?] Relief. B.T.D. up [?] [?] [?] [?]	
	21/5/18		A violent storm of [?] [?] afternoon. 14 o/r to Hosp. no hostile shelling.	
	22/5/18		Pistol distribution of Battn in St Ft. B.T.D. arrived in [?] 6 to 2/Lts R + L + [?]	
			Coming [?] from shelling with Yellow Cross Casualties, Major B. [?] Br + [?]	
	23/5/18		4 Capt + O.M. Hale to OC. 4/o [?] Alts exchange Lt. W.R. Straight joined the Battn.	B 75

WAR DIARY or INTELLIGENCE SUMMARY

Army Form C. 2118.

Place	Date	Hour	Summary of Events and Information	Remarks and references to Appendices
FRONT LINE	23/5/18		2t Boyd t/Hrs 16 of t/Hrs. Batt relieved in afternoon by 6th gordon Hrs & proceeded back to EURIE Camp. Very wet weather.	
	24/5/18		Wet & dry. Batt cleaning up after its 12 days in the line.	
	25/5/18		Lt of t/Hrs & working party of 400 to get up of the track to dig on POSTEUVE water bole. Fit eng R.E. Army suffered 17 casualties from mustard gas amongst party.	
	26/5/18		Batt resting. Voluntary church parade in evening.	
	27/5/18		Reinforcements 9 O/R. 40 men went down to Rifle Range at BRAY. C.O. visited transport lines & Q.M. stores in ECOURES.	
	28/5/18		All officers & NCOs of the 2nd in Com & CRS 51st Division. Training in camp. C.O. reconnoitred centre subsector GARUELLE Sector.	
	29/5/18		Batt relieved 7th Gordon Hrs in centre subsector of GARUELLE Sector. Dispositions A & C coys front line. D coy support (POSTEUVE) Bay Reserve (BROWN LINE)	
	30/5/18		Weather dry, hot. Very quiet on our front. No casualties. All company well in hand. Sent 2 patrols out at night.	
	31/5/18		Artillery more active than usual. FRONT & POST LINES shelled with 4.2s. No Casualties. 6 to hospital. Work on NEW FRONT LINE progressing. 2 Patrols out tonight.	

J.J. Binhorne Lt Col.
Commanding 1/4 Bn Gordon Hrs.

(6339) Wt. W160/M3016 1,500,000 10/17 McA & W Ltd (E 1898) Forms W3091. Army Form W.3091.

Cover for Documents.

Nature of Enclosures.

War Diary
for
JUNE 1918
of
4th Gordon

Notes, or Letters written.

SECRET.　　　　　　　　　　　O.101.

Headquarters
　154th Infantry Brigade.

Enclosed please find War
Diary of 1/4th Battalion The
Gordon Highlanders for
month of June 1918.

　　　　　　　　[signature]
　　　　　　　　Lt. Colonel.
　　Comdg. 1/4th Batt. Gordon Hrs.

30/6/18.

WAR DIARY
or
INTELLIGENCE SUMMARY.
(Erase heading not required.)

Army Form C. 2118.

Place	Date	Hour	Summary of Events and Information	Remarks and references to Appendices
TRENCHES	1	AM	Battalion in GAVRELLE SECTOR. Bn. H.Q. and Enemy area heavily shelled with 5.9's. Casualties 1 O.R. (wounded) 4 slightly wounded	
	2	AM	Back area heavily shelled 1 am – 3 am. Casualties nil. 1 green + gas shell.	
	3	AM	Bn. H.Q. moved to new quarters.	
	4	AM	Very hot & front trench & support line shelled slightly with 5.9's. Casualties 1 O.R. wounded. Inter Coy relief. B & D Coy relieved A & C Coy.	
	5	AM	Towy Alley shelled by enemy 4.2's. Preparatory shoot to a following ⟨ ⟩ B Coy 12th 4 minutes. A Coy 23. 12". D Coy 32. 25". C Coy 42. 5".	
	6	AM	Front line & Towy Alley shelled slightly. Hot + Dry.	

Army Form C. 2118.

WAR DIARY
or
INTELLIGENCE SUMMARY.
(Erase heading not required.)

Instructions regarding War Diaries and Intelligence Summaries are contained in F. S. Regs., Part II. and the Staff Manual respectively. Title pages will be prepared in manuscript.

Place	Date	Hour	Summary of Events and Information	Remarks and references to Appendices
FRONT LINE	7/6/17	PM	Suffolk one slightly shelled. Casualties 1.O.R. killed, accidentally by L.G.	
	8	AM	Hot & Dry very quiet.	
	9	AM	Trenches improved. Weather fine. Quiet.	
	10	AM	Batt. relieved by 1st Norfolks. Relief (prevails) to ECURIE WOOD CAMP. Relief quick & expeditious.	
	11	AM	Quiet. Batts & Scabies inspections.	
	12	AM	Bath Parade. Cerenine Drill for Infection by Cuba Commandant. Cleaning for wing & L.G. commenced. Lt LUNN transferred to D Coy.	
	13	AM	Range. Batt Sports. Fine & Hot.	
	14	AM	Brigade Parade. Medals presented. Lt Col D F. Jackson D.S.O. 2 Lt W PHILLIP M.C.	
	15	AM	Battalion digging a post LING. Left camp & returned 2 a.m.	

R. BOFER

WAR DIARY
or
INTELLIGENCE SUMMARY.

(Erase heading not required.)

Army Form C. 2118.

Place	Date	Hour	Summary of Events and Information	Remarks and references to Appendices
ECURIE WOOD CAMP.	15	AM	LT R STUART to B Coy. 3 Officers sent to Div. Course. Batt. Sports.	
	16	AM	Demonstration of gas projectors give response. Batt. to Bde Reserve in Roy Enclosure & Roy Sector. Working parties found.	
	17	AM	Hqrs & 3 Coy I.O.R. Rollers Work on SUPPORT & POST LINES entrained.	
	18	AM	Slightly shelling. 1 Bde H.Q. with People (Spec Coys) L.G.s received to 1 per Coy.	
	19	AM	Some shelling of Roy Enclosure I.O.R. wounded. A & B Coys Hutted.	
	20	AM	Hot & Fire. Quiet.	
	21	AM	Post LINE smartly heavily shelled. Hostile T.O.R. C & D Coys Hutted.	
	22	AM	Casualties 4 O.R. wounded. Some shelling of BROWN LINE. Batt relieved 7 A & S.H. in Line A & C Coy FRONT B & D Coy SUPPORT Omits	

WAR DIARY
or
INTELLIGENCE SUMMARY.

Army Form C. 2118.

Place	Date	Hour	Summary of Events and Information	Remarks and references to Appendices
FRONT LINE	23	PM	Fext SOS Rockets. Capt MACKINTOSH rejoins Coy. 2Lt MILLER killed by	
			I gone to Hotfire. P.U.O.	
	24	PM	Lifted by bus to FRONT LINE, 7.15 am. Fine, very quiet. Work unknown — were a few strafes.	
	25	PM	Very quiet. Intense Cy relief. B & D Coys to relieve A & C Coys in front line.	
	26	PM	Reserve Coys (A & C) Battery. Shelling slight. Quiet.	
	27	PM	Daylight picture and with good results. 2nd/Lt ROBERTSON HOSPITAL P.U.O. 2 O.R.	
	28	PM	Bttn relieved by 6th Suffolk Regt. Quiet. During the tour in trenches 1 were R, were lit up. in 12 days.	

WAR DIARY
or
INTELLIGENCE SUMMARY.

(Erase heading not required.)

Army Form C. 2118.

Place	Date	Hour	Summary of Events and Information	Remarks and references to Appendices
ECURIE WOOD	29	AM	Bty in camp. Btn. Ass. Conf. Returns & other dispatches. Relieved returns to camp P.	
CAMP	30	AM	Church Parade 10.30 am. Tree Div. Band Played in afternoon	

S.J. Bickmore Lt. Col.
Commanding 4th Bde. Le Gard West

154th Brigade

51st (Highland) Division

1/4th.Battn. THE GORDON HIGHLANDERS

JULY, 1918

154/51

96241

WAR DIARY

VOLUME No. 41.

JULY 1918

1/4th Battalion The Gordon Highrs.

WAR DIARY
or
INTELLIGENCE SUMMARY.
(Erase heading not required.)

Army Form C. 2118.

Place	Date	Hour	Summary of Events and Information	Remarks and references to Appendices
ECURIE	1/7/18	A.M.	Companies at disposal of Company Commanders for training. Weather very hot and fine.	
WOOD				
CAMP	2/7/18	A.M.	Battalion parade 10.30 am	
	3/7/18	A.M.	Parades as usual. Conference of O.C. Companies at distance. for training	
	4/7/18	A.M.	Battalion moved to Point 90 Subsector (right subsector of left sector) relieving 7th R.W.F. ECURIE WOOD CAMP left 2.30 pm. Relief complete 5.8 pm. Dispositions C Company right front. A Coy left front. D Coy Right Support. B Coy Left support. S.P. coy in Reserve taking over Trenches good.	
	5/7/18	P.M.	Quiet Relief. Both on defended localities carried out by A Coy. C Coy continued wiring in front of DEAD END SAP. Wiry difficult owing to great scarcity of wire and much sniping. Patrols find ground to lead to our troops in Pickets	

Army Form C. 2118.

WAR DIARY
or
INTELLIGENCE SUMMARY.
(Erase heading not required.)

Instructions regarding War Diaries and Intelligence Summaries are contained in F.S. Regs., Part II. and the Staff Manual respectively. Title pages will be prepared in manuscript.

Place	Date	Hour	Summary of Events and Information	Remarks and references to Appendices
FRONT LINE	5/7/18	A.M.	Quiet day. Some considerable shelling of MAISON BLANCHE DUMP with 5.9's. Work on defended locality continued.	
	6/7/18	A.M.	Wire in front of DEAD END SAP continued. Considerable shelling of MAISON BLANCHE Dump & Bn. HQ during morning. Work & wiring continued.	
	7/7/18	A.M.	The Coy relieved D Coy. C Coy relieved B Coy. relieved A Coy. Quiet relief.	
	8/7/18	A.M.	Quiet day. Work continued. DEAD END SAP wiring finished. Improvement to fire bays in right Suffolk Coy sector completed.	
	9/7/18	A.M.	Some slight shelling in rear of Battalion. Work continued.	
	10/7/18	A.M.	ditto	
	11/7/18	A.M.	Batt relieved in POINT DU JOUR subsector by 75th Batt. 4th Canadian Division, relief commenced 2 p.m. Quiet. Battalion proceeded to ANZIN	

Army Form C. 2118.

WAR DIARY
or
INTELLIGENCE SUMMARY.
(Erase heading not required.)

Instructions regarding War Diaries and Intelligence Summaries are contained in F. S. Regs., Part II. and the Staff Manual respectively. Title pages will be prepared in manuscript.

Place	Date	Hour	Summary of Events and Information	Remarks and references to Appendices
ANZIN	12/7/18	MN	Batt entrained midnight 11/12th July 1918 at ARTILLERY corner and proceeded to HANCHY-BRETON detrained were in early morning and marched to billets at OSTREVILLE	
OSTREVILLE	13/7/18	MN	day spent resting and cleaning	
	14/7/18	MN	Church parade and inspection of Battalion by C.O.	
BRYAS	15/7/18	MN	at 12 midnight 14/15th Batt marched to BRYAS and entrained 2 a.m. remainder of day and night spent on journey	
NOGENT	16/7/18	MN	Batt detrained at 6 a.m. at NOGENT-SUR-SEINE. at 6 p.m. Batt entrained	
CHAVILLY	17/7/18	MN	at 1 a.m. Batt detrained at wood on outskirts of CHAVILLY where day was spent. day spent resting at CHAVILLY	
BELLEVUE	18/7/18	MN	Battalion marched to wood at BELLEVUE, ¾ mile N. of CHAVILLY leaving CHAVILLY 6 a.m.	

WAR DIARY or INTELLIGENCE SUMMARY

Army Form C. 2118.

Place	Date	Hour	Summary of Events and Information	Remarks and references to Appendices
20/7/18	20/7/18	7 am	156 Bde ordered to attack. Batt Batt marched from BELLEVUE via ST IMOGES, a short distance S. of DANTOEUL. Batt struck W. to assembly position. Batt to take second objective passing through 4th Seaforth Highlanders. Batt attack to start at Zero + 40 minutes. 2nd Objective ESPILLY - NAPPES - LA CARBONNERIE. Zero hour 7.40am. At 8.20 am Batt attacked. Coys from right to left A.B.D. C Coy being in Batt reserve. At about 10.30 am Lt.Col D.J. BICKMORE was wounded and taken prisoner. At 3.30 pm Major HENDERSON 4th Seaforth Highlanders took command and reorganised. Casualties heavy. CAPT H MURRAY (A/Adj) see Lt D LUND (a/c D Coy), CAPT J BROWN (see staff) acting 2nd command killed.	

WAR DIARY
or
INTELLIGENCE SUMMARY.
(Erase heading not required.)

Army Form C. 2118.

Instructions regarding War Diaries and Intelligence Summaries are contained in F. S. Regs., Part II. and the Staff Manual respectively. Title pages will be prepared in manuscript.

Place	Date	Hour	Summary of Events and Information	Remarks and references to Appendices
	21/7/18		Some shelling of Batt H.Q.	
	22/7/18	AM	At 3.30 am Heavy enemy Barrage of S.O.S. & field guns. Suspected preliminary to attack. Have developed distinct smoke screen on right. D Coy on left. A & B Coy distinct forward field to left. Line advanced by artillery smoke barrage of five mins & moved forward line. When up in Bois DE COURCELLY A Coy right front. B Coy left front. C & D Coy respectively.	
	23/7/18	AM	Concerning A & B Coy Batt relieved by A & Seaforth Highlanders & withdrew to Brigade reserve. Relief began 8pm interrupted by heavy enemy Barrage. Thirty gas casualties. Disposition in Reserve. Batt H.Q. at X roads 1 km	
	25/7/18	AM	EA N.W. of ST. DENIS. Order A Coy rifle C left B.A.C.D	

WAR DIARY
or
INTELLIGENCE SUMMARY.

Army Form C. 2118.

Place	Date	Hour	Summary of Events and Information	Remarks and references to Appendices
	25/7/18		Some heavy shooting from field guns.	
	26/7/18		Batt relieved by 7th RW and marched back to woods 1 mile N of ST. IMOGES very wet.	
	27/7/18	At 12 noon	orders received for Batt to take up line from PUVERCY - MARFAUX Road through BULLIN FM to Point 84 ½ kms S.S.W of BULLIN FM. Batt moved off 12.45 p.m. Given two Enemy repeated retiring rapidly. Line taken up under of Cups right & left A.I.B.C. Heavy jerry with mixed gasses about 3 p.m. Batt took over front line.	
	28/7/18		Some gas shells	
	29/7/18		Some gas shells during day	
	30/7/18		Batt relieved by 4th Leics Batt & marched to huts	

1.30 a.m. 1/8/18

A Birdwhistle Lt Colonel

REPORT ON OPERATIONS
19/7/18 – 31/7/18.
by
1/4TH BATTALION THE GORDON HIGHLANDERS.

Map Reference:- JONCHERY – Scale 1/20,000.

On the Night of 19th July the Battalion took up positions in BOIS DE COURCY from POURCY on the right to a point about 1000 yards SSW as shown by a French guide.

The following morning at 8.40 a.m. the Battalion moved off to take up the jumping off positions. These were to be slightly in rear of the first objective (from CHAUMET to a point 300 yards left of the L of LA CARBONNERIE). "A" and "B" Companies moved off along the valley of the River ARDRE. "C" and "D" Companies and Battalion Headquarters moved off by a track leading to ESPILLY, NAPPES and left of LA CARBONNERIE.

"C" and "D" Companies and Battalion Headquarters, however, came in contact with the enemy in considerable numbers holding Machine Gun Posts along road running through the U of BULLIN to point 247.9. "C" and "D" Companies immediately deployed and attacked, causing the enemy to take up positions in the wood in rear of this road. On attacking both Companies met with strong opposition and sustained severe losses from Machine Gun fire. As "D" Company Officers had become casualties the Commanding Officer sent the Officer Commanding "C" Company to lead "D" Company. The Commanding Officer then personally took command of the two Companies. While leading his men to the attack the Commanding Officer was wounded by a Bomb.

At this moment strong resistance was met with and extremely heavy reserved fire from Machine Guns was encountered. The attack was broken. When the Stretcher Bearers returned to carry the Commanding Officer back, the ground on which he was left was found to be in enemy hands. The strong presumption is that he is a prisoner in enemy hand owing to wounds sustained while leading the Battalion.

"D" Company pushed forward on the left of "C" Company, but before going more than 200 – 300 yards both Companies were held up and eventually were forced to fall back and take up positions along the road on which they originally deployed.

"A" and "B" Companies met with similar opposition and after strong resistance had been made they were driven back somewhat disorganised.

On this line we got in touch with the 153rd Infantry Brigade on our left and the 7th Argyll and Sutherland Highlanders on our right.

Between 3 and 4 p.m. Major Henderson, 4th Seaforth Highlanders, took command of the Battalion and reorganised it with "C" Company on the right, "D" Company on the left and "A" and "B" Companies pushed out on a track leading from the left flank.

On the night of 20th – 21st July the Battalion remained on line held on the 20th. "A" and "B" Companies in front in the BOIS DE COUTRON and "C" and "D" Companies in support on the road running from the U in BULLIN to point 247.9. Touch was established with the supporting troops of 153rd Infantry Brigade (7th Black Watch) on the left and the 7th Argyll and Sutherland Highlanders on the right.

(Note): Road running from U in BULLIN to point 247.9, will be hereafter described as road X.

HISTORY OF OPERATIONS.
SHEET IX.

On the 21st - 22nd July "A" Company took over portion of the front held by 153rd Infantry Brigade - from point 263.7. 700 yards West of ROAD X and running in a N.E. direction to point 243.6. "B", "C" and "D" Companies pushed forward through the BOIS DE COUTRON and established themselves on the right of "A" Company, touch being established with the 8th Royal Scots on the left and the 7th Argyll and Sutherland Highlanders on the right. Throughout these days the Battalion attempted to push forward through the wood but no advance could be made on account of heavy Machine Gun Fire.

At 6 a.m. on the 23rd July the 152nd Infantry Brigade was ordered to attack, 4th Gordons and 7th Argylls having to push forward and keep touch with the advance. The Battalion was withdrawn to the forming up line (ROAD X), but when the attack started our own barrage and also the enemy's fell heavily on this road, again causing heavy casualties to the Battalion. The Battalion attacked but was again held up by severe Machine Gun Fire, and the line was established as originally, i.e. 700 yards in front of ROAD X and running in a N.E. direction till touch was gained with the 7th Argylls.

On the 24th July the 4th Gordon Highlanders and 7th Argyll and Sutherland Highlanders attempted to establish a line from the second L of ESPILLY to point 252.7. Battalion Scouts pushed forward to the road and reported all clear. One post on the extreme left was established, but when a second post was being placed in position it was met by severe Machine Gun and Rifle Fire and Bombs, the enemy being strongly entrenched in posts about 15 yards in rear of this road. Subsequently the original line was handed over to the 4th Seaforths on the night of 24th - 25th July - the Battalion going into Brigade Reserve.

On the 26th July the 154th Infantry Brigade was relieved by the 153rd Infantry Brigade, the 7th Black Watch relieving the 4th Gordons in Brigade Reserve.

On the 27th July the 154th Infantry Brigade was ordered forward, 4th Gordons establishing a Battalion Headquarters at BULLIN FARM and the Battalion remaining in Artillery Formation 300 yards in advance of this point.

On 28th July the Battalion moved forward to BOIS DE L'AULNAY and on the night of 28th - 29th July the Battalion relieved the 153rd Infantry Brigade. After some difficulty a front line was established from point 137.4. (700 yards E. of BOIS DES MELISSES and 600 yards S.E. of Y in CHAMBRECY) and running E. to edge of BOIS DES MELISSES - the 14th (French) Division being on the left and the 4th Seaforth Highlanders on the right. A support line was also established in rear of this position.

On the 29th July the Battalion was ordered to keep in touch with 14th French Division and 62nd Division should an advance be made. No advance was made however. Our patrols pushed through CHAMBRECY and found it unoccupied.

On the 30th July the orders remained the same as for the 29th - the French, however, making no attempt to advance. A patrol pushed forward to MICHEL RENAUT FERME, but when within 70 yards of this point, a light gun started shelling the farm and gradually working towards the patrol. The patrol was also subjected to a certain amount of Machine Gun Fire.

On the 31st July the Battalion was relieved by a Battalion of the 44th French Regiment and marched back to the CHAMPILLON area.

HISTORY OF OPERATIONS.
SHEET III.

In this action the casualties were approximately:-

        12 Officers.
        380 O/Ranks.

The Battalion captured:-

        Trench Mortars......6
        Machine Guns........2
        Prisoners...........2

A.J. Welch
                  Lieut.Colonel,
Commanding 1/4TH BATTALION THE GORDON HIGHLANDERS.

AUGUST, 8TH, 1918.

SECRET

War Diary

Volume #3

9R 42

August 1918

1/4th Battalion The Gordon Hrs

August 1918.

WAR DIARY
or
INTELLIGENCE SUMMARY. 1/4 Bn Gordon Highrs

Army Form C. 2118.

Place	Date	Hour	Summary of Events and Information	Remarks and references to Appendices
NANTEUIL	1-8-18		Dull + showery: Left NANTEUIL; Bn bivouaced in woods near BELLEVUE. Bn Headquarters in CHAMPILLON.	
BELLEVUE	2-8-18		Dry + hot: Battalion cleaning + reorganizing	
	3-8-18		Dry + hot: Bn marched off at 5 am and entrained for new area at EPERNAY. Left EPERNAY at 11 am. Passed through outskirts of PARIS that night.	
	4-8-18		Bn travelling via ETAPLES and ABBEVILLE to BRYAS at which station we detrained. When leaving REIMS area from BRYAS, the Battn was conveyed by motor waggons to area around BERLES where the billets were exceptionally good	
BERLES	5-8-18		Bn cleaning + reorganizing — weather hot + sunny.	
do	6-8-18		Training commenced, under Coy. Commanders, 9 am to 12.30 pm. Armourers inspection + Bn. Repair Inspection. — weather good.	
do	7-8-18		Hot + dry: Bn. Training under Coy Commanders at as the 6th.	
do	8-8-18		Hot + dry: Coys under Coy Commanders 9 am to 12.30 pm. Reorganizing Specialists; Baths at SAVY. for A.B.Tc. Coys.	

Army Form C. 2118.

WAR DIARY
or
INTELLIGENCE SUMMARY.
(Erase heading not required.)

Instructions regarding War Diaries and Intelligence Summaries are contained in F.S. Regs., Part II. and the Staff Manual respectively. Title pages will be prepared in manuscript.

Place	Date	Hour	Summary of Events and Information	Remarks and references to Appendices
BERLES	9.8.18		Hot & dry; Training 9 a.m. – 12.30 p.m. as per Training Programme; Medical Inspection for whole Battalion; Bolmerols entertainment at schoolhouse 5.30 p.m.	
do	10.8.18		Hot & dry; C.O. Parade, followed by Divine Inspection; Training as per Programme; Transport Inspection by C.O. 2.30 p.m. with Major Stenwell (to/rev/?); Capt G.T. Burney; Lt. G.D. Shelley (¾ A.S.H.); 2/Lt A.E.S Moorhie who joined Bn on the 8.8.18 were posted to Coys.	
do	11.8.18		Hot & Dry; C.O. inspected billets; Voluntary Pres. Service at 10 a.m. (Rouge attendance). Major Wilson A.R.G (A+S.H.) joined Bn on Second in Command.	
do	12.8.18		Hot & Dry; Parades & Training as per programmes arranged 9 a.m. to 12.30 p.m. Battalion was paid out.	
do	13.8.18		Hot & Day; Parades & Training as per Programme; Capt. B.C. Brodie was appointed a/Adjutant from 23/3/18, vice Capt. J.R. Thomson (U.K.)	
do	14.8.18		Hot & Dry; Parade & Training as per Programme, 9 a.m. to 12.30 p.m. C.O. Lectures all officers & N.C.O. on "Fundamental Principles to extend Success," at 2 p.m.	
do	15.8.18		Hot & Day; Battalion entrained in Light Railway at SAVY and	

Army Form C. 2118.

WAR DIARY
or
INTELLIGENCE SUMMARY.
(Erase heading not required.)

Place	Date	Hour	Summary of Events and Information	Remarks and references to Appendices
Berles.	15.8.18		detrained at FOSSEUX; had tea & proceeded to line as Brigade Support in "GAVRELLE SECTOR." Bn relieved 1/7th Royal Scots. (52nd Div).	Apx
Trenches	16.8.18		Hot. Dry; Very Quiet; a few gas shells crumped A 67. 5 O.R's gassed. Works commenced on Dugouts under R.Es; work under Bn arrangement, repairing firesteps, parapets, latrines, clearing trenches and carrying parties. etc etc; 2 Lt BEDDIE & 2 Lt LEES joined Battn	Apx
"	17.8.18		Hot & dry; Very Quiet all day & night; Work continued on the 16th inst. very satisfactory; Casualties NIL.	Apx
"	18.8.18		Hot & day; Very quiet all day; Work continued as on 16th inst; wiring on support line by A.Coy. 2Lt Cruickshank joined Batty; Batty came out of Trenches & Lieut. C. Coy left in Brigade Reserve lines, and proceeded to ROCLINCOURT WEST CAMP, (arriving 10 pm)	Apx
ROCLINCOURT	19/8/18		Hot Day; about 20 H.V. shells landed round Camp. no casualties. Day spent in cleaning up and resting. A. Mitchell & 2Lt. Buchanan, joined Battn for duty.	Apx

WAR DIARY
or
INTELLIGENCE SUMMARY.

Army Form C. 2118.

Place	Date	Hour	Summary of Events and Information	Remarks and references to Appendices
ROCLINCOURT	20/8/18		Dull & Showery; Parades and Training 9am to 12.30pm under O.C. Coys. Lewis Gun classes continue; Battn held Baths in ECURIE; Slight hostile bombing during the night; Major Wilson (A+S.Hts.) left Battn for Base.	Hry
do.	21/8/18		Very hot & dry; B.+D. Coys at Range 9am to 12.30pm. A. Coy Training as on 20th; Lecture by Commanding Officer 6.30pm to Officers & N.C.Os. on "Information".	Hry
do.	22/8/18		Very hot & dry; A. Coy at Range; B. & D. Coy. Training 9am to 12.30pm. C. Coy came out of line rejoin Battn about 5pm. (no casualties from camp homecoming shells) during the night.	Hry
do.	23/8/18		Dull but dry; B. Coy at Range; A + D. Coy Training area & C. Coy Resting & Cleaning; Sixteen military medals awarded N.C.Os of the Battn for gallantry displayed between 26th & 30th July 1918. 2nd Lt. W.R. Hindle & 2nd Lt. M. Pott (both A+S Htrs) joined Battalion.	Hry
do.	24/8/18		Very hot & dry; C. Coy at Range; A.B.&D. Coy Training; Coy Comdrs reconnoitre the front line (Rt. B.n) GAVRELLE SECTOR. Battn weekly one hours notice as Div. Reserve.	Hry
do.	25/8/18		Hot & dry; Voluntary Church Service 10 a.m.; Battn proceed to trenches in support in 152. Brigade Sector on N. bank of SCARPE	Hry

WAR DIARY or INTELLIGENCE SUMMARY

Army Form C. 2118.

Place	Date	Hour	Summary of Events and Information	Remarks and references to Appendices
Trenches (North bank of SCARPE)	25/8/18		At 12 midnight companies held following positions: A & B Coy. TILLOY TR. C & D. Coys TILLOY SUPPORT. Batt H.Q. TILLOY TRENCH. (Heavy rain during the whole night.) Casualties NIL.	
Trenches (Div. Res)	26/8/18		Cloudy, bit day: Battn in same positions as in 25th inst.; 152nd & 153 Brigades advanced to the attack about 11:30 am. Objective CALICO TRENCH. Canadians attack S. of SCARPE; all objectives carried. Casualties light; Bn Casualties NIL.	
do.	27/8/18		Battn received orders to move to following positions Q.Coy – PUDDING TR. B.Coy. CABLE AVENUE; C.Coy. DEE TR.; D.Coy. CAMERON LANE. Move complete at 7 p.m.; Bn under orders to move at 5 min notice. Casualties NIL. —— (hot day).	
do.	28/8/18		Showery, dull; Battn takes over front line from 6th Gordons starting 8:15 p.m. A & D Coys front line, with C & B Coy Support; Move complete 1 a.m. 29th inst. Operation orders received for attack next morning. A. Coy on Right & D.Coy on Left; Casualties slight; Coy Commanders were:– A. Coy Lt Philip M.C. B.Coy Lt A. Gogg. Capt. Benney M.C. D.Coy. & Lt N.S Williamson	

Army Form C. 2118.

WAR DIARY
or
INTELLIGENCE SUMMARY.
(Erase heading not required.)

Instructions regarding War Diaries and Intelligence Summaries are contained in F. S. Regs., Part II. and the Staff Manual respectively. Title pages will be prepared in manuscript.

Place	Date	Hour	Summary of Events and Information	Remarks and references to Appendices
Front line Trenches	29/8/18		Batt. attacks on a nine hundred yards front to a depth of 1000X Zero hour 6.30 a.m.; Barrage lifts hundred yds every five minutes; by 7 a.m. Coy. capture first objective with little casualties; B & C Coys capture 2nd objective (GREENLAND HILL) by 8 a.m. Scheme time casualties slight. Enemy resistance feeble with little shelling; During afternoon further Prisoners taken; shelling very heavy but all Companies holed on. By 12 noon; at night C Coy relieved by A Coy; Casualties were:- Killed 1 Off. 11 OR; Wounded 2 Off + 70 OR; Missing 1 OR; (Officer Killed 2/Lt Murray, A; gassed + sick 11 OR. (This covers night of 29/30 as well) Officer wounded 2/Lt Murray A.	A.D.
do.	30/8/18		Weather dull but dry; Spent his organised outpost line & patrols pushed forward from A + B Coys to establish outpost line which was occupied by A + B Coys at night; Fairly heavy shelling by the day.	from
do.	31/8/18		S.9. 1 m.2.9. during the day; Weather cloudy with slight rain; The batt. evacuated our held trenches immediately in front of PLOUVAIN and took the ARRAS-DOUAI RAILWAY; R.B boundary being 100X south of Railway and	Apy

WAR DIARY
or
INTELLIGENCE SUMMARY.
(Erase heading not required.)

Army Form C. 2118.

Place	Date	Hour	Summary of Events and Information	Remarks and references to Appendices
			Right Boundary 800 yds North of Railway. The hill lying due the Eastern side of GREENLAND HILL. The front was heavily shelled through the day.	

W. Watt
Lt Colonel.
Commanding 1/4 Bn Gordon H'rs

1st Battalion The Gordon Highlanders

WAR DIARY

VOLUME 44

September 1918

September 1918.

Army Form C. 2118.

WAR DIARY
or
INTELLIGENCE SUMMARY. 1/4 Bn. The Gordon Highrs
(Erase heading not required.)

Instructions regarding War Diaries and Intelligence Summaries are contained in F. S. Regs., Part II. and the Staff Manual respectively. Title pages will be prepared in manuscript.

Place	Date	Hour	Summary of Events and Information	Remarks and references to Appendices
Front Line Trenches. GREENLAND HILL	1/9/18.		Very hot day; The Bn. were holding the line, one N. of the SCARPE. D. Coy. relieved A. Coy. on Rt. Front Section, went midnight. The hostile shelling was slight, although its Rt. Sector suffered from Gas shelling on different occasions. Casualties:- 12 O.R. wounded to Hospital. 3 O.R.: 1 2nd. Lt. McKean A.T. joined the Bn. from	
do.	2/9/18.		Very hot day; The enemy shelled the whole sector (with about {illegible} intervals) during the former day. D. Coy were ordered to push forward by peaceful penetration to the FRESNES LINE. A patrol was sent out to reconnoitre but were soon turned to co-operation by D. Coy. had to be received owing to large enemy numbers. Casualties: wounded 3 O.R. Rich to Hospital. Major E. W. Watt joined the Bn., also Lieut. T. Gray. D. McDonald	Jnsmi.
do.	3/9/18.		Bright day; The hostile shelling quietened down considerably. The Battn were relieved by the 7th Black Watch 153 Brigade. Relief complete by 1 a.m. (4th {illegible}) Casualties. N.L.	Jnsmi.

Army Form C. 2118.

WAR DIARY
or
INTELLIGENCE SUMMARY.
(Erase heading not required.)

Instructions regarding War Diaries and Intelligence Summaries are contained in F. S. Regs., Part II. and the Staff Manual respectively. Title pages will be prepared in manuscript.

Place	Date	Hour	Summary of Events and Information	Remarks and references to Appendices
ROCLINCOURT	4/9/18		Warn Bty: Bn on completion of relief proceeded to Roclincourt West Camp, arriving abt. 2.30 a.m., rather hot, sleepers were served out. Reveille 9 a.m. The remainder of the day was spent in resting, cleaning up. Sick to hospital: 8 O.R.	
do.	5/9/18		Bat. & Bty: The Bn. were bathed at Roclincourt Baths. Commanding Officer Parader at B.D. Camp. 10 a.m. & C. Coy. 12 noon. Training under Coy. Commanders. 2 Lts. Phillip, Sweden & Rhee were awarded M.C. for gallantry displayed on 20/30th July also 3 D.C.M. + 1 M.M. to O.Rs. Bn. painted out; sick to hospital & Off. (Lieut. Slater - Arth. atd.) & 4 O.Rs.	
do.	6/9/18		Duel Bvhery: warm with thunder; Commanding Officers lecture on "Attack formation" 9 - 10.30 a.m. Training under Coy. Comdrs. 12.30 p.m.; Specialists under their own Instructors. Sick to hospital, 6 O.R.; lecture on Artillery by Lt. Col. Davidson D.S.O. from	
do.	7/9/18		Showery but very warm; C.O. lecture 9 - 10.30 a.m. on "Attack formation".	

WAR DIARY
or
INTELLIGENCE SUMMARY.
(Erase heading not required.)

Army Form C. 2118.

Place	Date	Hour	Summary of Events and Information	Remarks and references to Appendices
ROCLINCOURT	7/9/18 cont.		Lecture by Lt. R.T.L. Mitchell on the use of German bombs.	Appx
do.	8/9/18		Lieut. A.K.H. BROWN joined Bn.; Sick to hospice Sports commenced; Football C.Bn. v D.Coy & B/Coy Beat A. Raw and very wet; Voluntary Church Service (Presj.) C. of E. & R.C.; Recruits inspected by CO.; Div. Band played in camp in the afternoon; Capt. R.T. GILES (1st Gordons) joined the Battn.; Sick to Hospital, 5. O.Rs.	Appx
do.	9/9/18		Showery and dull; Training under Coy. Commanders; 1 A.Coy allotted Range; Lecture on German bombs by R.T.L.Mitchell; Officers H.Q. Class in the afternoon; Inter Football Match between B.&C. Coys. (5:0 for C.Coy). Sick to hospital 6. O.Rs.	Appx
do.	10/9/18		Warm but very showery & dull; Parades & Training under Coy. Commdr's; A. & B. Coys. at the Range; Bombing & Gas lecture to N.C.O.'s officers by Lts. Mitchell & Beddie respectively. No. 201648. Sgr. W. Davidson. awarded Croix de Guerre for gallantry displayed on March 1918 at Cambrai; Sgt. Hospital 1 O.R.; Lt. N. Williamson & McGregor made a/Capts. while commanding D. + A. Coys respectively.	Appx

Army Form C. 2118.

WAR DIARY
or
INTELLIGENCE SUMMARY.
(Erase heading not required.)

Place	Date	Hour	Summary of Events and Information	Remarks and references to Appendices
ROCLINCOURT	11/9/18		Very wet & rather cold: C. & D. Coys at the Ranges but had to discontinue owing to rain; Orders received to move to Camp	
MONT ST. ELOY.			at MONT. ST. ELOY. Batt. left. ROCLINCOURT & pr. arrived in New area. 5.20 p.m. Camp in poor condition. B. Coy hut nearly flooded owing to heavy rain during the night. Sick to hospital: 1. O.R. [A & B. Coys. bathed before leaving Roclincourt)	
MONT ST. ELOY.	12/9/18		Dull but dry: Parades and Training 9.30 a.m. to 12.30 a.m. under Coy Commdrs.: Gas & Bombing Lectures arranged: Slight hostile Bombing about 10 p.m. Sick to hospital 1 O.R.	
do.	13/9/18		Showery but warm: Training as usual under Coy Commdrs including Specialists Training: Lewis Guns: Stretcher Bearers: Signallers: Bombers: Scouts: Gas. N.C.Os. Sick to Hospital 1. O.R.	
do.	14/9/18		Bright & warm: Commanding Officers' Parade 9.15 a.m.: (Training in Tactical Schemes: C. & D. Coys. at Batt. in the afternoon. Sick to Hospital: 1. O.R.	
do.	15/9/18		Bright and warm: Brigade Church Service at Seaforth Camp.	

WAR DIARY
or
INTELLIGENCE SUMMARY.
(Erase heading not required.)

Army Form C. 2118.

Place	Date	Hour	Summary of Events and Information	Remarks and references to Appendices
Mont.St.Eloy	15/9/18		contd. for Presbyterians at 10 a.m.; Camp Inspection by Comm'dg. Officer at 11.15 a.m.; Football Match between officers of 4th Sea forths and 4th Gordons. Score: a draw, one against one; Sick to hospital 1. O.R.	
do.	16/9/18		Bright & warm; A.B & C. Coys in Training Area practising Artillery formation & Final Stages of attack and the assault. D. Coy under Coy. Commdr.; Sick to hospital. Nil. Lt. R.A. Robertson, & 2 Lt. Sullivan & Douglas, joined Bat'n. from 3rd Res. Gardens.	
do.	17/9/18		Bright & warm; A & D. Coys Training under Coy. Commdrs.; C. Coy at Rouex; B. Coy. inspected by G.O.C. Division. 10 a.m. Sick to hospital 3. O.R.s; 2nd Lt. SILVER J.W. joined Bat'n. from	
do.	18/9/18		Bright & warm; D. Coy at La MOTTE Rouge; A.B & C Coys practising the attack & artillery scheme; Special classes as ---- afternoon (Bombers, Lewis Guns). Sick to hospital. 4. O.R. form	
do.	19/9/18		Showery & cold; Coys. Special Training on attack with demonstration	

Army Form C. 2118.

WAR DIARY
or
INTELLIGENCE SUMMARY.
(Erase heading not required.)

Instructions regarding War Diaries and Intelligence Summaries are contained in F. S. Regs., Part II. and the Staff Manual respectively. Title pages will be prepared in manuscript.

Place	Date	Hour	Summary of Events and Information	Remarks and references to Appendices
MONT ST. ELOY	19/9/16		At Tardes: The early morning training had to be cancelled owing to rain; Specialist classes as on the 18th inst; Lecture by Commanding Officer on Protection at 5pm; 7 ORs awarded the M.M. for gallantry displayed in GREENLAND HILL 29th August. Divisional Foot Ball Match, beside camp, 7th Black Watch, versus 7th A. & S. H. Score 4/1 for 7th A. & S. H. Sick to Hospital. Nil.	Mon
do.	20/9/16		Showery, dull; Training as on the 19th with Special Demonstration of Tanks, assisting Infantry; B. Coy. Test Box Respiration in Gas Chamber; Battle for Transport, R.A.T.B Coys. at Mont St. Eloy; Company Pail out: 2 Lt. H. C. Findlay, M. Gordon, James Booth. Sick to Hospital. Nil.	Mon
do.	21/9/16		Heavy Rain morn: Coys. Training cancelled owing to rain: Major John Ew. Hay. Wett. & Coy Commanders reconnoitre SECTOR, in line, North of the SCARPE, in accordance with marching orders to move up on 22nd; Battn. fin C.M.D. Egp in the afternoon; Specialists classes as usual; Sick to Hospital	Mon

A6945. Wt.W1122/N1160 350,000 12/16 D.D. & L. Forms/C/2118/14.

WAR DIARY
or
INTELLIGENCE SUMMARY

Army Form C. 2118.

(Erase heading not required.)

Place	Date	Hour	Summary of Events and Information	Remarks and references to Appendices
MONT. ST. ELOI.	22/4/18		Showery, but Bright. B2 under orders to move up to Line back. Cancelled; Voluntary R.C. Church Service 10 am; R.C. Services 9 am & 5 pm P. Te. Mitchell appointed Intelligence Officer; Sick 5; Hospital 2 O.R.	
do	23/4/18		Bright & very hot. Companies carry out training & movement of Platoons & Companies in the open; A.T.C, Corps S.B, R.s. testing; Specialist classes assemble; Sick 4; Hospital 1 O.R.	
do	24/4/18		Bright & warm. Battn relieved 4th K.O.Y.L.I. Right Sub Sector, left Sector (GREENLAND HILL); A.T.C. Coys in front line with B. & D. in Support. Very Quiet Relief. Sick to hospitals NIL.	
Trenches	25/4/18		Showery but clear; Shelling very moderate. Enemy aeroplanes were supporting the trenches & frontage when we in a bad condition; very little enemy activity. One Patrol out by C. Coys for information re posts occupied by enemy; Sick 5; Hospital — 1. O.R. Casualties NIL.	
GREENLAND HILL				

WAR DIARY
or
INTELLIGENCE SUMMARY.

Army Form C. 2118.

Place	Date	Hour	Summary of Events and Information	Remarks and references to Appendices
"TRENCHES" GREENLAND HILL	24/9/18		Weather clearing; Companies carry on improving trenches; Our artillery active but enemy quiet; Preparations made for "CHINESE ATTACK" to be carried out next day; Casualties: 1 O.R. wounded. Sent to hospital 1 O.R.	
do.	27/9/18		Heavy rain during the early morning otherwise dry; "A" CHINESE ATTACK carried out successfully ZERO hour being 5.35 a.m. very little enemy retaliation; Casualties: 1 O.R. wounded. Sent to hospital 3 O.R.S.; Inter Company relief B.D. Coys. take over from A & C Coys (very quiet relief).	
do.	28/9/18		Shelling and clear; Our artillery very active. Hostile shelling very slight; Companies continue the improvement of trenches; Casualties: 1 O.R. wounded. Sent to hospital 3 O.R.S.	
do.	29/9/18		Very showery dull; Companies carry on improvement of trenches; Very little hostile shelling. Gas projector and ext. enemy line at 11.30 p.m. (unsuccessful) Casualties 1 O.R. wounded at Duty; Sent to hospital 5 O.R.S.	

Army Form C. 2118.

WAR DIARY
or
INTELLIGENCE SUMMARY.
(Erase heading not required.)

Place	Date	Hour	Summary of Events and Information	Remarks and references to Appendices
TRENCHES. GREENLAND-HILL	30/9/18		Bright but Showery: Very little hostile Shelling; our artillery successfully cutting the wire in front of FRESNES-ROUVROY-LINE: Batt" was relieved by 7th R. S. Hrs and moved back to Brigade Support Casualties. 2. O.R. wounded. Sics to Agricostan.	

A.J. Welch
Lt Colonel
Commanding 1/4th Br. The Gordon Highrs

[Stamp: 1/4th BATT THE GORDON HIGHLANDERS Date 30.9.18]

1/4th Bn. The Gordon High[rs]
1st/5th

Vol 44

WAR: DIARY — October 1918

Volume: No 45.

1/4 Br (THE) GORDON HIGHRS

Army Form C. 2118.

WAR DIARY
or
INTELLIGENCE SUMMARY for OCTOBER 1918.

(Erase heading not required.)

Instructions regarding War Diaries and Intelligence Summaries are contained in F.S. Regs., Part II. and the Staff Manual respectively. Title pages will be prepared in manuscript.

Place	Date	Hour	Summary of Events and Information	Remarks and references to Appendices
GREENLAND HILL "SUPPORT. TR."	1/10/18		Heavy rain during the early morning. Bright afterwards; Bn. receive orders to move out of Support. Trenches and entrain at ATRIES for Mont. St. Eloi camp, arriving 5-30 p.m. when hot tea were served. Casualties. 1 O.R. (W.) to Hospital Sick. 5 O.Rs	John
Camp, Mont. St. Eloi	2/10/18		Bright but very cold; Day spent in cleaning up, resting; Companies period out; Baths; Will draw clothing for whole Battn.; Winter Blankets arrive; each man supplied with one; Sick to Hospital – NIL.	
do.	3/10/18		Bright but cold; Commanding Officers Parade 9 a.m.; Armourers, S.A. Inspection of Rifles; Scabies Inspection; Sick to Hospital. 2. O.R.	Jas.
do.	4/10/18		Bright but very cold; Commanding Officers Parade 9 a.m.; Return by Bn. Commander on Training area; Lecture in the army; Sick to Hospital. 1. O.R. Lieut. R.T.O. BRAKKEN joined Battn. posted to D Coy.	Jun.
do.	5/10/18		Bright but very cold; Battn. practice the attack: weather	Jun.

Army Form C. 2118.

WAR DIARY
or
INTELLIGENCE SUMMARY.
(Erase heading not required.)

Place	Date	Hour	Summary of Events and Information	Remarks and references to Appendices
CAMP. MONT. ST. ELOI			Major WATT: Battn. Sports in the afternoon.; Draft of 141 O.Rs. from 1/7th Gordons; Reinfts. Alexander & Robertson & 2/Lt FLINT joined Bn. from 1/7 Gordons, Jr.; Sick to hospital. NIL.	Jim.
do.	4/10/18		Dull, showery but cold.; Brigade Church parade for Regt. at 10 am.; Voluntary Communion Service 3 pm. Sick to hospital. 4.ORs.; 2nd Lieut. BRACKEN struck off strength on proceeding to Base. 2nd Lieut. W.J. ARCUS joined Battn.	Jim
do	7/10/18		Bright but very cold: Battn. moved in Buses to new area at INCHY: awrie to heavy roads the buses only arrived at 2 am. in the 8th inst. Sick to hospital. 4.ORs.	Jim
Inchy.	8/10/18		Cold + wintry. weather. Bn Genl RDGord.S sp. this augt. conforming to the own threats Relief City Batt also relieving the 47. Canadian Bn.; most of the new dug outs. Others under Canvas. Day spent in resting and cleaning. Sick to hospital. 2.ORs.	Jim
do	9/10/18		Dry but dull + cold.; Capt. Falconer Capt. + Lt. Heath remaining reinfts to BOURBON. WOOD. Training under Coy arrangements; Sick to Hospital. 2.ORs.	Jim

WAR DIARY
or
INTELLIGENCE SUMMARY.
(Erase heading not required.)

Army Form C. 2118.

Place	Date	Hour	Summary of Events and Information	Remarks and references to Appendices
INCHY.	10/10/18		Dull & cold, with rain; Batty. receive orders and move with the Brigade to new area at St. OLLE near CAMBRAI; Bn. arrive in Trenches there at 1 pm. Part of the Batty. in dugouts remainder under Canvas; Two observation Balloons brought down by Enemy aeroplane near camp; Huge explosion occurring in Enemy lines E. of Cambrai; Sick to Hospital - 3. O.R.	[signature]
IWUY.	11/10/18		Dull & cold with rain; Batty. receive orders and move with the Brigade forward; Batty. halted on west side E of ESCAUDŒUVRES, had dinners there, then proceeded to Support Trenches. (Billets in cellars etc.) on the west side of IWUY. Remarcables, quick relief; a Battn. relieved 25th Canadians; Casualties NIL. Sick to Hospital: 1. O.R. Transport Personnel on Main road S.E. of TATUN, St. MARTIN. Lieut. A.K.N. Brown. goes sick. Batt'n. goes into Line. Argylls Seaforth in front. Duck Showery; very cold; Division attacked successfully East with Batt'n. in Support;	[signature]
Support Trenches at Iwuy	7/10/18			

WAR DIARY
or
INTELLIGENCE SUMMARY.

Army Form C. 2118.

Place	Date	Hour	Summary of Events and Information	Remarks and references to Appendices
Support Trenches Tury.	12/10/18		Entry: this morning - ZERO. 12,00 hours: objective ST. AMAND (outskirts) reached. Battn. moved up to E. side of Tury. to new Support Positions. Casualties { 2nd Lt. FINDLAY wounded. ORS. NIL. Sick to Hospital. NIL. (Shelling fairly severe near, gas shells with H.Es.)	Appx.
Front Line (ST. AMAND)	13/10/18		Dull + cold; Shelling enemies but continuous; Companies opened the day improving shelters etc; Always W The Battn relieved the 7th B2 A & S.H. in front line: LEFT SUB SECTOR of Brigade Front; D.T.C. Coys in front, with A & B in Support; Very Quiet relief; Patrols went out, from A & B Coys but found ST. AMAND reoccupied by enemy. Pt. Buchanan wounded Sick to Hospital. NIL. Casualties, 4. ORS wounded 5. ORS.	Appx.
Front Line ST. AMAND.	14/10/18		Dull, Cold + Showery; Companies improve Trenches etc; Very heavy shelling during the day; Ground gained by Patrols continually cut; Battn relieved by 7th Bn The Black Watch; and now back to Billets in TATIN ST. MARTIN.; Hot meals on arrival Casualties, 9. ORS wounded Sick to Hospitals 5. ORS.	Appx.

WAR DIARY
or
INTELLIGENCE SUMMARY.
(Erase heading not required.)

Army Form C. 2118.

Place	Date	Hour	Summary of Events and Information	Remarks and references to Appendices
TAZIN ST. MARTIN	15/10/18		Heavy rain + cold; Batt'n. spent the day refitting + cleaning. Feet, Rifles + S.B.R. inspection; Sick to hospital, 2. O.R.s.	Appx.
do.	16/10/18		Wet + cold; Training by companies; German M.G. Class under Lewis Gun Officer; Kit inspection for whole Batt'n. Battle stores made up; Sick to Hospital 12. O.R.s.	Appx.
do.	17/10/18		Dull but dry; Batt'n. receive orders to relieve 5th Seaforth Hrs. in front line. AVESNES. Le. SEC. Reconnoitring party under 2nd.Lt. Arcus. (Intelligence Officer.) sent up the early morning.	Appx.
Trenches AVESNES. LE. SEC.			A. Coy. - Front line.; D.C. + D. Coys. Support Reserve; 1 Scouting Patrol sent out from E. Coy; Casualties. 2. O.Rs killed; 7. O.Rs. wounded, otherwise quiet relief; Sick to Hospital 1. O.R.	Appx.
FRONT. LINE	18/10/18		Weather very dull + foggy; cold; Heavy hostile shelling in village area It.5. Gas. No change in the situation. Casualties NIL; 2. O.Rs MISSING. 1 Patrol sent out from Coy + Capt Roberton + 1 O.R.	Appx.
AVESNES LE. SEC.				
do.	19/10/18		Weather cold + foggy with rain; Slight hostile shelling of Battalion area; During the afternoon enemy reports	Appx.

WAR DIARY
or
INTELLIGENCE SUMMARY.
(Erase heading not required.)

Army Form C. 2118.

Place	Date	Hour	Summary of Events and Information	Remarks and references to Appendices
			to be retiring on our left & patrols of neighbouring units pushing forward. Our scouts were kept up closely by H.G. fire but at 18.00 hrs a platoon under Lieut ALLARDYCE pushed forwards and occupied position held by hostile M.G., coming in conjunction with above, across the Batt'n pushed forward & Coy forming a defensive flank on right in touch with D. Coy on left who pushed forward again and captures the hamlet of FLEURY being reported by A Coy. Casualties:- Lieut A.W. Robertson (N.Y.D.Gas), wounded 4.0 p.m. MISSING 2.0 a.m. Weather dull + cold. Very heavy shelling during the day.	
Front line 28/9/18 FLEURY.			Consisting of H.E. + Gas; Batt'n spent the day consolidating our positions round FLEURY; At 14.00 hrs in a Patrol under 2 Lt. S. Lochrin advanced this; enemy position and remained thus until Church when F Br. Seaforths advanced across our front leaving our Bn in Support. Casualties:- MISSING. Lieut G.L. ALLARDYCE; + HQ.R. Wounded 6.0 a.m. Major GoSaville rejoined Batt'n on 19th in from S.O.S. Alarshot. Weather Fair but cold. Slight hostile Shelling.	
SUPPORT. FLEURY.	2/10/18		Much Overhead day	

Army Form C. 2118.

WAR DIARY
or
INTELLIGENCE SUMMARY.
(Erase heading not required.)

Instructions regarding War Diaries and Intelligence Summaries are contained in F.S. Regs., Part II. and the Staff Manual respectively. Title pages will be prepared in manuscript.

Place	Date	Hour	Summary of Events and Information	Remarks and references to Appendices
Support trench FLEURY.	22/6/18		for Battn:- Casualties Nil. Sick to Hospital:- NIL. Weather fair + fresh; Very little hostile shelling; Day spent in improving positions; Batt:n relieved by 1/6th A.+S.H'rs at night; Very quiet relief; Batt:n proceed to rear Billets at DOUCHY; Hot meals on arrival; Casualties 1.O.R. Sick to Hospital 5.O.Rs.	
DOUCHY.	23/6/18		Weather, Sunny fresh; Batt:n have baths with clean change Rifles, Sect & S.B.R. Inspections by Coys; Remainder of the day spent in reorganizing training. Batt:n shelled by hostile H.V. Gun. Casualties 1.O.R. wounded. Sick to Hospital 1.O.R.	
DOUCHY.	24/6/18		Weather Sunny + Bright; Many civilians returning to the village; Batt:n get sudden orders to move to the up position in front of FLEURY, acting support to 152nd Brigade which had just moved into Front line; Casualties Nil. Sick to Hospital:- ☒ ☒, A.R.H. Brown, Lt. + Capt. Robertson	

Army Form C. 2118.

WAR DIARY
or
INTELLIGENCE SUMMARY.
(Erase heading not required.)

Place	Date	Hour	Summary of Events and Information	Remarks and references to Appendices
Support in Front of FLEURY.	25/10/18		Weather Fair, but cold; The day passed uneventful: at 2300 hrs Battn. suddenly called upon to move & take over front line, in front of MAING. relieving 6'S Seaforths; B'TG Coy in front with A+D. Coys in Support. Casualties NIL. Sick to Hospital 1. O.R.	
FRONT. LINE, MAING.	26/10/18		Weather fine; At 10,00 hrs. Battn. attacked village of FAMARS. This was successful. A + D. Coys going through C+B. capturing the village: Prisoners taken. 1 Off + 121 o.Rs: At 1500 hrs the enemy made a heavy counter attack on our left flank which was unsupported owing to Battn on left failing to gain objective. This attack was beaten off. Village remained in our hands. Casualties Killed, 2Lt. I.C. Silver & 3 o.Rs. Wounded, Lieuts R.A. Robertson, + A.H. Salmon; 2nd Lieuts Batchelor. F.R; Hughson D. Sullivan B.J. + 77 o.Rs. N.Y.D. Gas. Capt. Kynoch D; 10 ofrs missing 1 gun	
Front. LINE	27/10/18		Weather Dull, cold; Heavy hostile shelling all day: At 11.30 hrs	
FAMARS.			enemy counter attacked again + occupied village. Coys across	

WAR DIARY
or
INTELLIGENCE SUMMARY.
(Erase heading not required.)

Army Form C. 2118.

Place	Date	Hour	Summary of Events and Information	Remarks and references to Appendices
			reorganized and cleared the village at the point of the bayonet. Civilians remained in the village through the battle and endured a trying time; Pats were re-established in front of the village; The Battn. was relieved in the evening by 6th Seaforths, and went into reserve in MAING. Casualties, killed, 2 ORS; Missing; Lieut. R.T.L. Mitchell + 2nd Lt. Clark + 19 ORS; Wounded. 30 ORS; Sick to Hosp. 2 ORS.	
Reserve MAING	23/10/18		Weather fair; At noon Battalion was rushed up to support Seaforths + R.S. Hrs in their attack on MONT HOUY which was successful; Continuous heavy hostile shelling all day; In the evening the Battn. was again drawn back to MAING. Casualties, wounded 10 ORS; missing 1 O.R. Sick to Stopifier NIL.	
MAING. – DOUCHY	20/10/18		Weather, Sunny + fresh; Heavy hostile shelling of MAING; At 10.00 hrs. Battn. left village + proceeded to Rest Billets at DOUCHY; Hot meals on arrival and Baths during	

Army Form C. 2118.

WAR DIARY
or
INTELLIGENCE SUMMARY.
(Erase heading not required.)

Instructions regarding War Diaries and Intelligence Summaries are contained in F.S. Regs., Part II. and the Staff Manual respectively. Title pages will be prepared in manuscript.

Place	Date	Hour	Summary of Events and Information	Remarks and references to Appendices
DOUCHY	30/10/18		the afternoon: Casualties killed NIL, wounded 9 O.Rs., 1 O.R. + 2 O.Rs. NIL, sick to hospital: 12 O.Rs. C.Y.D. Gas; Lieut. W.D. Chambers rejoined Battn. from U.K. Weather: Sunny, fresh: The Battalion spent the day resting and cleaning's Rifles, feet + S.B.R. inspections by Coys; General officer Commanding 51st Division, Troubled + congratulated the Battalion on the excellent fighting during the recent tour in the line; Sick to hospital. 2 O.Rs. N.Y.D. Gas + 1 O.R. sick.	(Sgn.)
DOUCHY	31/10/18		Weather: Sunny, fresh; Battn. proceeded to rest area near CAMBRAI, starting from DOUCHY 08.10 hrs, arriving 12.30 hrs; Billets moderately comfortable; Sick to hospital: 1 O.R. N.Y.D. Gas.	(Sgn.)

Mhuinta Kent
Lt. Colonel.
Commanding 1/4th Bn. THE GORDON HIGHRS.

1/4TH BATTALION THE GORDON HIGHLANDERS.

HISTORY OF OPERATIONS

24/10/18 - 29/10/18.

BEING THE ATTACK ON AND CAPTURE OF THE VILLAGE OF FAMARS AND

HIGH GROUND COMMANDING THE RHONELLE RIVER.

---oOo---

1/4TH BATTALION THE GORDON HIGHLANDERS.
Map Reference:- HAINS, 1/20,000.
HISTORY OF OPERATIONS
24/10/18 - 29/10/18.
BEING THE ATTACK ON AND CAPTURE OF THE VILLAGE OF FAMARS AND
HIGH GROUND COMMANDING THE RHONELLE RIVER.

---oOo---

For the purpose of the narrative the account of operations will be divided into four phases as under:-

PHASE I.	READINESS	24/10/18 - 10.00 hrs., 26/10/18.
PHASE II.	ATTACK AND CONSOLIDATION.	10.00 hrs. 26/10/18 - 17.30 hrs. 26/10/18.
PHASE III.	COUNTER-ATTACK.	17.30 hrs. 26/10/18 - 23.45 hrs. 27/10/18.
PHASE IV.	RESERVE.	23.45 hrs. 27/10/18 - 10.00 hrs. 29/10/18.

The dispositions of the Battalion during above phases are shown as under on attached trace to be superimposed on HAINS, 1/20,000 Map.

PHASE I.........BLUE.
PHASE II........RED.
PHASE III.......GREEN.
PHASE IV........BROWN.

Various moves of Companies during phases are shown by numerals.

---oOo---

PHASE I. READINESS.

24/10/18.
15.15 hrs. On 24/10/18 the 1/4th Battalion The Gordon Highlanders were in billets at DOUCHY. At 15.15 hrs. orders were received to move at once to positions marked blue on attached trace.

16.00 hrs. The Battalion marched out at 16.00 hrs. and took up positions indicated, Battalion Headquarters being established at WATSON ROWE, I.36.a.3.3.
From this time the Battalion was under the orders of 152 Infantry Brigade.

25/10/18. These dispositions remained unaltered until the late afternoon of 25/10/18, when "D" and "B" Companies were ordered to positions of readiness in sunken road J.28/a. and c.

17.00 hrs. At 17.00 hrs. "A" and "C" Companies moved up and joined "D" and "B" Companies in sunken road. Positions are shown on attached trace and coloured blue and black and numbered "2".

: 2 :

23.00 hrs.   At about 23.00 hrs. Orders were received for the Battalion to relieve the 6th Battalion Seaforth Highlanders in the line East of MAING and to participate in operations on the succeeding day. During night 25th/26th the Battalion moved and occupied the jumping off positions by 08.00 hrs. 26/10/18.   Zero hour was to be 08.00 hrs.

The dispositions of the Battalion were:-

"D" Coy.........Right Front.
"C" Coy.........Left Front.
"A" Coy.........Right Support.
"B" Coy.........Left Support.

The dispositions are shown on attached trace and coloured blue and yellow and numbered "3".

PHASE II.   ATTACK.

The objectives of the attack are shown on attached trace and are coloured as under:-

1st Objective........Black dotted.
2nd Objective........Blue and red dotted.

At the 1st Objective a leap-frog was to be made, the supporting Companies being ordered to take the Final objective.

The object of the attack was to secure the high ground and village of FAMARS and to establish posts East of the village commanding the crossings of the River RHONELLE at AULNOY.

The attack was to be made under a barrage in conjunction with the 6th Battalion The Gordon Highlanders on the right and with the 6th Black Watch on the left.

Zero hour was altered from 08.00 hrs. to 10.00 hrs.

26/10/18.   At Zero hour the barrage opened and the Battalion advanced to the
Zero,10.00 hrs.   attack at 10.05 hrs.
10.05 hrs.

The enemy did not put down a heavy barrage and for a distance of about 400 yards little resistance was met with.   On reaching this point, however, heavy Machine Gun fire was met with on the left flank and from HOUSE WOOD on the right.   Progress was slow and advance could only be made by a series of short rushes.

Some of the Machine Gun Posts were compelled to retreat by the heavy barrage, some were disposed of by the advancing Battalion and some

26/10/18.
11.00 hrs.
were taken prisoners and at 11.00 hrs. the crest of the hill was gained and advance made on the village. Here again heavy fire was met from Machine Guns, but the first objective was gained by "B" Company on the right and "C" Company on the left.

The barrage paused 200 yards in front (East) of the first objective, and "A" Company on the right and "D" Company on the left leap-frogged over "B" and "C" Companies and advanced on the final objectives.

A considerable number of prisoners were taken (see SCHEDULE "B" attached hereto).

26/10/18.
11.30 hrs.
The final objective was gained at about 11.30 hours.

A series of posts were formed East of the village. Positions are shown on attached trace and coloured red and green.

Touch was found with the 5th Gordon Highlanders on the right and with the 6th Black Watch on the left at N.8.c.8.8., who, having met with strong resistance had been unable to reach their objectives. The result of this was to leave a comparatively unprotected flank to the Left Front Company ("D").

During the period of attack the enemy shelling was not heavy, but during consolidation and the succeeding phases intense enemy shell fire was maintained on the village of FAMARS, accompanied by large quantities of gas.

PHASE III. COUNTER-ATTACK.
    (a) By enemy.
    (b) By the Battalion.

27/10/18.
17.30 hrs.
(a) During the late afternoon it was thought that the enemy was massing for counter-attack, and at 17.30 hrs. a counter-attack developed on the Right flank of the front held by the Bn — "A" Coy. on the Right (which had lost all its officers) fell back and "D" Company on the left, thus having both flanks in the air, was also compelled to withdraw. The two front Companies and half the Left Support Company and elements of the Right Support Company withdrew to the Railway, but after reorganisation went forward. The tide of the attack was stemmed, however, and by 23.00 hrs. the line was restored as formerly held. As, however, the re-organisation had to take place in the dark, some difficulty was experienced in satisfactorily adjusting it owing to the somewhat disorganised condition of Companies. The Left Front Company was reinforced by two platoons from the Left Support Company and by one platoon of 7th Argyll and Sutherland Highlanders.

A relief by 7th Argyll & Sutherland Highlanders was intended, but could not take place owing to visibility being good.

The line was held thus for the remainder of the night and succeeding morning.

4

27/10/18.
10.00 hrs.
(b) During the early morning enemy movement was suspected in front, and at 10.00 hrs. a strong counter-attack began to develop, coming from a North Easterly direction, the main counter-attacking force coming from NOYT HOUY against the exposed flank. The counter-attack was made under a very heavy barrage which rested on the village and on the support line.

10.30 hrs. At 10.30 hours the enemy Infantry advanced to the attack which was launched with great violence, bending the Front and Support Companies lines to the West side of the village. Enemy Machine Gun Posts were established in the village.

The organisation of a counter-attack was at once begun and parties were at once put out round the flanks of the village to out-flank the enemy, time having been given to these to work forward. Our Counter-attack swept through the village, overrunning all opposition, the enemy evincing great energy and resolution. A Lewis Gun was fired on the enemy, who were at one point massed in the street, inflicting very heavy casualties and dispersing the remainder.

The line was immediately re-adjusted and the positions held before were taken up again.

21.00 hrs.
27/10/18.
At 21.00 hrs. the Battalion was relieved by the 8th Battalion Seaforth Highlanders and was withdrawn to HAING.

PHASE IV.   RESERVE.

10.00 hrs.
28/10/18.
At 10.00 hrs. 28/10/18 orders were received for the Battalion to take up positions in area K.7.b. and d., having one Company forward. These positions are shown on the attached trace and are coloured brown and yellow and marked "G".

These positions were held during the day and in the late evening one Company more was put forward.

01.00 hrs.
28/10/18.
Orders were received for the Battalion to withdraw at HAING at 01.00 hrs. 28/10/18.

10.00 hrs.
29/10/18.
At 10.00 hours 29/10/18 the Battalion marched to DONCHY to billets.

REMARKS.

Communication back was bad. A visual signalling post was established, but owing to low visibility this was useless.

Casualties are shown on attached SCHEDULE "A".

Prisoners are shown on attached SCHEDULE marked "B".

Capt. & Adjt.
1/4th Bn. The Gordon Highlanders

Lieut-Colonel,
Commanding 1/4TH BATTALION THE GORDON HIGHLANDERS

OCTOBER 30TH, 1918.

SCHEDULE "A".

CASUALTIES.

Officers:- KILLED.   1.   2/LIEUT. J. W. SILVER.

WOUNDED   6.   LIEUT. A. H. SALMON, M.C.
                 LIEUT. R. A. ROBERTSON,
                 2/LIEUT. E. J. JOLLY,
                 2/LIEUT. D. HENSHAW,
                 2/LIEUT. F. R. BATCHELOR,
                 2/LIEUT. W. J. SULLIVAN.

MISSING   2.   LIEUT. R.T.L. MITCHELL,
                 2/LIEUT. A. CLARK.

N.Y.D.GAS 1.   CAPTAIN D. J. KYNOCH, M.C.
           ──
           10

O/Ranks:-

	"A"	"B"	"C"	"D"	H.QRS.	TOTAL
KILLED	2	3	1	1	-	7
WOUNDED	25	45	33	27	2	130
WOUNDED AT DUTY	-	-	3	3	-	6
MISSING	7	1	3	22	1	34
WOUNDED & MISSING	-	-	-	1	-	1
	34	47	40	54	3	178
N.Y.D.GAS	1	3	1	5	1	11
N.Y.D.N.	2	1	3	5	1	12
	37	51	44	64	5	201

──

SCHEDULE "B".

PRISONERS:-   Officers..............1
                   O/Ranks..............121
                                       ────
                               Total   122.

1/4th BATTALION THE GORDON HIGHLANDERS.

REPORT ON OPERATIONS.

11/10/18 - 14/10/18.

On the 11/10/18 the 4th Battalion THE GORDON HIGHLANDERS marched from the neighbourhood of ST.OLLE - WEST of CAMBRAI - to THUN-ST.-MARTIN, 1 km. WEST of IWUY, and relieved the 29th Battalion Canadian Infantry, in support to the 7th Argyll & Suth'd. Highlanders on Left, and 4th Battalion Seaforth Highlanders on the Right. The Battalion being disposed on the West Bank of the stream, N.34 and T.5. "D" Co: - N.34.d., "C" Co: - T.4.b., "B" Co:- T.4. central, "A" Co: - T.10.b.

At ZERO (12.00 hours) the Brigade attacked, and in the late afternoon the Battalion moved forward to the N.E. Corner of IWUY.

Companies were disposed as under:-

"D" Co. in trenches N.29.b.
"B" " " " N.29.a.8.3. (area)
"C" " " cellars N.35.b.3.7.
"A" " " " Near Chateau, N.29.c.50.00 (area).

On 13/10/18 at 19.00 hours the Battalion moved up into the Left Front Sector to relieve 7th Battalion Argyll & Suth'd. Highrs. Companies were disposed as under:-

"D" Co. Right Front, N.12.d. and O.13.a.
"C" " Left Front, N.12.c. and d.
"A" " Right Support, N.18.b.
"B" " Left Support, N.18.a.

The line was held by a series of posts.

During the night 13th/14th and day of 14th patrols were continually being pushed out to ascertain if LIEU ST. AMAND was occupied, but on each occasion they were compelled to withdraw owing to heavy machine gun fire.

The shelling both H.E. and Gas during the day was heavy both on Front and Support Lines.

On night 14th/15th the Battalion was relieved by 7th Black Watch, and marched back to THUN-ST.-MARTIN.

CASUALTIES.

Officers. Wounded. 2/Lieut. H. C. FINDLAY.
2/Lieut. J. F. BUCHANAN.

O/Ranks. killed. 9 Other Ranks.
wounded. 10 " "
missing. 1 " "
N.Y.D. Gas. 2 " "
N.Y.D. Neurasthenia. 3 " "

(Sgd) B. C. BRODIE, Capt. & Adj.
1/4th Bn. Gordon Highrs.
for Lieut.Colonel,
Commanding 1/4th Bn. The Gordon Highlanders.

October 17th, 1918.

1/4th Bn. The Gordon Highlanders.
=*=*=*=*=*=*=*=*=*=*=*=*=*=*=*=

HISTORY OF OPERATIONS.

17th - 22nd Oct.

Being the account of the advance from AVESNES-LE-SEC and the Capture

of the Village of FLEURY.

For the purposes of the narrative of the advance the account will be divided into three phases.

PHASE 1.   The taking over of the line from the 5th Bn. Seaforth Highlanders and reorganization of the line, 20.00 hours 17/10/18 - 21.00 hours 19/10/18.

PHASE 2.   The advance on our occupation of FLEURY, 21.00 hours 19/10/18 - 06.45 hours 20/10/18.

PHASE 3.   The advance from FLEURY and period of Battalion in Support 06.45 hours 20/10/18 - 16.00 hours 22/10/18.

The dispositions of the Battalion are shown on the attached trace to be superimposed on Maps, 1/20,000 Sheets, 51.A. S.W.,N.W., S.E., N.E., and coloured as under:-

> PHASE 1........BLUE.
> PHASE 2........RED.
> PHASE 3........GREEN.

PHASE 1.

On the 17th October, 1918, the 1/4th BATTALION THE GORDON HIGHLANDERS was resting in THUN-ST-MARTIN. The Battalion marched out in the evening to AVESNES-LE-SEC to relieve the 5th BATTALION SEAFORTH HIGHLANDERS in the Right Sub-Sector of the Brigade Sector, having the 1st Battalion Hants Regiment of the 4th Division on the Right and the 7th Argyll & Sutherland Highlanders on the Left.

The line was held by one Company ("A") in a system of posts, "B" Company being in close support; "C" and "D" Companies in support in depth. The dispositions are shown on attached trace and coloured blue.

All positions were shelled during the night 17/18th and day of the 18th. Two other ranks were killed and seven wounded from the Support Companies. The shells were chiefly H.E. with a considerable intermixture of gas.

No action was taken during the 18th or night 18/19th with the exception of patrolling, which was carried out by day and night. and resulted in the location of enemy Machine Gun Posts in the WHITE HOUSE, O.22.b.99.90. and O.16.d.20.45., O.16.c.7.6., and in areas O.17.

On the 19th the post at WHITE HOUSE was reported to have been vacated.

At 14.00 hours Battalion Headquarters moved forward about 600 yards and during the evening new dispositions were made preparative to an attack under a barrage for which orders were received.

/This

PHASE 1 (Cont.).

This caused a readjustment of the Battalion, the three left posts being taken over by the 7th Argyll and Sutherland Highlanders, and the Battalion takin over three posts occupied previously by the 1st Hants.

"B" Company moved up to the Right Front Company Sector.
"A" Company retained its position as Left Front Company.
"C" Company moved to support "B" Company, and
"D" Company to support "A" Company.

These dispositions are shown on attached trace and coloured blue and yellow.

During the early night reports were received that the enemy was retreating on the front covered by the Battalion on the left and that they were advancing.

PHASE 2.

At 21.00 hours the Battalion was ordered to advance in co-operation with the Left Battalion. As, however, the Battalion on the right had orders not to advance but to remain in their jumping off positions, it was necessary to form a defensive flank on the Right and to advance in conjunction with the 7th Argyll and Sutherland Highlanders on the left. Orders were therefore issued that the right half Battalion should advance to the black dotted line in the attached trace, the right half Front Company and the Right Support Company forming a defensive flank to the right, while the left half Battalion advanced to the black dotted line on the left in conjunction with the 7th Argyll and Sutherland Highlanders.

No opposition was met, and no machine gun or shell fire encountered.

The advance on the left continued, but no advance of any kind was made on the right.

Orders were issued that the right half Battalion should continue to form a defensive flank, while the left half Battalion pushed on and occupied FLEURY. At 23.00 hours the advance continued.

The left Front Company ("A"), however, lost direction and struck the River SELLE somewhere about 0.12.a.60.20. On striking the river the Officer Commanding Company decided to work down stream and attempt to effect a crossing between the front where they were and FLEURY. He moved down stream, i.e., Northwards, and finding the old poles of a destroyed bridge somewhere about 0.12.a.4.8. a crossing was attempted over an improvised bridge of a few planks, but after about one hour's work only eight men had been got across with great difficulty, arising chiefly from the muddy nature of the banks and from the fact that sufficient bridging material was not available to make a bridge sufficiently stable to allow of men in Battle order, and carrying Lewis Guns, to cross. Operations were much impeded by the extremely muddy nature of the river banks. The Officer Commanding Company decided to push on towards FLEURY.

On reaching FLEURY "A" and "D" Companies found touch on the river bank, coming under heavy Artillery fire and some machine gun fire. O.C. "A" Company, deciding that too many men were disposed in a small area and in order to avoid casualties, decided to withdraw. This he did immediately before daybreak, taking up position in close support marked 2 on attached trace.

/Meanwhile

Meanwhile O.C. "D" Company, realising that a crossing must be effected, organised a bridging party, and, having collected straw, branches, beds and beams, formed a bridge.

At 06.45 FLEURY was occupied, some machine gun fire being encountered from bank at Crossroads O.6.c.8p.98.

Considerable credit is reflected on Officer Commanding "D" Company (Lieut. R.T.L. MITCHELL) who, by his resource in improvising a bridge and by his resolution in pushing forward, succeeded in occupying the village in face of considerable opposition, and thereby formed a bridgehead for the Battalion and numerous batteries who crossed later.

PHASE 3.   At 08.00 hours 20/10/18, Supporting Companies were moved FORWARD forward to positions shown on attached trace and coloured green.

These positions were occupied during the day (20th). A patrol of one platoon found by Company in Support was pushed forward to P.1.b.2.6., but before reaching the that point it came under heavy Machine Gun fire, and being unable to move during the day, lay there returning at dusk.

At 04.30 hours 21/10/18 the advance was continued. One Company ("C") was pushed through "D" Company in FLEURY and took up position in P.1.d. "B" Company was disposed on the left . "A" Company in close support and "D" Company in Support in FLEURY. Battalion H.Q. moved to FLEURY. All these positions are shown on attached trace and coloured green and brown.

The Battalion was now in support, as, during the occupation of FLEURY, the 4th Seaforth Hrs crossed the River SELLE at NOYELLES SUR SELLE and took up position in J.26, J.32, and P.2 a and b.

Later in the day one Company (B) was withdrawn to FLEURY under cover.

On 22/10/18 the Battalion was relieved by 6th Arg.& Suth. Hrs and marched back to DOUCHY.

The weather was bad, being both cold and wet during the whole period.

REMARKS ON OPERATIONS
The following points were noted:-

1.   In open fighting of this kind prismatic compasses are of the greatest importance. If more use had been made of these, loss of direction, as that which occurred in the case of "A" Company, would not be possible.

2.   Communication back was bad. The importance of information even if only of negative value, cannot be too often impressed on Company Commanders.
Mounted despatch riders were found to be of the greatest value and it is suggested that the number (2) allotted to Battalions should, if possible, be increased to four. In addition to two men of N.Z.M.R., mounted Battalion orderlies were used.

3.   Pack animals carrying hot tea wrapped in wet hay and carried in packs were found to be most useful. By these means hot tea was taken to platoons in the front line at all hours; the tea always arriving hot. Six to eight tins can easily be carried.

1/4th Battalion The Gordon Highlanders.

Map Reference - MAING, 1/20,000.

History of Operations.

24/10/18 - 29/10/18.

Being the attack on and capture of the Village of FAMARS and High Ground commanding the RHONELLE River.

For the purpose of the narrative the account of operations will be divided into four phases as under:-

PHASE 1.	READINESS.	24/10/18 - 10.00 hrs. 26/10/18.
PHASE 11.	ATTACK AND CONSOLIDATION.	10.00 hrs. 26/10/18 - 17.30 hrs. 26/10/18.
PHASE 111.	COUNTER-ATTACK.	17.30 hrs. 26/10/18 - 23.45 hrs. 27/10/18.
PHASE IV.	RESERVE.	23.45 hrs. 27/10/18 - 10.00 hrs. 29/10/18.

The dispositions of the Battalion during above phases are shewn as under on attached trace to be superimposed on MAING, 1/20,000 Map.

PHASE 1........BLUE.
PHASE 11.......RED.
PHASE111.......GREEN.
PHASE IV.......BROWN.

Various moves of Companies during phases are shown by numerals.

****

PHASE 1.   READINESS.

24/10/18
15.15 hrs.   On 24/10/18 the 1/4th Battalion The Gordon Highlanders were in billets at DOUCHY. At 15.15 hrs. orders were received to move at once to positions marked blue on attached trace.

16.00 hrs.   The Battalion marched out at 16.00 hrs. and took up positions indicated, Battalion Headquarters being established at MAISON ROUGE, I.36a.3.3.
From this time the Battalion was under the orders of 152nd Infantry Brigade.

25/10/18.   These dispositions remained unaltered until the late afternoon of 25/10/18, when "D" and "B" Companies were ordered to positions of readiness in Sunken road J.28.a. and c.

17.00 hrs.   At 17.00 hrs. "A" and "C" companies moved up and joined "D" and "B" companies in Sunken road. Positions are shewn on attached trace and coloured blue and black and numbered "2".

23.00 hrs.   At about 23.00 hrs. Orders were received for the battalion to relieve the 6th Bn. Seaforth Highrs. in the line East of MAING and to participate in operations on the succeeding day. During night 25th/26th the battalion moved and occupied the jumping off positions by 05.00 hrs. 26/10/18.

/Zero

—2—

Zero hour was to be 08.00 hours.

The dispositions of the Battalion were -

"B" Company.........Right Front.
"C" Company.........Left Front.
"A" Company.........Right Support.
"D" Company.........Left Support.

The dispositions are shown on attached trace and coloured blue and yellow and numbered "3".

PHASE 11.   ATTACK.

The objectives of the attack are shown on attached trace and are coloured as under:-

1st objective............Black dotted.
2nd   "   ....Blue and Red dotted.

At the 1st objective a leap-frog was to be made, the supporting companies being ordered to take the final objective.

The object of the attack was to secure the high ground and village of FAMARS and to establish posts East of the village commanding the crossings of the River RHONELLE at AULNOY.

The attack was to be made under a barrage in conjunction with the 6th Bn. Gordon Highrs. on the right and with the 6th Bn. Black Watch on the left.

Zero hour was altered from 08.00 hrs. to 10.00 hrs.

26/10/18
Zero
10.00
hrs.

At Zero hour the barrage opened and the battalion advanced to the attack at 10.05 hours.

The enemy did not put down a heavy barrage and for a distance of about 400 yards little resistance was met with. On reaching this point, however, heavy M.G. fire was met with on the left flank and from ROUGE MONT on the right. Progress was slow and advance could only be made by a series of short rushes.

11.00
hrs.

Some of the Machine Gun Posts were compelled to retreat by the heavy barrage, some were disposed of by the advancing battalion and some were taken prisoners and at 11.00 hours the crest of the hill was gained and advance made on the village. Here again heavy fire was met from M.G's, but the first objective was gained by "B" Company on the right and "C" Company on the left.

The barrage paused 200 yards in front (East) of the first objective, and "A" Company on the right and "D" Company on the left leap-frogged over "B" and "C" Companies and advanced on the final objectives.

A considerable number of prisoners were taken (see SCHEDULE "B" attached hereto).

11.30
hrs.

The final objective was gained at about 11.30 hrs.

A series of posts were formed East of the village. Positions are shown on attached trace and coloured red and green.

Touch was found with the 6th Gordon Highrs. on the right and with the 6th Black Watch on the left at K.8.c.8.8. who, having met with strong resistance had been unable to reach their objectives. The result of this was to leave a comparatively unprotected flank to the left front company (D).

/During

During the period of attack the enemy shelling was not heavy, but during consolidation and the succeeding phases intense enemy shell fire was maintained on the village of FAMARS, accompanied by large quantities of gas.

PHASE III   COUNTER-ATTACK.

    (a) By enemy.
    (b) By the Battalion.

27/10/18.
17.30 hrs.

(a) During the late afternoon it was thought that the enemy was massing for counter-attack, and at 17.30 hrs. a counter-attack developed on the right flank of the front held by the battalion.
"A" Company on the right (which had lost all its Officers) fell back and "D" Company on the left, thus having both flanks in the air, was also compelled to withdraw. The two front companies and half the left support company and elements of the right support company withdrew to the railway, but after re-organization went forward. The tide of the attack was stemmed, however, and by 23.00 hrs. the line was restored as formerly held. As, however, the re-organization had to take place in the dark, some difficulty was experienced in satisfactorily adjusting it owing to the somewhat disorganized condition of companies. The left front company was reinforced by two platoons from the left support company and by one platoon 7th Argyll & Sutherland Highrs.

A relief by 7th Argyll & Suth'd. Highrs. was intended, but could not take place owing to visibility being good.

The line was held thus for the remainder of the night and succeeding morning.

10.00 hrs.

(b) During the early morning enemy movement was suspected in front, and at 10.00 hrs. a strong counter-attack began to develop, coming from a North Easterly direction, the main counter-attacking force coming from MONT HOUY against the exposed flank. The counter-attack was made under a very heavy barrage which rested

10.30 hrs.

on the village and on the support line. At 10.30 hours the enemy Infantry advanced to the attack which was launched with great violence, bending the front and support companies lines to the West side of the village. Enemy M.G. posts were established in the village.

The organization of a counter-attack was at once begun and parties were at once put out round the flanks of the village to outflank the enemy, time having been given to these to work forward. Our counter-attack swept through the village, over-running all opposition, the enemy evincing great energy and resolution. A Lewis Gun was fired on the enemy, who were at one point massed in the street, inflicting very heavy casualties and dispersing the remainder.

The line was immediately re-adjusted and the positions held before were taken up again.

21.00 hrs.

At 21.00 hours the Battalion was relieved by the 6th Bn. Seaforth Highrs. and was withdrawn to MAING.

PHASE IV.   RESERVE.

10.00 hrs.
28/10/18.

At 10.00 hours 28/10/18 orders were received for the Bn. to take up positions in area K.7.b. and d., having one company forward. These positions are shown on the attached trace and are coloured brown and yellow and marked "2".

These positions were held during the day and in the late evening one company more was put forward.

01.00 hrs.

Orders were received for the battalion to withdraw at MAING at 01.00 hours 29/10/18.

/ At

10.00 hrs. 29/10/18.	At 10.00 hours 29/10/18 the Battalion marched to DOUCHY to billets.
REMARKS.	Communication back was bad. A visual signalling post was established, but owing to low visibility this was useless.
	Casualties are shown on attached SCEDULE "A"
	Prisoners are shown on attached SCHEDULE marked "B".

                                                (Sgd) B. C. BRODIE.
                                                       Capt. & Adjt.
                                        for Lieut.Colonel,
                        Commanding 1/4th Bn. Gordon Highrs,

October 30th, 1918.

SCHEDULE "A".

CASUALTIES.

Officers.   Killed   1.   2/Lieut. J. W. SILVER.

            Wounded   6.   Lieut. A. H. SALMON, M.C.
                           Lieut. R. A. ROBERTSON.
                           2/Lieut. E. J. SOLLY.
                           2/Lieut. D. HENGHAN.
                           2/Lieut. F. R. BATCHELOR.
                           2/Lieut. W. J. SULLIVAN.

            Missing. 2.   Lieut. R. T. L. MITCHELL.
                           2/Lieut. A. CLARK.

            N.Y.D. Gas 1. Capt. B. J. KYNOCH, M.C.
                      ―――
                       10

Other Ranks.	"A"	"B"	"C"	"D"	Hqrs.	Total.
Killed.	2	3	1	1	-	7
Wounded.	25	43	33	27	2	130
Wounded at duty.	-	-	3	3	-	6
Missing.	7	1	3	22	1	34
Wounded and Missing.	-	-	-	1	-	1
	34	47	40	54	3	178
N.Y.D. Gas	1	3	1	5	1	11
N.Y.D.N.	2	1	3	5	1	12
	37	51	44	64	5	201

SCHEDULE "B"

PRISONERS.   Officers..........1
             O/Ranks...........121
                              ―――
                              122

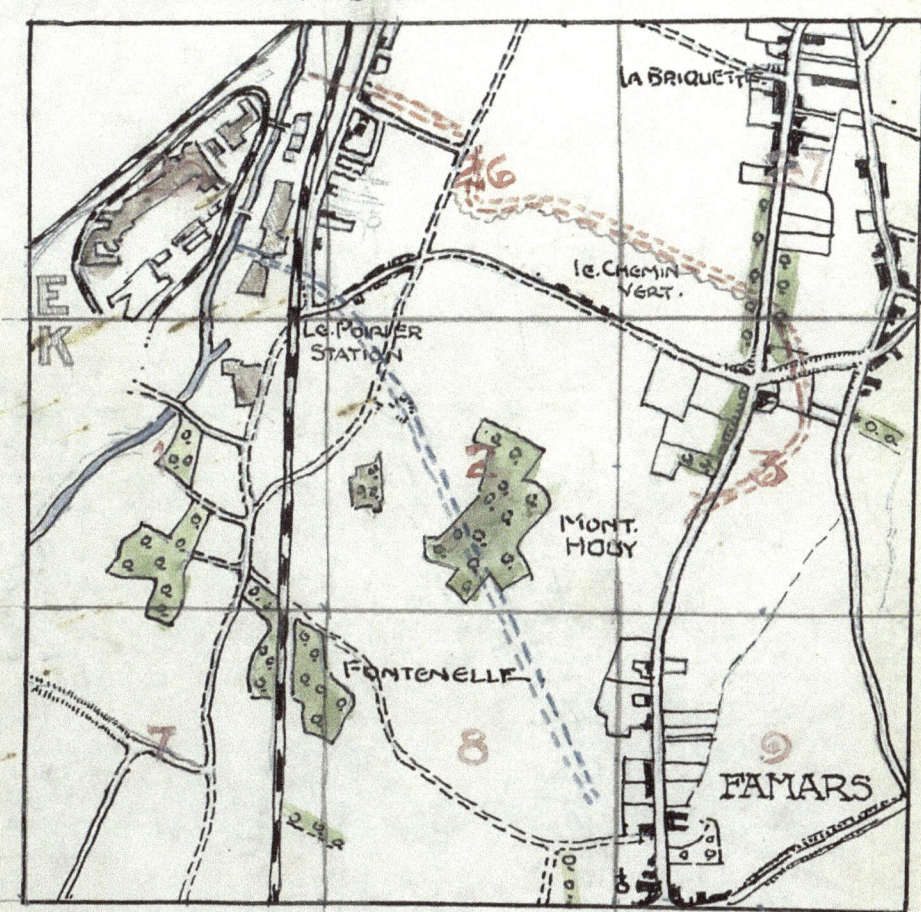

DISPOSITION MAP.
4th SEAFORTH HIGHLANDERS.

REFERENCE. MAP.
SHEET. 51A. N.E
...... 1 : 20,000 ......

LEGEND.

OBJECTIVES
 FIRST -----
 FINAL -----

MAP No. 2

154/51
Vol 45

WAR DIARY
of
1/4TH BATT. THE GORDON HIGHLANDERS
from
1ST NOVEMBER to 30TH NOVEMBER 1918
VOLUME No. 46.

November 1918.

WAR DIARY or INTELLIGENCE SUMMARY. 1/4 Bn The Gordon H'rs

Army Form C. 2118.

Place	Date	Hour	Summary of Events and Information	Remarks and references to Appendices
CAMBRAI.	1/11/18		The weather was cold & frosty. The Bn. marched to billets at CAMBRAI. on the 31st of Oct. The day was spent in resting & cleaning. Billets very good. Lewis partially demolished houses. Armourer Sgt inspected rifles. Major J.H.M. GORDON M.C. is re-appointed Second in Command. Sick to hospital. 2. O.Rs.	
do.	2/11/18		Cold, showery & dull. The Batn. spent the day re-organising & cleaning. All civilian property was carefully checked & stored by all companies. Sick to hospital. NIL.	W.D.B.
do.	3/11/18		Cold, dull, frosty. The Brigade paraded for divine service (Pres) at 10.00 hours. R.C.'s service at St. Roch. 10.00 hrs. The remainder of the day was spent in resting. 2nd Lieuts GORDON and MURDOCH. joined from U.K.	W.D.B.
do.	4/11/18		Cold showery & dull. Reorganisation continues. Kit inspection by companies. between 0900 & 1100 hrs. Medical Inspection after 11 o'ka. To hospital sick. 1. O.R.	W.D.B.
do.	5/11/18		Showery but mild. Training commenced under officer training	W.D.B.

Army Form C. 2118.

WAR DIARY
or
INTELLIGENCE SUMMARY.
(Erase heading not required.)

Instructions regarding War Diaries and Intelligence Summaries are contained in F. S. Regs., Part II. and the Staff Manual respectively. Title pages will be prepared in manuscript.

Place	Date	Hour	Summary of Events and Information	Remarks and references to Appendices
	(contd) 5/11/18		Programme: Specialists Training during the afternoon. Lieut Shatter reported from Div. Canteens. Sick to hospital. NIL.	
			Draft of 13th O.R.s joined.	ASB.
CAMBRAI	6/11/18		Cold + frosty. Trained by Companies off in accordance with Training Programme. Specialists as on the 5th. Lecture by Capt Perkins. Chemical Advisor at 18 cohoure on "Science". Sick to hospital 1. OR. Reaching room opened for all OR. Off. Col. A.J.GARDNER. qua. au Frewer leave. Major Gordon taking over Baton. Very wet week. Owing to bad weather Lectures had to be substituted for parades. Batta. assembled for whole Baton. at. ESCAUDOEUVRES. D. Coy working on range.	ASB.
do	7/11/18		Sick to Hospital: NIL	WSB.
do	8/11/18		Cold, frosty day. Training as per Programme. Specialists also as per Programme. The G.O.C. divisions drives that formation for Column of Route. Other than an Ceremonial Parade will be used instead of fours: much discussion throughout the Baton. On informed that German delegates are crossing the line to	WSB.

WAR DIARY
or
INTELLIGENCE SUMMARY.
(Erase heading not required.)

Army Form C. 2118.

Place	Date	Hour	Summary of Events and Information	Remarks and references to Appendices
CAMBRAI.	8/11/18		arrange ARMISTICE with Allies; Free show of the "Balmoral" for Batn. at 18 hours; To Hospital sick 2 O. Ranks; Rejoined from Hospital, Lieut. A.W. Robertson.	
do	9/11/18		Bright but very frosty; Battn. Parade at 0900 hrs; Coy. Training during the remainder of the forenoon; D. Coy. inspected by Commanding Officer at 14.15 hrs; Five N.H.'s awarded to the Batn. for gallantry during operations from the 12th to 28th of FLEURY. To U.K. sick Lieut A.K.H. Braum; Sick to hospice Nil.	MB.
do	10/11/18		Brighter + frosty; Divine Service in Factory at 11.30 hrs. R.C.s at St. ROCH at 10.30 hrs; Brief kit Inspection by C.O. at 09.45 hrs; VALENCIENNES is passed out of Bermans; Battn. informed of the internal condition of Germany; employing the field at Keil etc.; Sick to Hospice 3 O.Rs. Runes A. DRUMMOND & STEWART Ar.S. 1180. alld.?	MB.
do	11/11/18		Brighter + frosty; The Commanding Officer informs all ranks that an ARMISTICE has been signed by Germany; The	MB.

Army Form C. 2118.

WAR DIARY
or
INTELLIGENCE SUMMARY.
(Erase heading not required.)

Place	Date	Hour	Summary of Events and Information	Remarks and references to Appendices
CAMBRAI	11/11/18		men make no effort to rejoice. Such a day is difficult to realize. All Parades cancelled. The day is regarded as a holiday. Sick to Jafalac I.O.R.	
do	12/11/18		Bright, frosty; Companies carry out Ceremonial, Close order & Saluting Drill, after Commanding Officers Parade at 09.00hrs; Div. Commander's Parade at 12.00hrs when he thanked all ranks for their devotion to duty which serving under him and give promise of an early visit to Germany; Adjutant lectured all N.C.O's on Reconstruction; 2 Lieut. C. Davidson joined from U.K.	MSB
do	13/11/18		Bright & clear but frosty; The day was regarded as a holiday to celebrate the 2nd anniversary of BEAUMONT — HAMEL; A special dinner tea is provided to all ranks; Div. Cross Country Run at 11-00hrs; Sports in the afternoon for the Battn; 2 Lieut W. Bruce Joined Battn from BASE; Sick to Jafalac NIL.	MSB

Army Form C. 2118.

WAR DIARY
or
INTELLIGENCE SUMMARY.
(Erase heading not required.)

Place	Date	Hour	Summary of Events and Information	Remarks and references to Appendices
CAMBRAI	14/1/18	a.m.	Bright but frosty + cold. Commanding Officers Parade at 09.00 hrs. Saluting by all companies during the afternoon. D. & C. Coys. have baths and clean clothing under Bn. arrangements. F.G.C.M. held at Bn. H.Q. to continue case of Pte. P. CROWNIE. Sick 10 — Hospital 1 O.R.	
do.	15/1/18		Bright but cold. Commanding Officers Parade at 09.15 hrs. Remainder of day spent in cleaning and refitting under Company arrangements. Inspection of Transport at 14.30 hrs. "A" and "B" Coys. have baths and clean clothing under Bn. arrangements. Restriction as to the use of cameras are [struck] relaxed. Sick to hospital Censorship regulations are cancelled. Sick to hospital Lt. O.R. Capt. J. GILES reported from 1st Army Inf. School.	NB
do.	16/1/18		Bright but frosty. "A" Coy. have baths. "B" Coy. paraded on Training Area for Ceremonial and Close Order drill. "C" Coy. engaged in selecting and "D" Coy. on range. Inspection of Q.M. Stores by Commanding Officer at 15.00 hrs. Lieut. T.H. WATSON, 2nd Lt. D.J. CRUICKSHANK and A.S. LAWSON	NB

Army Form C. 2118.

WAR DIARY
or
INTELLIGENCE SUMMARY.
(Erase heading not required.)

Instructions regarding War Diaries and Intelligence Summaries are contained in F. S. Regs., Part II. and the Staff Manual respectively. Title pages will be prepared in manuscript.

Place	Date	Hour	Summary of Events and Information	Remarks and references to Appendices
	6/16		Joined from U.K. Sick to Hospital NIL.	W.B.
Cambrai	17/1/18		Bright and frosty. Divine Service in Factory at 10.05 hrs. R.C.s. at St Roche at 10.00 hrs. Gifts Church Parade. Staff on hand to clean up roads in front of Billets. Sick to Hospital NIL.	W.B.
do.	18/1/18		Frosty and Wintery cold. Companies carry out Training according to programme with the exception of "C" Coy which was selecting. Inspection of "A" Coy by the Commanding Officer at 14.00 hrs. Specialist Training at 15.15 hrs. Major E.W. Watt delivered a lecture on "EDUCATION" in the Recreation Room at Brigade Transport Lines. 2/Lieut. P.M. SMALL joined from U.K. Lieut.Col. A.J. Dutch returned from Rest Leave.	W.B.
do.	19/1/18		Companies carry out Training and saluting on foot and drill. Inspection of "C" Coy by Commanding Officer. Inspection of Armourer Sgt. AITKEN at Training Area. Lecture to officers by 2/Lieut. R.F. GRANT at 14.00 hrs. 15.00 hrs. on "The Care and Inspection of Arms." Joined from U.K. Sick to hospital 2 O.R.	W.B.

Army Form C. 2118.

WAR DIARY
or
INTELLIGENCE SUMMARY.
(Erase heading not required.)

Place	Date	Hour	Summary of Events and Information	Remarks and references to Appendices
	Con'd			
Cambrai	20/1/18		Very cold and foggy. Baths at ESCAUDOEUVRES allotted to all Coys. "C" Coy on Range during the forenoon and "B" Coy during the afternoon. "D" Coy. salving Vaux CUVILLERS. Sick to hospital 2 O.Rs.	
Cambrai	21/1/18		Bright but cold. "A" Coy carried out Ceremonial and Company drill. "B" + "C" Coys. salving. "D" Coy. Route march. Inspection during the afternoon (14.00 hrs) of "B" Coy. by the Commanding Officer, also N.C.O.s Physical Training Class. At 15.00 hrs. The Commanding Officer to Officers C.S.M's, and C.Q.M.S.'s. on "Billeting". There was also a Medical Inspection of all Coys. Capt. G.T. BURNEY M.C. rejoined from Course. Sick to Hospital 3 O.Rs.	
do.	22/1/18		Fine but cold. "A" + "B" Coys. employed in filling in trenches. "B" + "C" Coys. on route march. Baths allotted to the Battalion at ESCAUDOEUVRES. During the afternoon those companies not at Baths paraded for Physical Training. At 10.00 hrs. the Divisional Commander inspected all animals on the Bn. establishment. Sick to Hospital Nil.	

WAR DIARY
or
INTELLIGENCE SUMMARY.

Army Form C. 2118.

Place	Date	Hour	Summary of Events and Information	Remarks and references to Appendices
Cambrai	Dec. 23/18		Frosty but bright. Commanding Officers parade on Training Area at 10.15 hr. Reinforcements of 49 O.R. arrived. Sick 16. Hospital Nil.	W.D.3
do.	24/18		Frosty and bright but very cold. Battalion paraded for Divine Service in factory at 09.05 hr. R.Cs at St Roch at 10.00 hr. after church parade the Commanding Officer inspected the Battalion billets. Sick 16. Hospital 1. O.R.	W.D.3
do.	25/18		Cold and damp. "A.C." + "D" Coys. carry out Training as per programme. "B" Coy. fill in shell holes and bury dead horses. "C" Coy. also engaged in salving. Capt. C. McGREGOR struck off strength.	W.D.3
do.	26/18		Dull and damp. "A" + "D" Coys. filling in trenches and salving in Training Area. "B" + "C" Coys carry out Close Order Drill - Saluting etc. Sick to Hospital - 2. O.Rs.	W.D.3
do.	27/18		Dry but cold. Battalion proceeded by Route March to the Divisional Sports ground at Thun L'Eveque to attend the first day of the Divisional Sports, which were heavily enjoyed by all ranks. Lieut. Col. A.J. WELCH proceeded 16 Brigade H.Q.	W.D.3

WAR DIARY
or
INTELLIGENCE SUMMARY.

(Erase heading not required.)

Army Form C. 2118.

Place	Date	Hour	Summary of Events and Information	Remarks and references to Appendices
	contd.		in command of 152 Infantry Brigade. Sick to Hospital Nil.	WD3.
CAMBRAI	28/11/18.		Cold and wet. Special programme of work for to-day was issued by Bn, owing to pct smaller men being confined to billets for a considerable time. Sick to Hospital 4. O.R.	WD3.
"	29/11/18.		Damp and cold. A & B Coys carried out close order drill. Coln Drill and saluting in the vicinity of billets. Bn's "C" and "D" Coys were allotted to 7th Battalion as follows:— "C" and "D" Coys during the forenoon, and "A" and "B" Coys during the afternoon. At 10:30 hrs. football match between the 1st Gordon & the 7th Gordon Highlanders (Cyclist Bn). Highrs (Cyclist) Battalion and the Gordon Highrs (Cyclist) Bn. was attended by all available men. Lieut G. Duguid offr- for Course in U.K. Sick to Hospital 3. O.R.	
"	30/11/18.		Cold clay and foggy. Battalion proceeded by route march to its Divisional Sports. Keen competition was shown by all units. This being St Andrew's Day miniature Scottish National Flags were issued to all ranks. These were worn about the Badge	WD3.

Army Form C. 2118.

WAR DIARY
or
INTELLIGENCE SUMMARY.
(Erase heading not required.)

Place	Date	Hour	Summary of Events and Information	Remarks and references to Appendices
CAMBRAI	30/11/18	contd.	to the Balmoral. Sick to Hospital NIL.	WB.
			James A Gordon Major	
			Commanding, 1/4th Bn. The Gordon Highlanders	
	1-12-18			

Confidential.

98 45

1/4. Battalion The Gordon Highlanders.

War Diary

for

December 1918.

Volume No. 50

Army Form C. 2118.

WAR DIARY
or
INTELLIGENCE SUMMARY.
(Erase heading not required.)

Place	Date	Hour	Summary of Events and Information	Remarks and references to Appendices
CAMBRAI	1/12/18.		Dry but very cold. The Battalion paraded at 10.05 hrs for Divine Service. By arrangement with the Senior Chaplain Church of England men attended the Presbyterian Service. Roman Catholic Service was held in the Church Hy.	
			St ROCH at 10.00 hrs. Inspection of billets by the Commanding Officer after church parade. Sick to Hospital 3. O.Rs.	W.S.F
do.	2/12/18.		Dry and cold. Training carried out in accordance with Training Programme during morning and afternoon. "A" Coy filled in trenches in Training Area. "B" Coy carry out Close Order Drill, Arm Drill, Saluting etc. "C" Coy Ceremonial, Roll and Guard Duties. "D" Coy. Route March. Sick to Hospital 2. O.Rs.	W.S.F
do.	3/12/18.		Dry and mild. Training carried out as follows. "A" Coy Ceremonial + Guard duties. "B" Coy Route March, "C" Coy Route March, "D" Coy Ceremonial + Guard duties. Capt. J.M. G.A. GREVE reported from leave. Sick to Hospital 1. O.R.	W.S.F
do.	4/12/18.		Dry but cold. Training carried out in accordance with Training Programme. "A" Coy - Close Order Drill, "B" Coy - Range, "C" Coy - Filling in Trenches. "D" Coy - Range. Capt. D.KYNOCH M.C. granted 20 days sick leave 12/11/18.	W.S.F

A6943 Wt. W11422/M1160 350,000 12/16 D. D. & L. Forms/C,2118/14.

Army Form C. 2118.

WAR DIARY
or
INTELLIGENCE SUMMARY.
(Erase heading not required.)

Place	Date	Hour	Summary of Events and Information	Remarks and references to Appendices
(contd.)				
Cambrai	5/7/18		Lieut. A.J. McLEAN proceed to U.K. on leave. Sick to Hospital NiL.	M.M.
			Bny + cold. Battalion paraded at 09.00 hrs for Route March.	
			Route CAMBRAI - NAVES - CAGNONCLES - CAMBRAI. Capt. G.T. BURNEY	
			M.C. rejoined to 6/7 Bn. Gordon H'rs. Major J.H. McI. GORDON, M.C.	
			proceeded to U.K. on leave. Sick to Hospital 2 O.R. (Apt. D.) Kynoch rejoined	M.M.
	6/7/18		from sick leave. Training as per programme. "B" Coy - Ceremonial + Guard	
do			Duties; "B" Coy - Close Order Drill and Saluting; "C" Coy - Close	
			Order Drill, Arms Drill and Saluting; "D" Coy - Saluting, Drills etc at	
			7.20. B.O.S. Baths allotted to 16 Platoon. Sick to Hospital 2 O.R.	
do	7/7/18		Cold and damp. Training as follows: "A" Coy - Route March; "B" Coy.	M.M.
			Saluting Drills in S.29, B.O.O near MORENCHIES; "C" Coy - Range;	
			"D" Coy - Close Order Drill etc. Lecture at 17.30 hrs at Lecture	
			Hall Brigade Transport Lines by Lt. Col. P.A. GUTHRIE on	
			"CANADA AND AFTER THE WAR PROBLEM". No 200398 Sgt. W. FRENCH	
			awarded the "MEDAILLE MILITAIRE" by the French Government.	
			Sick to Hospital 2 O.Rs. Lt. Col. WELCH struck off strength 23/7/18.	M.M.

Army Form C. 2118.

WAR DIARY
or
INTELLIGENCE SUMMARY.
(Erase heading not required.)

Instructions regarding War Diaries and Intelligence Summaries are contained in F. S. Regs., Part II. and the Staff Manual respectively. Title pages will be prepared in manuscript.

Place	Date	Hour	Summary of Events and Information	Remarks and references to Appendices
CAMBRAI.			Rev. W. J. Sym, Presbyterian Chaplain joined for duty. Sick to Hospital 2. O.R.	
do.	8/12/18		Bright & Frosty. The Bn paraded for Divine Service (Pres) at 10.30 hrs; C. of E. at 10 hrs; The commanding officer inspected billets at 11.45 by Officers meeting re Education Scheme at 17.00 hrs. Sick to Hospital 1. O.R.	n.sut
do.	9/12/18		Bright & fresh. Parades & Training as per programme. C. Coy Saluting, "LINE". Shells marked "safe"; Lewis Gun classes continue; Officers HOCK BALL MATCH at 14.30 hrs. Sick to Hospital NIL.	n.sut
do.	10/12/18		Duel & Showery. Parades & Training as per programme; C. Coy Saluting; Lecture at 17.30 hrs by Major WILLCOCKS. D.S.O. M.C. on "Battle of FAMARS. 1793". Crickets to value of £20 received were proceeds of the sale of German Iron Cross (a gift of a Private of this Batt.). Sick to Hospital 1. O.R.	
do.	11/12/18		Continuous Rain; Training parades cancelled; to carry out Interior Economy; Officers French Class started at 17.00 hrs under Lt. REIS	n.sut

Army Form C. 2118.

WAR DIARY
or
INTELLIGENCE SUMMARY.
(Erase heading not required.)

Instructions regarding War Diaries and Intelligence Summaries are contained in F.S. Regs., Part II. and the Staff Manual respectively. Title pages will be prepared in manuscript.

Place	Date	Hour	Summary of Events and Information	Remarks and references to Appendices
CAMBRAI	11/12/18 contd.		Capt. Lynch M.C. + Capt. Philip M.C. and 5 O.Rs. proceed to ABERDEEN for Battn. Colours; 11 ORs Demobilized; 2 sick to Hospital NIL.	
do	12/12/18		Duller day Showery. Training started as per programme but cancelled owing to weather. Sewage work also covered. 8 O.R's Demobilized; Sick to Hospital 1 O.R. Officers Shorthand Course commences under Capt. GRIEVE.	
do	13/12/18		Dry, dull, windy; O.R. exp. sewing; all exp. Battled; Sick to Hospital 1 O.R.;	
do	14/12/18		Surprised & Sunny; all Companies on Saluting & Sports for all Coys. at 14:30 hrs; Cmdr. W. Philip M.C. awarded Bar to M.C.; Sgt. F. McHardy + G. Hardie + Cpl. A. McCombie awarded D.C.M.; 10 ORs Demobilized; Sick to Hospital 3 ORs.	
do	15/12/18		Mild and bright; the Battn. paraded for divine service (Pres) at 10:05 hours; C/O 09:30 hrs. R.C. 10:00 hours. the Commanding Officer in- spected billets of "A" and "B" Coys at 11:45 hrs. O/C "C" and "D" Coys ins- pected billets of their own Companies. Lt. Col. WELCH reported as C.O.	

WAR DIARY or INTELLIGENCE SUMMARY

Army Form C. 2118.

Place	Date	Hour	Summary of Events and Information	Remarks and references to Appendices
CAMBRAI	16/12/18		Mild & showery. "A" "B" & "D" Coys. Saluting at hills. "C" Coy. Training Area. Medical Inspection of all Coys. from 13.45 hrs. to 15.15 hrs. Major R.J. GARDNER struck off strength on proceeding to RUSSIA (Auth. A.G. 2158/9176(a) 12/12/18.) Lieut. D. McDONALD rejoined from No1 Army Training Camp, MATRINGHEM.	
do.	17/12/18		Evacuated for demobilization – 1 OR. Reinforcements 2 OR. to Transportation Troops Base Depot, CALAIS 1 OR. Conducting duty 1 Officer. Mild & dry. "B" Coy. Saluting at hills. "A" "C" & "D" Coys. Training as per programme. afternoon strike.	
do.	18/12/18		Still & showery. "A" "B" "C" Coys. Saluting shells. "D" Coy. Firing at Range. to Hospital 1 OR. Base for demobilization 1 OR. to Prison 1 OR. to Railhead AUDRICQ as Room Sergeant 1 OR. Reinforcement 1 OR.	
do.	19/12/18		Very cold. All companies saluting hills. Lecture at 14.00 hours by the Commanding Officer to all Officers and N.C.O's on "The GALLIPOLI Campaign". Reinforcements 1 OR. Rejoined from leave 1 Officer.	
do.	20/12/18		Very wet & stormy. Salvage work ("D" Coy.) and training "A" "B" & "C" started but was cancelled on account of the weather. Interior	

WAR DIARY
or
INTELLIGENCE SUMMARY.
(Erase heading not required.)

Army Form C. 2118.

Place	Date	Hour	Summary of Events and Information	Remarks and references to Appendices
CAMBRAI	20/12/18		Economy carried out by all Coys. A Gift of Hankety Sweets and 10,000 Cigarettes has been received by ABERDEEN CITY WAR WORK ASSOCIATION. Sick to Hospital 1 O.R.	
do	21/12/18		Coy Drills. "B" Coy taking shells. "A" Coy firing on Range. "C" & "D" Coys Ceremonial Drill at training Area. Sick to Hospital 1 O.R.	
do	22/12/18		Cold + Showery. Bath: paraded for Divine Service – Pres. at 11.05 hours, C. of E. 11.30 hours. R.C. 10.00 hours. All C. Coys. carried out Inspection of Billets under Coy arrangements. Proc. for Demobilization 1 O.R. Sick to Hospital 1 O.R.	
do	23/12/18		Cold + Showery. Training in accordance with Programme. "A" Coy Ceremonial Drill. "B" Coy Saluting. "C" Coy Inspection of Arms by Armourer Sgt. Kit Inspection. "D" Coy Close Order Drill + Arm Drill. Proc. for Demobilization 3 O.R. Reinforcements 7 O.R.	
do	24/12/18		Dry + Frosty. Training as per programme. "A" Coy. Inspection of arms by Armourer Sgt. Kit Inspector. "B" Coy Ceremonial Drill. "C" Coy Close Order Drill + Arm Drill. "D" Coy Saluting Shells. Sick to Hospital 3 O.Rs.	

Army Form C. 2118.

WAR DIARY
or
INTELLIGENCE SUMMARY.
(Erase heading not required.)

Instructions regarding War Diaries and Intelligence Summaries are contained in F. S. Regs., Part II. and the Staff Manual respectively. Title pages will be prepared in manuscript.

Place	Date	Hour	Summary of Events and Information	Remarks and references to Appendices
CAMBRAI	25/12/18		A voluntary service (Xmas) was held at 10.00 hours. A Roman Catholic service in Church Fcy St Roch at 10.00 hours. C of E Service at 09.30 hours. Major J.H. McI. GORDON, M.C. reported from leave. Evacuated for demobilization 1 O.R.	
do	26/12/18		Bright & frosty. Training as per programme. "A" Coy. balance of kit. "B" Coy. Close Order Drill & Arm Drill. "C" Coy. Ceremonial Drill. "D" Coy. Armourer Sgts Inspection of Arms. Kit Inspection. Evacuated for demobilization 10 O.R. To Calais as A.M.L.O. Guard 1 Officer. Colour Party returned with the Colours to the Battalion. Hospital 1 O.R.	
do	27/12/18		Very wet & cold. All training cancelled in consequence. Bn. carry on Interior Economy. To 1st Army Rifle Training Camp. 1 Officer.	
do	28/12/18		Field & Showery. "A" Coy. & "D" Coy Salvage Shells. "B" Coy Ceremonial Drill. "C" Coy. Close Order Drill and Arm Drill. Evacuated for demobilization 1 O.R.	
do	29/12/18		Mild and dull. The Battalion paraded for Divine Service at 09.10 hours (Presbyterian.) C of E Parade 09.30 hours & R.C. at 11.00 hours.	

WAR DIARY
or
INTELLIGENCE SUMMARY.
(Erase heading not required.)

Army Form C. 2.

Place	Date	Hour	Summary of Events and Information	Remarks and references to Appendices
CAMBRAI	29/12/18		Coln the Commanding Officer inspected Billets of all Companies, starting with "A" Coy at 10.00 hours. Sick to Hospital 1 O.R.	
do	30/12/18		Full dressing day. Parades & training as laid down in Programme of Work. "A" Coy – Range. "B" & "C" Coys to bury "D" Coy – Route march. Sick to Hospital – 2 O.R. Proceeded on Special leave to U.K. (14/1/19 – 30/1/19) 1 Officer.	P.235
do	31/12/18		To-day was observed as a Holiday throughout the Division. The Divisional Cross Country Run took place, starting from the Divisional Sports Ground at THUN LEVEQUE at 1100 hours. Rft from Hosp 1 O.R.	

1/4th Battalion The Gordon Highlanders.

War Diary

1-31 January, 1919.

WAR DIARY
or
INTELLIGENCE SUMMARY.
(Erase heading not required.)

Army Form C. 2118.

Place	Date	Hour	Summary of Events and Information	Remarks and references to Appendices
CAMBRAI	1/1/19		Cold but dry. To-day was observed as a holiday throughout division and was devoted to sports.	W.J.
CAMBRAI	2/1/19		Cold and showery. Battalion paraded at 0900 hours for Route march. Dress:- Full marching Order, Jerkins and Gloves. Proceeded on leave (31/12/18 - 14/1/19) Capt. B.C. BRODIE, M.C. Sick to Hospital 2/Lt.	W.J.
CAMBRAI	3/1/19		Very cold but dry. Parades and training as per programme. "A" Ceremonial Drill. "B" Ceremonial Drill. "C" Close Order Drill. "D" Range. Reported from Course at Oxford - 2/Lieut. E. DUGUID.	W.J.
CAMBRAI	4/1/19		Cold and dry. "A" Coy. on Leave. Remainder - Education - Payment of Benevolent Letters and Post cards discontinued in accordance with G.R.O. 5941 dated 29/12/18. Evac. to Sennelager S. of P. Church of Scotland, on apptt. as Staff Captain to 154th Infantry Brigade - Lieut. W.C. BROWNLIE, M.C.	W.J.
CAMBRAI	5/1/19		The Battalion paraded for Divine Service (Presbyterian) at 10.00 hrs. C. of E. Service at 11.30 hrs in "A" Squash Highrs." Recreation Room R.C. Service in Church of ST. LOUIS at 10.00 hrs. Sick to Hospital 2/Lt.	W.J.

Army Form C. 2118.

WAR DIARY
or
INTELLIGENCE SUMMARY.
(Erase heading not required.)

Instructions regarding War Diaries and Intelligence Summaries are contained in F. S. Regs., Part II. and the Staff Manual respectively. Title pages will be prepared in manuscript.

Place	Date	Hour	Summary of Events and Information	Remarks and references to Appendices
CAMBRAI	6/1/19		Bright but cold and windy. "A" Coy Close Order Drill. "C" Coy Lectures. "B" & "D" Coys Kit Inspection & Interior Economy. Sick to Hosp. 2 O.R.	NSW
CAMBRAI	7/1/19		Cold and cloudy. Baths were allotted to "B" Coy 0900 - 10.15 hours. "C" Coy 10.15 - 11.30 hours. "D" Coy 11.30 to 12.45 hours. Transport and Headquarters 12.45 - 13.30 hours. "A" Coy. 15.30 to 16.45 hours. Sick to Hospital 2 O.R. Proceeded on Leave (9/1/19 - 23/1/19) 2/Lieut. W.D. BEDDIE.	NSW
CAMBRAI	8/1/19		Bright and sunny. Battalion paraded for Church March at 0900 hrs. Dress - Full Marching Order, Jerkins and Gloves.	NSW
CAMBRAI	9/1/19		Very wet day. All parades were cancelled and interior economy carried out instead. Proceeded on Special Leave (10 - 24/1/19) - 2 Lieut. Reinforcements to 2 O.R. D. MCDONALD. Sick to Hospital 1 O.R.	NSW
CAMBRAI	10/1/19		Cold but dry. Training Programme for today was cancelled, and the day was devoted to preparations for move to new area. Sick to Hospital - 1 O.R.	NSW
HOUDENG	11/1/19		The Battalion moved to Houdeng area in accordance with Operation Order No. 93 attached. Report on Conducting duty. - 2/Lt. W.R. MURDIE.	NSW

Army Form C. 2118.

WAR DIARY
or
INTELLIGENCE SUMMARY.
(Erase heading not required.)

Place	Date	Hour	Summary of Events and Information	Remarks and references to Appendices
HOUDENG	12/1/19		Bright and dry. The Church Parades were held today. The Battalion spent the day in settling down and an improvement of billets and billeting area. Reinforcements - 2 O.R.	
HOUDENG	13/1/19		Very cold and showery. Companies were at the disposal of Coy. Commanders. Evac. for demobilization - 6 O.R. Joined Depl. of Agri. W.J. MORRISON, Lt. Q.M.C. (Auth A.G. 2158/645A(0) d. 3/1/19). Struck off Strength - Lieut-Col A.J. WELCH (Auth A.G. 2158/645A(0) d. 13/1/19).	
HOUDENG	14/1/19		Very cold but dry. Companies were at the disposal of Coy. Commanders from 0900 - 1100 hours. The Battalion paraded on Battalion Parade Ground at 11.30 hours dress - drill order. Belts and side arms only. This will be the dress for future parades unless otherwise ordered. Evac for demobilization 2nd Lieut W. REID and 3 O.R. Sick to Hospital 1 O.R.	
HOUDENG	15/1/19		Still and showery. Battalion paraded at 0900 hours for Route march. 2nd Lieut H.J. DOUGLAS has been appointed Battalion Tire Master a/c from 14th Jan 1919. Sick to Hospital 1 O.R. Rejoined	

Army Form C. 2118.

WAR DIARY
or
INTELLIGENCE SUMMARY.
(Erase heading not required.)

Place	Date	Hour	Summary of Events and Information	Remarks and references to Appendices
HOUDENG	15/11/19		Rejoined from leave - Capt. B.C. BRODIE, M.C.	W.E.L
HOUDENG	16/11/19		Bright, Sunnyday. Parades 09.30 to 12.30 hours. Inspection by O.C. Corps. of Arms, Equipment, Clothing &c. and Billets, from 09.30 - 11.00 hrs. 10.00 - 11.00 hours - Saluting and squad drill. 11.00 - 12.00 hrs. Battalion Arm drill under the R.S.M. Companies under the C.S. Major. Battalion Parade Ground. 12.00 - 12.30 hrs. Musketry under Company arrangements. Awards - the following officers and other ranks have been "cited" and awarded the Croix de Guerre by the Fifth French Army:- Croix de Guerre avec Palme. "B" Coy. 301772 Piper P. PATTERSON. Croix de Guerre, Gold Star. Lieut. H.M. FRASER, att'd. 154th Inf. Bde. Croix de Guerre Silver Star. Rev. J.M.K. MURRAY, C.F. "A" Coy. 200398 Sgt. W. FRENCH. Croix de Guerre, Bronze Star - Capt. D. FALCONER, M.C., "A" Coy. 6771 R.S.M. W. WATT, "D" Coy. 200942 L/Cpl. ANDERSON, W. Lieut. H.C. BROWNLIE, M.C. (October on strength. (Auth. 51st. [H]. D. 20/a.) Lt. Col. W.J. MORRISON, M.C. to U.K.	W.E.L.
HOUDENG	17/11/19		Bright but very cold. Parades 09.00 - 12.30 hours + 14.00 - 16.00 hours &c./	W.E.L.

Army Form C. 2118.

WAR DIARY
or
INTELLIGENCE SUMMARY.
(Erase heading not required.)

Instructions regarding War Diaries and Intelligence Summaries are contained in F. S. Regs., Part II. and the Staff Manual respectively. Title pages will be prepared in manuscript.

Place	Date	Hour	Summary of Events and Information	Remarks and references to Appendices
HOUDENG.	17/1/19	Cont.	Saluting and squad drill. 10.00 to 11.00 hours. Guard duties.	*
			11.00 to 12.00 hours - At disposal of Company Commanders. 12.00 to 12.30 hours - musketry under Company arrangements. Evacuated for observation 2 O.R. Reinforcements 6 O.R. 2nd Lieut. ARCUS re-joined from leave.	nil
HOUDENG.	18/1/19		Showery and very cold. Baths were allotted to the Battalion today as follows:- "D" Coy. 08.30 - 10.00 "C" Coy. 10.00 to 11.30 hours. "B" Coy. 11.30 to 12.30 and 13.30 to 14.00 hours. "A" Coy. 14.00 to 15.30 hours. Transport 15.30 hours onwards. Blankets were issued. Sick to Hospital 2 O.R.	
HOUDENG.	19/1/19		Bright and frosty. The Battalion paraded for Divine Service at 09.45 hours. Dress:- Drill Order without arms. Belts and side arms only. Leather jerkins and gloves. R.C. Service at 09.30 hours in Church at Frand Place, HOUDENG. Church of England Service at 2/15th (H) Field Ambulance, HOUDENG at 10.30 hrs. Lt. Col. G.G. CRUICKSHANK to course at 1st Army Rifle Training School.	nil

A6945 Wt. W11422/M1160 350,000 12/16 D. D. & L. Forms/C. 2118/14.

Army Form C. 2118.

WAR DIARY
or
INTELLIGENCE SUMMARY.
(Erase heading not required.)

Place	Date	Hour	Summary of Events and Information	Remarks and references to Appendices
HOUDENG	20/1/19		Bright and frosty. Parades 09.30 - 11.00 hours. Close order and Alm drill under Company arrangements. 11.30 hours - Cross Country Run. Evac. for Demobilisation to OR Lieut A.S. STEWART transferred to T. A. L.D.H. (Vide S.C. 109 d/d 18/1/19) to Hospital 2 O.R.	
HOUDENG	21/1/19		Education Classes were resumed at 09.00 hours. Parades 09.30 to 12.30 hours. "A" and "B" Coys. the M.O. Lectured to these Coys. at 09.30 and 10.00 hours respectively. 10.30 to 12.30 hours - Close Order Arm drill and musketry under Coy. arrangements. "C" and "D" Coys. 09.30 - 10.00 hours Saluting and squad drill. 10.00 - 11.00 hours Guard Duties. 11.00 to 12.30 hrs Arm drill and musketry. Lieut A.RULE, M.C. and 6 O.R evacuated for demobilisation. Lieut W.C. BROWNLIE, M.C. struck off strength as from 24/12/16 (Auth. A.G. 5505/(a) d/d 16/1/19)	
HOUDENG	22/1/19		Very cold. Lukdrys. No Education classes held today. The Bath Paraded at 09.30 hours for Route March. Dress - full marching order, jerkins and gloves were worn. Fine for demobilisation. 7 O.R.	

Army Form C. 2118.

WAR DIARY
or
INTELLIGENCE SUMMARY.
(Erase heading not required.)

Place	Date	Hour	Summary of Events and Information	Remarks and references to Appendices
HOUDENG	22/1/19	Cont.	Lt. Col. W.T. MORRISON, M.C. struck off strength (Auth. A.G. 2154/ 2734 (0) dtd. 16/1/19.	
	23/1/19		Very cold, with slight showers of snow. Baths at St Joseph School were allotted as follows:- For those not attending Educational Classes "A" Coy. 08.30 – 09.30 hours. "B" Coy. 09.30 – 10.30 hours. "C" Coy. 10.30 – 11.30 hours. "D" Coy. 11.30 to 12.30 hrs. For those attending Educational Classes + Headquarters 13.30 – 15.00 hrs. Transport 15.00 – 15.30 hours. Sick to Hospital 3 O.R.	
HOUDENG	24/1/19		Frosty and bright. Parades and Training 09.30 – 12.30 hours. First half hour devoted to Physical Training and Games. Thereafter the Companies were at disposal of Company Commanders. Evacuated to C.C.S. 2 O.R. Proceeded on leave to U.K. Major E.W. WATT and 2/Lieut. H.C.W. FLINT.	
HOUDENG	25/1/19		Mild frosty. No Education Classes and Training. Platoons at the disposal of their Commanders for purpose of carrying out Sports Training and Practice. Evac. to Remob. Brigadier 6 O.R. Sick to Hospital 1 O.R.	

Army Form C. 2118.

WAR DIARY
or
INTELLIGENCE SUMMARY.
(Erase heading not required.)

Place	Date	Hour	Summary of Events and Information	Remarks and references to Appendices
HOUDENG	26/1/19		Snowy day. The Battalion paraded for Divine Service at 10.45 hours dress, drill order with belts and side arms only. Leather jerkins and gloves. Roman Catholic Service in Church of St Gery, HOUDENG at 09.30 hours. C. of E. Service at 2/1st (H) Field Ambulance at 11.00 hrs. 2/Lt A. DAVIE and 6 O.R. evacuated for demobilization. Keep to Hospital 2 O.R.	7 O.R.
HOUDENG	27/1/19		Very cold. Parades 09.30 - 12.30 hours. 09.30 - 10.30 hrs Physical Recreational Training. 10.30 - 12.30 hrs. Platoon + Company drill to C.C.S. 3 O.R. for C. for demobilization to O.R.	3 O.R.
HOUDENG	28/1/19		Bright and frosty. Parades 09.00 - 12.00 hours. 09.00 to 09.45 hrs Physical and Recreational Training. 09.45 to 12.00 hours Sports under Company arrangements. H.R.H. The Prince of Wales visited the Battalion today. Several Officers and N.C.O.s were presented to Him.	7 O.R.
HOUDENG	29/1/19		Very cold and snowy. Baths were allotted at St Joseph's Institute as follows:- "A" Coy. 06.30 - 09.45 hrs. "B" Coy. 09.45 - 11.00 hours	7 O.R.

WAR DIARY
or
INTELLIGENCE SUMMARY.
(Erase heading not required.)

Army Form C. 2118.

Place	Date	Hour	Summary of Events and Information	Remarks and references to Appendices
HOUDENG	29/1/19	Cont'd	"C" Coy. 1100 to 1230 hours. "D" Coy. 13.30 to 14.45 hours. Headquarters 14.45 – 16.00 hours. Transport 14.00 – 16.30 hours. Capt. G.A. GRIEVE (Quartermaster), 2/Lt. R. NEWALL and A9. O.R. Over for demobilization.	
HOUDENG	30/1/19		Very frosty. Parades 0900 – 1200 hours, 0900 – 10.00 hours Physical and Recreational training. 10.00 to 12.00 Under Coy arrangements in preparation for inspection by G.O.C. 2/Lt. D.J. CRUICKSHANK to R.E. Workshops, MONS for duty. Sick to Hospital 1 O.R.	
HOUDENG	31/1/19		Very cold. Parades 0900 – 1200 hours. 0900 – 1000 hours – Physical training and Games 1000 – 12.00 hours Under Coy. arrangements in preparation for inspection by G.O.C. Sick to Hospital 1 O.R.	

signature
Capt. & Adjt.
1/4th Bn. The Gordon Highlanders

signature
Lt. Colonel
Commanding
1/4th Batt. The Gordon Highlanders

COPY NO 9.

1/4TH BATTALION THE GORDON HIGHLANDERS.

OPERATION ORDER NO. 93.

Reference Maps :-- BRUSSELS)
NAMUR) 1/100,000.

1. The 4th Battalion Gordon Highlanders, less 150 all ranks of "D" Coy., will move from CAMBRAI on 11th January 1919 to HOUDENG Area by bus.

2. The Battalion (less 150 ranks of "D" Coy) will parade on Rue de Quesnoy at 07.50 hours; Battalion Headquarters on the right (at Schoolroom) - "A", "B", "C", "D" Companies.
    Hqrs., and Coys., will be told off into parties of 25 & each party will be in charge of an Officer or N.C.O. who will be responsible for discipline etc., during the journey. Care must be taken that tarpaulins etc., are not damaged.

3. DRESS: Full marching order.
    Balmorals will be worn. Steel Helmets will be strapped to back of packs. One blanket per man carried on pack. Jerkins and Greatcoats will be worn.

4. Remaining Blankets will be rolled in bundles of ten and will be at Quartermaster's Stores at 06.00 hours. Each bundle will be labelled with the names of men owning blankets, and with the number of the platoon and the letter of the Company.

5. Orderly Room Boxes, Officers Valises etc., will be at Q/M Stores by 06.30 hrs., Mess Boxes by 07.15 hours.
    All spare boxes and kit will be sent to Q/M. Stores by 14.00 hours today.
    "D" Company will detail Guard over blankets of 1. N.C.O. & 3 men to be Q.M. Stores at 06.00 hours.
    Baggage guard for journey will be found by Q.M. Staff.
    O;C. "D" Company will arrange meals for this party.

6. Lewis Guns will be carried by Companies and Headquarters, also 4 magazines per gun.

7. On debussing Companies will march in threes and will be numbered off in this way before embussing.

8. Colours will be handed in their box to the Q.M. whose baggage guard will be responsible for them.

9. Returns as shown in Table Z attached will be rendered.

10. Each Company will detail one runner to report to the A/Adjutant in front lorry of Battalion Convoy immediately the Company has completed embussing.

11. Officers in Command of Companies will travel in first lorry of those allotted to Coy.
    Second in Command of Companies in last lorry of those allotted to Coy.

12. REAR PARTY
    O.C. "D" Company will ensure that all billets are clean; finding necessary parties.

13. No baggage will be carried on the convoy.

Copy No. 9.

1/4TH BATTALION THE GORDON HIGHLANDERS.

AMENDMENT TO OPERATION ORDER NO. 83.

Reference Para 3. Line 3.

    For:- "One blanket per man carried on pack".
    Read:- "One blanket per man carried in pack".

Reference Para 15.

    Delete - "Limber will proceed to new area on 12th instant under orders of O.C. 8th Royal Scots.
    and insert:- "Limber will join 8th Royal Scots at PAVILLY on evening of 11th inst."

ACKNOWLEDGE.

    (Sgd) A. DRUMMOND, Captain & A/Adjutant,
    1/4TH BATTALION THE GORDON HIGHLANDERS.

JANUARY 10th 1919

Copy No. 1..........Commanding Officer.
Copy No. 2..........O.C. "A" Company.
Copy No. 3..........O.C. "B" Company.
Copy No. 4..........O.C. "C" Company.
Copy No. 5..........O.C. "D" Company.
Copy No. 6..........Headquarters.
Copy No. 7..........Quartermaster.
Copy No. 8..........File.
Copy No. 9..........War Diary.

COPY NO.

1/4TH BATTALION THE GORDON HIGHLANDERS.

OPERATION ORDERS NO. 95

ADMINISTRATIVE ORDERS.

1. Unexpended portion of days ration will be carried on the men.

2. Water bottles will be filled before starting.

3. All indents from Companies for material required in New Area will be rendered as early as possible and in no case later than as shown in Table 2, serial 6, column ii.

4. Runners from Battalion Headquarters will travel with Company H.Q. (one per Coy). One runner from each Company will travel with Battalion Headquarters. These will ascertain position of Companies and Battalion Headquarters respectively, on arrival in New Area. Having done this they will report to Battalion and Companies respectively.

5. ACKNOWLEDGE.

(sgd) A. DRUMMOND, Captain & A/Adjutant,
1/4TH BATTALION THE GORDON HIGHLANDERS.

JANUARY 10TH 1919.

OPERATION ORDER NO. 93.

-2-

14.   The journey will take approximately 7 hours.
      The Convoy will halt for 15 minutes, one and a quarter hours after starting and after every subsequent two and a quarter hours.

15.   150 all Ranks of "D" Company will remain behind and at 14.00 hours 11/1/19 will proceed to IWUY where billets will be found under arrangements of O.C. "D" Company.
      Two G.S. Wagons from 8th Royal Scots will report at 14.00 hours for conveyance of blankets etc.,
      This party will embus on 13th instant from IWUY at 08.25 hours at IWUY CHATEAU GATES, and will carry two blankets on the man.
      A limber will be provided to draw rations from 8th Royal Scots at ESTRUN for above party for consumption up to 14th January 1919 inclusive.
      Limber will proceed to new area on 12th instant under orders of O.C. 8th Royal Scots.

16.   ACKNOWLEDGE.

                          (Sgd.) A. DRUMMOND, Captain & A/Adjutant,
                          1/4TH BATTALION THE GORDON HIGHLANDERS.

JANUARY 10TH 1919.

              Copy No. 1............Commanding Officer.
              Copy No. 2............O.C. "A" Coy.
              Copy No. 3............O.C. "B" "
              Copy No. 4............O.C. "C" "
              Copy No. 5............O.C. "D" "
              Copy No. 6............Headquarters.
              Copy No. 7............Quartermaster.
              Copy No. 8............File.
              Copy No. 9............War Diary.

TABLE Z

COLUMN	I	II	III	IV	V
Serial No	NATURE OF RETURN	TIME	TO WHOM RENDERED	PLACE OF RENDERING	BY WHOM RENDERED
1.	Casualties of identification parties	immediately coy is involved	adjutant	Hub of Bttn. Convoy	O.C. Coys & M.Os.
2.	Inspection of animals in lines	Immediately coy has arrived	Orderly Room	Orderly Room	Coys
3.	Return of sick in hospital nursing numbers in each Coy Hosp. returns	10.00 hrs 12/1/19	ditto	ditto	ditto
4.	Location of Regimental Aid Post Location Return weekly	18.00 hrs 13/1/19	M.O. and O/C Sqn	ditto	ditto
5.	Location of Coy H.Qrs.	20.00 hrs 1/1/19	Orderly Room	ditto	M.O.s
6.	Summary	12.00 hrs 15/1/19	ditto	ditto	ditto
7.	Location of W.O. rank	16.00 hrs 17/4/19	ditto	ditto	Q.M.

Original

W 48 27

Confidential

War Diary

of

1/4th Gordon Highlanders

Vol

From 1st Feb 1919 To 28 Feb 1919.

WAR DIARY
or
INTELLIGENCE SUMMARY. 1/4 Bn London Bns.

Army Form C. 2118.

Place	Date	Hour	Summary of Events and Information	Remarks and references to Appendices
HOUDENG	1.2.19		Very hard frost. Parades - Sports under company arrangements. Evacuated for demobilization 1 O.R.	[illeg]
HOUDENG	2.2.19		Snow and frost. The Battalion paraded for Divine Service at 09.45 hours (Presbyterians). Dress - Drill order without arms, Belt and side Arms only. Leather Jerkins and Gloves. C of E Service at 2/1st (H) Field Ambulance, HOUDENG, at 11.00 hrs. Roman Catholic Service at 09.30 hours in Parish Church, HOUDENG.	[illeg]
HOUDENG	3.2.19		Dull with showers of snow. Parades and training. "A" and "B" Coys. 10.00 - 11.00 hrs. Practice of drill &c. for Inspection by G.O.C. "C" "D" Coys. 11.00 - 12.00 hours - 11-1200 hours. Company Drill. "C" "D" Coys. 11.00 - 12.00 hours. Practice of drill &c. for inspection by G.O.C.	[illeg]
HOUDENG	4.2.19		Mostly. Baths for the Battalion were allotted as follows:- "B" Coy 08.30 - 09.45 hrs. "C" Coy. 09.45 - 11.00 hrs. "D" Coy. 11.00 - 12.30 hours. "A" Coy. 13.30 - 14.45 hrs. Headquarters 14.45 - 16.00 hrs. Transport 16.00 - 16.30 hours. Interpreters rejoined from Army of occupation - 2 O.R. Sick to Hospital 3 O.R.	[illeg]

Army Form C. 2118.

WAR DIARY
or
INTELLIGENCE SUMMARY. 1/4 Bn Gordon Hrs.

(Erase heading not required.)

Instructions regarding War Diaries and Intelligence Summaries are contained in F. S. Regs., Part II. and the Staff Manual respectively. Title pages will be prepared in manuscript.

Place	Date	Hour	Summary of Events and Information	Remarks and references to Appendices
HOUDENG	5/2/19		Heavy fall of snow in the evening. Parades and training. "A" & "B" Coys. Practised drill to formation by G.O.C. from 10.00 - 11.00 hours. "C" & "D" Coys from 11.00 to 12.00 hours. "A" & "B" Coys. from 11.00 - 12.00 hours. Company drill. Jerob while on leave to U.K. 1 O.R.	
HOUDENG	6/2/19		Bright and frosty. Parades and training 0900 - 12.00 hours. Companies at disposal of Company Commanders. Sick to Hospital 1 O.R. Proceeded on Special Leave - 2/Lt. R.F. GRANT 2d course at OXFORD (4.2.19) 2/Lt. W.G. GORROD.	
HOUDENG	7/2/19		Very cold but dry. Parades. Companies at disposal of Company Commanders. Special attention directed to cleaning of arms and equipment. Evacuated for demobilization - Capt. W. PHILIP, M.C. Lieut. W. PHILIP, M.C. 2/Lieut. G. DUGUID, and 64 O.R.	
HOUDENG	8/2/19		Clear and frosty. Companies at disposal of Company Commanders. Special attention directed to clothing, equipment and arms. Struck off strength and taken on strength of Bde. H.Q. 1 O.R. (24/12/15) Evacuated for demobilization 2/Lieut. W.G. ARCUS, 2/Lieut. H.J. DOUGLAS, & 67 O.R.	

WAR DIARY
or
INTELLIGENCE SUMMARY.

1/4 Bn. Gordon Hrs.

Army Form C. 2118.

Place	Date	Hour	Summary of Events and Information	Remarks and references to Appendices
HOUDENG	8.2.19 Contd.		ÉTAPLES for attachment with 2/14th LONDON REGIMENT, 10 Officers and 200 O.R. Taken on strength from 154th Trench Mortar Battery (disbanded) 2/Lieut. J. McD. SCOTT and 11 O.R. sick to Hospital 4 O.R.	
HOUDENG	9.2.19		Very hard frost. Church Parade. Presbyterian. The Battalion paraded for Divine Service at 10.30 hours. Evac. for demobilization 1 O.R. (Attd. Bde. H.Q.) to Hospital from course 1 O.R.	
HOUDENG	10.2.19		Very frosty and bright. Parades. The draft proceeding to join the 1st Bn. the Gordon Highrs. paraded at 10.00 hours. Evac. to C.C.S. 1 O.R. Sick to Hospital 1 O.R.	
HOUDENG	11.2.19		Still very cold. The party detailed to proceed to 1st Bn the Gordon Highrs. (new) paraded at 10.30 hours for 1/2 hour dress drill order with arms. Baths at St Joseph's Institute were allotted as follows:- "A" Coy. & H.Q. 13.30 to 14.30 hours. "B" Coy 14.30 to 15.40 hours. "C" Coy. 15.40 to 16.15 hours. "D" Coy. (including Transport) 16.15 to 17.00 hours. An Officer proceeded with each party.	

WAR DIARY
or
INTELLIGENCE SUMMARY. 1/4 Bn. Gordon Hrs

Army Form C. 2118.

(Erase heading not required.)

Place	Date	Hour	Summary of Events and Information	Remarks and references to Appendices
HOUDENG	11.2.19		Cath. sick to Hospital 1 O.R. Evac. to C.C.S. 1 O.R.	
HOUDENG	12.2.19		The composite Company under orders to proceed to 1st Bn. The Gordon Highlanders paraded at 10.00 hours under orders of O.C. Company. Reported from leave - Lieut. A.W. ROBERTSON and 2/Lieut. M.C.W. FLINT. Evac. to C.C.S. 3 O.R.	
HOUDENG	13.2.19		Still very frosty. The composite Company paraded as yesterday. Reported from leave - Major E.W. WATT. Evac. to C.C.S. 1 O.R. Proceeded on leave - Capt. R.J. GILES. Demobilized while on leave 70 O.R. Evac. for demobilization 70 O.R. and 1 O.R. A.O.C. attd.	
HOUDENG	14.2.19		Fresh and rainy. The composite Company paraded as yesterday. Evac. for demobilization 6 O.R.	
HOUDENG	15.2.19		The Composite Company paraded under orders of the O.C. Coy. and carried out the following training :- 0930 - 10.00 hours Physical Training. 10.00 - 10.30 hours Arm drill. Demobilized while on leave 1 O.R. sick to Hospital 1 O.R.	
HOUDENG	16.2.19		Mild and dry. The Battalion paraded for Divine Service at	

WAR DIARY
or
INTELLIGENCE SUMMARY. 1/4 Bn. Gordon Hrs.
(Erase heading not required.)

Army Form C. 2118.

Place	Date	Hour	Summary of Events and Information	Remarks and references to Appendices
HOUDENG	16.2.19	Sunday. 11.00 hours	11.00 hours in the Battalion Hall. Dress:- drill order without arms. Belt and side arms only. Leather Jerkins. Sick to Hospital 1 O.R.	
HOUDENG	17.2.19		Dull & showery. Parades 09.30 to 11.00 hours 3/4 hour Physical and Recreational Training. 1/2 hour Arm drill. 1/4 hour Saluting. Reinforcements 2 O.R. Sick to Hospital 3 O.R. Struck off strength on being 7 days in Field Ambulance – 2 O.R.	
HOUDENG	18.2.19		Cold and dry. Parades 09.30 hrs Physical & Recreational Training. 10.00 hours – Arm drill. 10.30 hours Companies carried out Kit inspection under Coy. arrangements to C.C.S. 1 O.R. demobilized while on leave 1 O.R. Reinforcements 1 O.R.	
HOUDENG	19.2.19		Forenoon devoted to cleaning and refitting. Baths were allotted as follows:- J. Coy. & Transport 13.30 to 14.30 hours. "C" Coy. 14.30 to 15.40 hours "B" Coy. 15.40 to 16.15 hours. "A" Coy. and H.Q. 16.15 to 17.00 hrs. Sick to Hospital 3 O.R.	
HOUDENG	20.2.19		Bright, dry day. Companies cleaning and refitting. Evacuated	

WAR DIARY
OR
INTELLIGENCE SUMMARY. 1/4 Bn. Gordon Hrs.

Army Form C. 2118.

Place	Date	Hour	Summary of Events and Information	Remarks and references to Appendices
HOUDENG	20.2.19 (contd)		for demobilization 90 O.R. to 6/7th Bn. The Gordon Highlanders & struck off strength - 65 O.R. (11 on detached duty.) Evacuated to C.C.S. 3 O.R. Proceeded on concentrating duty and leave to U.K. Lieut EUNSON and 2/Lieut BRUCE. Taken on strength from No. 7 Concentration Camp - 22 O.R. Posted from 6/7th Bn The Gordon Highlanders and taken on strength 10 Officers and 170 O.R. Position of this draft on detached duty is 6 Officers and 68 O.R.	
HOUDENG	21.2.19		Very rainy and cold. The day was spent cleaning and refitting. Special attention being paid to the correct method of fitting equipment. Evacuated to C.C.S. 1 O.R. Taken on strength of 154th Infantry Brigade - 1 O.R. Struck off strength on proceeding for de- mobilization (previously shown as detached) 5 Officers. 315 O.Rs. Struck off strength - Capt. W.J. SYM, C.F. Sick to Hospital 1 O.R. Posted from 6/7 Bn Gordon Highrs. and taken on strength - 7 Officers & 228 O.R. Portion of this draft on detached duty 6 Officers & 6 O.R.	

Army Form C. 2118.

WAR DIARY
or
INTELLIGENCE SUMMARY.   1/4 Bn Gordon Hrs
(Erase heading not required.)

Instructions regarding War Diaries and Intelligence Summaries are contained in F. S. Regs., Part II. and the Staff Manual respectively. Title pages will be prepared in manuscript.

Place	Date	Hour	Summary of Events and Information	Remarks and references to Appendices
HOUDENG	22.2.19		Reveillé 04.30 hours. The Battalion commenced the journey to the Second Army, but owing to the non-arrival of the train at MANAGE, billets were procured for the night.	
MANAGE	23.2.19		The Battalion entrained at 11.30 hours.	T.S.W.
VLATTEN	24.2.19		The Battalion detrained at MECHERNICH at 11.00 hours and proceeded to billets in VLATTEN previously occupied by the 2/4th K.O.Y.L.I., 187th Infantry Brigade, 62nd (W.R.) Division.	T.S.W.
VLATTEN	25.2.19		2 Field Ambulance 3.O.R. Evacuated to C.C.S. 1.O.R. Evacuated to 3.O.R.	T.S.W.
VLATTEN	26.2.19		Dull and Showery. The day was spent cleaning and re-organising on lines laid down by the Commanding Officer at Company Commanders' Conference. 1.O.R. to Hospital. 1.O.R. Baths were allotted as follows: "A" Coy 09.30 to 12.00 hours. "B" Coy 14.15 to 16.15 hrs. "C" Coy 12.30 & 13.45 to 16.45 onwards. H.Q. 13.00 hours.	T.S.W.
VLATTEN	27.2.19		Cold and wet. The day was devoted to cleaning and reconstruction. All equipment was washed. Baths were allotted as follows: "C" Coy 09.30 hrs to 12.30 hrs. "D" Coy 13.45 hrs onwards.	T.S.W.

WAR DIARY
or
INTELLIGENCE SUMMARY.

Army Form C. 2118.

1/4 Bn. Gordon Hrs.

Place	Date	Hour	Summary of Events and Information	Remarks and references to Appendices
VLATTEN	27.2.19	6.0th	Sick to Hospital 3 O.R.	
VLATTEN	28.2.19		Cold but dry. The day was spent in re-organising and cleaning. Special attention being paid to cleanliness and correct fitting of equipment. Demobilised from 51st Division H.Q. 1 O.R. Sick to Hospital 1 O.R.	

James A. Cooper.
Lieut Colonel
Commanding 1/4 Bn. The Gordon Hrs.

1/3/19.

Confidential

War Diary
of
1st Bn Gordon Highlanders

from 1st March 1919 to 31st March 1919

Volume

Army Form C. 2118.

WAR DIARY
or
INTELLIGENCE SUMMARY.
(Erase heading not required.)

Instructions regarding War Diaries and Intelligence Summaries are contained in F. S. Regs., Part II. and the Staff Manual respectively. Title pages will be prepared in manuscript.

Place	Date	Hour	Summary of Events and Information	Remarks and references to Appendices
VLATTEN	1.3.19	AM	Cold and rainy. The day was spent in cleaning and re-organising under orders of Company Commanders. Inoculation Parade of 'A' & 'B' Coys, who had not been inoculated against Typhoid during the past 12 months was carried out at 1600 hours. The following postings are made to take effect as from today:- Lieut. H.I. CLAPPERTON, M.C. to 'B' Coy. Lieut. G. MACLEAN to 'A' Coy. Evacuated to C.C.S. 2 O.R. "Summer time" commenced at 2300 hrs.	
VLATTEN	2.3.19	AM	Dry cold day. C. of E. service, VLATTEN, 07.15 hours. Holy Communion at 11.00 hours. Voluntary Service, HERGARTEN at 19.30 hours. Sick to Hospital 2 O.R.	
VLATTEN	3.3.19	AM	Cold and showery. The day was spent in cleaning and reorganising under Company arrangements. The Battalion was medically inspected from 11.00 to 12.00 hours, sick to Hospital 2 O.R. Struck off strength on being over 7 days in Field Ambulance - 11 O.R.	
VLATTEN	4.3.19	AM	Cold and wet. The day was devoted to re-organising under	

WAR DIARY
or
INTELLIGENCE SUMMARY.

Army Form C. 2118.

(Erase heading not required.)

Place	Date	Hour	Summary of Events and Information	Remarks and references to Appendices
VLATTEN	4.3.19		Coy Company arrangements except as follows. Baths were allotted to H.Q. 09.30 to 11.00 hours and to "A" Coy. 11.00 hours onwards. There was a demonstration at 10.30 hours giving examples of the correct and incorrect method of fitting equipment. All N.C.Os and Subaltern Officers attended. The Rev. W.A. ELLIS lectured in Cinema at 11.00 hours on "CAIRO to the CAPE" with lantern slides. The following attended:- 2 Officers per Coy. "A" Coy. 70 OR. "C" Coy. 70 OR. "D" Coy. 70 OR. H.Q. 40 OR. March to Field Ambulance for Field to Garrison General Hospital - 1 OR. (27.2.19.)	
VLATTEN-BUIR	5.3.19		Mild sunny day. Reveille 04.15 hours. The Battalion paraded in full marching order ready to march off at 06.30 hours in order of march "D","C","A","H.Q.","B" Coys. The Battalion moved by track route to ZULPICH, and there entrained for BUIR. Billets previously occupied by the 2nd Battalion The Royal Scots were taken over. Sick to Hosp. 1 OR.	

WAR DIARY or INTELLIGENCE SUMMARY

Army Form C. 2118.

Place	Date	Hour	Summary of Events and Information	Remarks and references to Appendices
BUIR.	6.3.19	AM	The day was spent in reorganising, cleaning and re-allotment of billets. 3 Field Ambulance 10R. Rejoined from Staff. 1 OR.	*
BUIR.	7.3.19	AM	Mild and showery. The day was spent in re-organising and cleaning. The Commanding Officer inspected all billets from 1000 to 1200 hours. Rejoined from Hospital 3 O.R. Joined from 1st Bn. the Gordon Highlanders and taken on strength 10 Officers, 167 other ranks. Joined and taken on strength, Capt. H. TAYLOR, Chaplain to the Forces.	
BUIR.	8.3.19	AM	The day was devoted to cleaning and re-organising, all web equipment was washed under company arrangements. 2 Field Ambulance 5 O.R. Rejoined from 51st Amb. 1 O.R. Taken on strength 1 Pte. from R.A.S.C. Interpreter to Joined and taken on strength Capt. & Quartermaster T. KEAY, M.C.	1
BUIR.	9.3.19	AM	Dry and mild. Church service was held in Recreation	

Army Form C. 2118.

WAR DIARY
or
INTELLIGENCE SUMMARY.
(Erase heading not required.)

Instructions regarding War Diaries and Intelligence Summaries are contained in F. S. Regs., Part II. and the Staff Manual respectively. Title pages will be prepared in manuscript.

Place	Date	Hour	Summary of Events and Information	Remarks and references to Appendices
BUIR	9.3.19	Contd	Room at 1000 hours. The following attached. All officers, 100 O.R. per coy, 50 O.R. per headquarters. Dress: drill order without Arms. Belt and side-arms only. 2 Field Ambulance 1 O.R. Rejoined from Field Ambulance 1 O.R.	
BUIR	10.3.19		Dull and mild. Parades and training in accordance with Training Programme revised to Companies. Platoons from "C" Coy worked on miniature Range under orders of their Coy Commander.	
BUIR	11.3.19		Training in accordance with Training Programme. Work on Miniature Range continued. "C" Coy relieves "D" Coy on Bridge Guard. Cinema open 18.30 h.	
"	12.3.19		Training in accordance with Programme. Cold and dull.	
"	13.3.19		Parades and Training according to Programme. 2Lt. D. McDonald struck off strength, demobilised. Went on leave.	
"	14.3.19		Training. Hurdles & Arms 2 Section drill. Cold and dull. Work on Assault Course.	
"	15.3.19		Coy devotes to Cleaning and Kit Inspection. Blanco made for order of	

Army Form C. 2118.

WAR DIARY
or
INTELLIGENCE SUMMARY.
(Erase heading not required.)

Instructions regarding War Diaries and Intelligence Summaries are contained in F. S. Regs., Part II. and the Staff Manual respectively. Title pages will be prepared in manuscript.

Place	Date	Hour	Summary of Events and Information	Remarks and references to Appendices
BUIR.				
" M	14/3/19		Brigadier was for the first time – successful	
" M	16/3/19	–	Church Service in Recreation Room at 09:45 hrs. 1 W.O.R. to Cpl. R.C. at GOIZHEIM. Numbers C/E GOIZHEIM 110th.	*
" M	17/3/19		Training in accordance with Training Programme. Cold and dull. Retreat to be sounded at 18.30 hrs. Rate 3 B/c Guards cease wearing steel helmets.	
" M	18/3/19		Inspection of Rifles and L.G. by Armourer Sgt. Ile Perlin Fortress. 1 Pelton keep 3 Pelton. 13 Pelton v 14 Pelton.	
" M	19/3/19		Medical Inspection Battalion reported remarkably free of Scabies and vermin. In "D" Coy only 1 re-cast found vermin 3. 1 case of scabies only in whole Battalion.	
" M	20/3/19		Training in accordance with Training Programme. Foden Disinfector dismissed. A. & B. Coys blankets. Nos J Stafft. R Henry R.C Lindsey. A.W. Gregor V.L. Davies. T.W. Steward. Mr. E.C. McDonald. A. Rae taken in strength 9. 12 O.O.R. all from 6/17 = R.R. Le Gnd Infanterie.	*
" M	21/3/19		Training in accordance with Training Programme.	

WAR DIARY
or
INTELLIGENCE SUMMARY.
(Erase heading not required.)

Army Form C. 2118.

Place	Date	Hour	Summary of Events and Information	Remarks and references to Appendices
BUIR 22/3/19	22/3/19	AM	Coy and Posft. Training as details in Training Programme. W.D. to D.Diff. strength on attached on Ph.t 6/7" Beh. Yte. gain Hrs.	*
"	23/3/19	AM	Church Parade in Recreation Room 0915 hrs. 10.0.R R Cny 30.0.R fm HQ	
"	24/3/19	AM	Repairs to Defective rifle by Armourer. Training in accordance with Training Programme. Very cold.	
"	25/3/19	AM	Training in accordance with Training Programme. Battalion Bakery Started — Jam Rolls issued to Coys. Amongst the first to issue or isse of Oat Cake daily. Dance 18.30h	
"	26/3/19	AM	Training in accordance with Training Programme. 4/5 CRANSTON 7 updates from (1st Scottish Rifles) is posted to "A" Co. Training and work in Arsenal Camp continued. Cold.	*
"	27/3/19	AM	Route March cancelled owing to bad weather.	
"	28/3/19	AM	27.O.R. went to COLOGNE to see 2nd Army Football Cup (Final) very cold. Some snow.	

Army Form C. 2118.

WAR DIARY
or
INTELLIGENCE SUMMARY.
(Erase heading not required.)

Place	Date	Hour	Summary of Events and Information	Remarks and references to Appendices
BUIR	29/3/19	AM	Day devoted to cleaning and Kit Inspection. very cold and intermittent snow storms. Lecture at HERZEWICK by Major A Ratcliffe Dugmore F.R.G.S. 1700 hrs on "Stalking African Big Game with a Camera". Dance 1830 hrs in Recreation Room.	
"	30/3/19	AM	Church Parade in Recreation Room 10.15 hrs. Billet inspection (D and B Coys) by C.O. at 1100 hrs. Cold with intermittent snow storms.	
"	31/3/19	AM	Training to accordance with Training Programme	

James S. Oxton, M Col
Commanding
4th Bn. The Gordon Highlanders.

www.ingramcontent.com/pod-product-compliance
Lightning Source LLC
Chambersburg PA
CBHW080838010526
44114CB00017B/2333